Spice Islands Forts

An illustrated history

and catalogue

SIMON PRATT

This is an IndieMosh book

brought to you by MoshPit Publishing
an imprint of Mosher's Business Support Pty Ltd

PO Box 147
Hazelbrook NSW 2779

indiemosh.com.au

A catalogue record for this work is available from the National Library of Australia

NATIONAL LIBRARY OF AUSTRALIA

https://www.nla.gov.au/collections

Title:	Spice Islands Forts
Subtitle:	An illustrated history and catalogue
Author:	Pratt, Simon (1965–)
ISBNs:	978-1-922440-61-7 (paperback)
Subjects:	HISTORY: Asia/Southeast Asia; Military/Wars and Conflicts; Maritime History and Piracy

Cover design and layout by Ally Mosher at allymosher.com

Cover photos (front and rear) © Nur Alam

Artwork of fort (rear cover) © Lucas Kukler at kukler.com/

Acknowledgements

Thanks to kind assistance from:

Dr Laode Muhammad Aksa
   Director, Bureau for the Protection of Cultural Heritage, Ternate

Charles Blackwood
   Publications Coordinator, Fortress Study Group, UK

Hans Bonke
   Netherlands Menno van Coehoorn Society

Dr Florentina Rodao Garcia
   Complutense University of Madrid

Pierre Joppen
   Paulus Swaen Map Auctions & Gallery

Manuel Lobato
   University of Lisbon

Marco Ramerini
   colonialvoyage.com

Febriyanti Suryaningsih
   Executive Director, Pusat Dokumentasi Arsitektur, Indonesia

Illustrations

Unless otherwise acknowledged, photos and artwork are from the author's collection. Many thanks to my brilliant Indonesian photographer, Nur Alam Mochammad Noer (instagram.com/nuralammn), whose talent graces these pages.

Contents

Timeline

Date	Event
1721 BC	Cloves originating from the Spice Islands were in use in Syria.
Pre-1500	Chinese, Arab and Malay traders regularly visited the Spice Islands for centuries before Europeans arrive, exchanging gold, cloth and foodstuffs for nutmeg, mace and cloves.
1200–1400	Various travellers, adventurers and traders, including Marco Polo, write accounts of their journeys to Asia. An account by Venetian Nicolo Conti appearing around 1447 gives us the first European glimpse of the Spiceries.
1415	Portugal storms Ceuta in North Africa—the first step in an empire which would stretch to China.
Mid 1400s	Islam arrives in the Spice Islands via Arab and Malay traders.
1457	First Spice Island appears on a European map—an anonymous Genoese world map shows Banda.
1488	Portuguese Bartholomew Dias is the first to round southern Africa and find the route into the Indian Ocean.
1492	Italian Christopher Columbus in the service of Spain crosses the Atlantic and arrives in the Bahamas, 'discovering' the Americas while searching for the Indies.
1494	With papal blessing, Spain and Portugal divide the undiscovered world between themselves at the Treaty of Tordesillas.
1510	Italian, Ludovico de Varthema publishes an unconvincing account of his supposed travels to the Spice Islands five years earlier.
1511	Portugal captures Malacca, spice emporium of the East. The first expedition to find the Spice Islands is dispatched from here later that year.

Date	Event
1512	Portuguese locate the Bandas, Ambon and Ternate.
1519	The Ottomans conquer the Mameluke kingdom of Egypt, bringing them into direct conflict with Portugal in the Indian Ocean for the first time.
1521	Portuguese Ferdinand Magellan, in the service of Spain, leads the first fleet across the Pacific seeking the Spice Islands, but is killed in today's Philippines.
1521	November: remnants of Magellan's Spanish fleet arrive at Tidore, and meet a Portuguese who voyaged from the east, thus encircling the globe for the first time.
1522	First Spice Island fort, the Portuguese Fort St John the Baptist (referred to as Kastella in this account), is commenced on Ternate.
1527	Spanish build their first fort on Tidore.
1529	Portugal commences Fort Nassau on Banda, but abandon it after resistance from the locals.
1529	The Treaty of Zaragoza between Spain and Portugal awards the Spice Islands to Portugal in return for 350,000 gold ducats. A few months later, Portuguese troops storm the Spanish defences on Tidore.
1536–1539	Governorship of Antonio Galvao on Ternate.
1545	Spanish surrender their Moluccan positions to Portugal and leave the Spice Islands.
1551	Portugal destroys the Jailolo kingdom on Halmahera.
1558	Portugal builds a fort on Bacan; much later it becomes Fort Barneveld.
1568	Start of the Eighty Years War between the Dutch and Spain.
1570	Portuguese murder Ternate's Sultan Hairun in Kastella. His son Babullah takes the crown and embarks on a holy war against them. Kastella is besieged.
1571	Spanish capital of the Philippines, Manila, is established.
1575	The starving Portuguese defenders on Ternate surrender to Sultan Babullah, vacate Kastella and flee to Ambon.

Date	Event
1576	Portugal commences what later becomes Fort Victoria at Ambon.
1578	Fort Reis Magos, built by Portugal on Tidore.
1578	Portugal's King Sebastian dies in battle in Morocco leaving no heirs.
1579	English privateer Francis Drake arrives at Ternate during his circumnavigation.
1580	Spain absorbs Portugal after Sebastian's uncle, King Henry I, dies—the Iberian adversaries are now on the same side.
1581	Seven Dutch provinces declare independence from Spain.
1591	Spain bans the sale of Iberian spices at Amsterdam, encouraging the Dutch to seek the Spice Islands on their own.
1596	First Dutch expedition reaches Java.
1599	First Dutch fleet reaches the Spice Islands.
1600	Portuguese fort at Ambon attacked by the Dutch.
1602	First English fleet reaches Java and the Spice Islands.
1603	First English trading lodge in the Spice Islands built on Run, Banda Islands.
1605	A Dutch fleet captures Fort Victoria at Ambon and then Fort Reis Magos on Tidore from Portugal.
1606	A Spanish counterattack from Manila storms locally held Kastella on Ternate; Spanish defences on Ternate and Tidore are strengthened; Fort Nova built.
1607	Fort Malayo (later Fort Orange) built by the Dutch on Ternate.
1609	Fort Willemstadt built by the Dutch over a local work at Tacome, Ternate.
1609	Fort Nassau built by the Dutch on Banda over Portuguese foundations.
1609	Fort Marieco built by Spanish on the western side of Tidore.
1610	Fort Tohula commenced by Spanish on the eastern side of Tidore.

Date	Event
1611	Fort Belgica built above Fort Nassau on Banda by the Dutch.
1611	Fort Tolucco built by Spanish on Ternate, but quickly abandoned to the Dutch.
1612	Fort Mauritius built on Makian by the Dutch.
1613	The Dutch capture Forts Marieco and Fort Reis Magos on Tidore.
1613	Spanish build Fort Tomarina south of now Dutch Marieco, on Tidore.
1616	The Dutch defeat the English-supported Ai rebels in the Bandas and build Fort Revenge.
1618	Forts Rum, Kalomata, St Lucia built on Ternate and Tidore.
1624	The Dutch build Fort Hollandia on Banda Besar.
1630	The Dutch build Fort Concordia on Banda Besar.
1642	The Dutch build Fort Kayu Merah over an older fort on Ternate.
1648	The Peace of Munster ends the Eighty Years War between Spain and the Netherlands.
1663	The Spanish abandon and partially destroy their forts in the Moluccas.
1667	The Treaty of Breda, signed between the Netherlands and England, ends the Second Anglo–Dutch War. Dutch exchange Manhattan in return for Run Island in the Bandas. The Dutch are now the sole masters of the Spice Islands.
1683	English East India Company abandons base at Bantam, Java.
1795	Fifth Anglo–Dutch War. Britain captures Cape Town, Ceylon and Malacca.
1796	Fort Victoria and Ambon fall to the British, followed by the Bandas.
1799	The VOC collapses and its interests are taken over by the Dutch state.
1801	Fort Orange and Ternate fall to the British East India Company.
1803	The Spice Islands are restored to Dutch rule.

Date	Event
1810	Sixth Anglo–Dutch War. British Captain Cole storms Fort Belgica. Ambon and Ternate also captured.
1817	The Spice Islands are restored to Dutch rule once again.
1817	Indonesian hero Pattimura storms Fort Duurstede on Saparua.
1942	The Spice Islands captured by Imperial Japan.
1944	The US invades Morotai in the northern Spice Islands.
1949	Indonesian independence.
1950	The secessionist RMS is defeated at Fort Victoria on Ambon.
1974	The last World War II Japanese soldier surrenders on Morotai.

Introduction

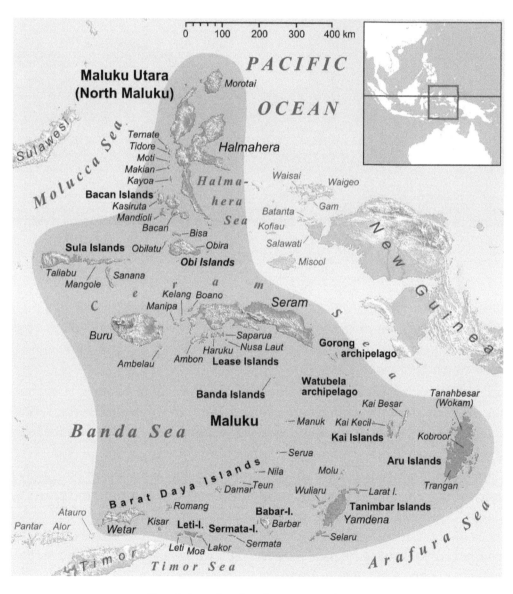

1. The Spice Islands of Eastern Indonesia.
Image credit: Lencer CC BY-SA 3.0

2. Fort Belgica on Banda silhouetted against the equatorial dusk.

Astride the equator and on the far south-eastern edge of Asia, a line of jungle-clad volcanos rise steeply out of tropical seas. Their lava-blackened peaks often shake and smoke with anger. From these islands alone across history's pages came cloves. They were known as the Moluccas.

Four hundred nautical miles to the south are the Banda Islands, a scattering of ancient volcanos amid reef-fringed turquoise waters. In the entire world, nutmeg and mace, two precious parts of the same rare plant, grew only on this remote handful of islands.

In between these two isolated and mysterious archipelagos lies Ambon, a deep, safe harbour, focal point of the region. These three localities combine to form the Spice Islands or 'Spiceries', once part of the Dutch East Indies, today the Indonesian provinces of Maluku and Maluku Utara. Other exotic spots, like Zanzibar and Grenada, also today call themselves 'spice' islands, but these are newcomers to the game, pretenders to the historic title.

History owes much to these real Spice Islands. The Age of Discovery, where European navigators mapped the globe from 1450 onwards 'discovering' the lands of the Indian and Pacific Oceans and the Americas, kicked off with a desire to find these Spiceries of the Indies, and reap their rewards.

Bartholomew Dias was seeking them when he was the first to round Africa and enter the Indian Ocean in 1488. Christopher Columbus was looking for them when he instead bumped into the Americas in 1492. And the great circumference of the earth was first closed in the Spice Islands in 1521 when survivors of Ferdinand Magellan's Spanish expedition, crossing the endless Pacific from the Americas, ran into a Portuguese trader on Ternate who had arrived there on the long haul around Africa, from the west.

Whether nutmeg and mace from Banda, cloves from the Moluccas, pepper from Sumatra, cinnamon from Ceylon, or sandalwood from Timor, trade in spices like these changed our world forever. The spice trade created the world's first transoceanic merchants, led directly to the first global mercantile system, encouraged the formation of credit-based commercial structures, gave birth to the first global corporation (the Dutch *Vereenigde Oostindische Compagnie*, or VOC), and led to the establishment of the very first links between the European, Middle Eastern, Indian and Chinese worlds. Concentrated rather than bulky, easily transportable, imperishable, handily divisible and highly sought after, spices were the perfect trade product.

From before Classical times these spices were used for flavouring and preserving bland food, for freshening breath and for medicinal purposes. They were even reputed as a defence against the plague, which had devastated Europe in medieval times. The profits involved in the trade were immense for those who could cut out the multitude of middlemen that ferried the aromatic cargos from eastern Asia to China, India, the Middle East and Europe.

The Portuguese, combining this desire for profit with their advanced nautical technology and experience, were the first to put the Spice Islands on the map, in 1512. But they had no intention of giving their location away, and were zealous with maintaining the secrecy of their sea charts. Determined to safeguard their investment, they built the first of the Spice Islands forts on Ternate in 1522. But soon the lure of spice profits saw forts—and conflict—multiply across the region.

Spaniards from Magellan's fleet were invited by Ternate's rival, the Sultan of Tidore, to help fortify his capital as a counter to the newly combined power of Ternate and Portugal, but they were very soon defeated in the first of the colonial Spice Islands wars.

Subsequent Spanish voyages across the Pacific all sustained catastrophic losses of men and ships, with the survivors seeking refuge from Portuguese retribution on Tidore and the jungle ports on nearby Halmahera. Time and again, the Spanish enclaves were destroyed by the muskets and cannon of Portugal and the warriors of Ternate. After a generation of conflict, Madrid admitted defeat and accepted an enormous payment of gold from Portugal to relinquish its claims to the Spiceries.

3. The empty battlements of Fort Kalomata on Ternate—most important of the clove islands—keep watch on the volcanos of Tidore and Maitara. Once on the frontline between the Spanish and Dutch enclaves, Kalomata was later stormed by British marines.

Portugal's problems, however, continued. Its limited resources and substantial adversaries always left its Spice Islands operations denuded of the support needed to exert proper control over the spice trade. It was perpetually fighting, from Mozambique to the Gulf to India to Malaya to China, taking on the regional superpowers of the Middle East and Asia, not one at a time, but all at once. And it never had nearly enough men and galleons in the theatre to match its extravagant aspirations.

Endlessly assailed by besiegers at its capitals of Goa and Malacca, with a long and tenuous supply route around the Cape, its Indies empire was starved of funding from Lisbon, despite providing a good part of the royal revenue. At the very far edge of the empire, the incompetent captains of Kastella—at the fortress on Ternate—managed to alienate the local elites and when that boiled over, Portugal lost its foothold there in 1575, just 63 years after arriving.

Ternate then became the prime regional power, uniting the disparate sultanates under the banner of Islam, while the Portuguese held onto small forts on Ambon and Tidore only with difficulty. But the next phase of the spice wars was just beginning.

First, Spain absorbed a kingless Portugal, then banned the Dutch from distributing the Indies spices out of Amsterdam. The newly combined provinces of the Netherlands had smelt the spice profits and were at war with Spain in Europe. They decided to seek the spices at the source. In 1605 Dutch fleets captured both Portugal's remaining Spice Islands forts, at Ambon and Tidore. The Eighty Years War in Europe spread to the clove volcanos and the nutmeg plantations of the Indies.

For the next three decades, Spanish bases in the Philippines,[1] Portuguese ones in India and Malacca, and the Dutch strongholds on Java all poured men and fleets into the Spice Islands to maintain and expand their positions. Forts were built to hold garrisons, to protect spice stores and plantations, as a base for maritime power, to pacify local populations and to guard areas of strategic significance.

The main arena of conflict was in the Moluccas. The clove crop represented far more worth than the nutmeg equivalent and the Spanish and Dutch went head-to-head on the main islands of Ternate and Tidore for more than a decade. Some of their forts were just a few hundred metres apart. The battles extended across the monsoon-stippled adjacent seas, and the forests and jungles that hosted the clove trees.

In the Bandas too, there was a long struggle for control of the nutmeg plantations, but mostly between the VOC and the Bandanese. The islanders handed the Dutch some stinging defeats, but eventually paid the price as the resources of the VOC swamped their resistance. The English arrived in the spice game too late; by then only the most remote of the Bandas, Run Island, was still unclaimed, and they held that with difficulty for just a few years before bowing out to Dutch pressure. Run was eventually swapped for Manhattan in 1667, as part of a peace treaty that ended one of a seemingly endless series of Anglo–Dutch wars.

Slowly spices became less important, seeds were smuggled out and the unique plants came to grow elsewhere, in other tropical climes. The Spanish were more focused on maintaining the Philippines, and they too abandoned the game in 1663, leaving all the Spiceries to the Dutch. Apart from a couple of minor interludes, they held onto the Spice Islands and the East Indies until World War II. The new nation of Indonesia now counts the clove and nutmeg islands among the 18,000 that make up its lands.

---

[1] The Philippines, 'discovered' by Magellan in 1521, were named in 1543 in honour of the ruling Spanish monarch, King Phillip II.

The Dutch built the most colonial forts, with the Spanish close behind. The English and Portuguese had a handful each. Local sultans, rajahs and princes ruling the hundreds of societies spread between New Guinea and the Philippines also built many forts, both before the colonial era and during it. Even the Japanese in World War II built a few fortifications, mostly on Ambon.

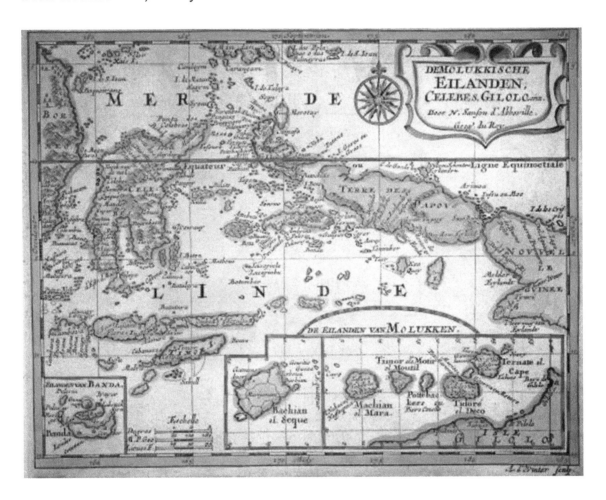

4. A French view of the Spice Islands from Sanson d'Abbeville printed in Paris in 1683 showing what is now Eastern Indonesia with the principal islands of the Moluccas and Bandas shown in an inset along the base of the map. Note how poorly understood were major islands such as New Guinea, Sulawesi and Borneo, whereas the Spice Islands are located and drawn with much greater accuracy.

Many of the forts were contested and changed hands, some a number of times. There were five main fortresses responsible for commanding the adjacent regions. For the Spanish up to 1663 it was Kastella on Ternate and Tohula on Tidore. For the Dutch it was Malayo (or Orange) on Ternate, Victoria on Ambon and Belgica on Banda. All five can still be seen today, in varying degrees of integrity.

Fort Victoria on Ambon had one of the most convoluted histories of Spice Islands forts. It was originally built by the Portuguese, who beat off a number of attacks by local forces until surrendering to the Dutch in 1605. They expanded the fort considerably, but it fell twice to the English, in 1796 and 1810, reverting to Dutch control both times. With Ambon as a key point of the Dutch defences in 1942, Fort Victoria was quickly overrun by the Japanese, who used it as a headquarters. This invited substantial allied bombing in the last years of World War II, which severely damaged the defences that had already suffered centuries of earthquakes. Following Indonesian independence, Fort Victoria was used briefly as a stronghold for successionist rebels before being recaptured in bitter fighting. It remains in use by the Indonesian military today.

5. The very active volcano of Gunung Api (Fire Mountain) seen from Bandaneira, the main settlement of the nutmeg-endowed Banda Islands. The ramparts of Fort Belgica are in the foreground, while a Pelni liner comes alongside Banda's tiny wharf.

Only a few forts are restored to glory, most notably Fort Belgica. Many stand crumbling into the jungle, fighting against centuries of exposure to the tropics, indifference, vandalism and neglect. Some are lost forever, buried under the modern towns they once dominated with their cannon. Today, a traveller can take in around 15 forts scattered over the Spice Islands that are both sufficiently accessible and of historical interest, but they are spread across three archipelagos and traversing the 'wild East' of Indonesia can be challenging.

Nowadays there is still nutmeg grown in the Bandas and cloves in the Moluccas, but the original habitats of the world's most famous spices are no longer household names and they have drifted off the radar for all but the most determined travellers.

The thunder of the guns has long been silenced. The galleons and the traders have passed into history. But amidst the towering volcanos and turquoise waters of the picturesque islands, centuries-old crumbling battlements and earthquake-shattered ramparts draped with creepers and shaded by coconut palms remain as a testament to the endeavours of long forgotten pioneers who charted the world's oceans chasing down the elusive Islands of Spice.

The Moluccas, Ambon and Banda remain remote and seldom visited, a forgotten corner of the globe, racked by volcanos and earthquakes, beset by ethnic tensions. They have little to show for their glory days. On the border between Asia and the Pacific, at the frontline of the old empires of Spain, Britain and the Netherlands, amidst the volcanos of the Pacific ring of fire, they slumber, forgotten by the world they were central to defining.

1. Spices and the spice trade

6. Enduring image from the Spice Islands: volcanos and forts. This is Fort Kalomata with Ternate's towering 1700-metre Gammalamma volcano shrouded in steam and sulphur behind.

It was a couple of hours after dawn on Ternate in 1522, and already the jungle steamed under a burning sun in a cloudless sky. Ardi, a wiry old spice picker, crouched in a patch of shade braced against the slope of the mountain, sipped a little water and regarded his next tree; tall, bushy and difficult, but its harvest would complete his work for the day. It stood around five times his height, wide and luxuriant with a full suit of glossy dark green leaves, the branch tips heavy with cloves. Each year he took 20 kilograms of buds just from it. Ardi was old, 30 seasons of picking behind him, but this tree had seen five like him come and go, and other kings of the forest nearby, ten. His leathery forehead wrinkled as he squinted up at the high flowers, checking that he wasn't too early or too late, that the little pungent buds were just on the edge of ripeness.

7. Perhaps a descendant of Ardi:
a modern clove picker on Ternate dries his buds in the sun.

Deep under his feet, the island rumbled. He glanced up at the peak, soaring above him, clouds of sulphur venting lazily from its cauldron, but the thunder died away and the mountain gods slumbered again. Across the narrow strait to the south at Tidore, a half dozen outriggers pulled out for a raid across turquoise water unruffled by breeze, but they were headed east, not a threat to Ternate, and his attention returned to his tree. When his sack was full, he'd lay the buds in the sun to dry in the village and tomorrow exchange them for two reams of cloth and a week's rice at the fort of the strange new white men. Not bad for a morning's work, he thought.

To Ardi and the Ternateans these new Europeans were just the latest in a long line of outsiders who eagerly sought the only product of value in their tiny landfalls.

8. Mace (left) and nutmeg. Across the whole globe they were found only in the Banda Islands.

First to arrive, thousands of years ago, had been traders from Java, two week's sail to the west. Later, around 300 BC, Chinese merchants found the islands, sailing also via Java. But from the 1400s, the Chinese preferred to wait at Malacca for others to deliver the spices to them, so that when the Portuguese arrived in 1512, it was the Malays who shipped most of the cloves from the northern Moluccan islands, and nutmeg from the southern Banda Islands back to Malacca, the thriving entrepot perfectly located between the seas of China and India.

The trade in spices enriched individuals, sultans, companies and empires, but it was never very bountiful to the Spice Islanders themselves. All land suitable for agriculture on the islands was devoted to either nutmeg or clove trees, and so they relied on food imports to survive. All other trade goods—textiles for clothing, iron cookware, knives, axes, nails, mirrors, scissors and metal for weapons—also had to be exchanged with the traders who took away the spices. Naturally, the prices of these essentials were set very high by foreign traders. The rulers of the various Spice Islands generally applied an export tax on their cloves and nutmeg, and this filled their treasuries, but not much of this trickled down to Ardi and his kin.

9. A mature clove tree could yield up to 20 kg of spice annually. For an unremarkable tree, it produced an amazingly unique fruit. Of the same Myrtaceae or Myrtle family as the eucalypt, the guava and the allspice, clove trees can live upwards of 400 years.

Cloves, most famous of all sixteenth century spices, came only from a line of five volcanos soaring out of the equatorial sea just off the coast of Halmahera, itself perched in between Sulawesi and New Guinea. The unique sharpness and versatility of these little black sprigs saw them prized from China to India to Europe. The struggle to supply such far-flung markets with a relatively tiny output—assailed as all other agricultural commodities by the vagaries of climate, pests, disease and mismanagement—quite naturally led to elevated prices.

Used as a medicine, a flavouring, for religious ceremonies, for freshening breath, as a preservative and as a delicacy, cloves were also credited with curing headaches, assisting digestion, improving vision, arousing lust and even warding off the plague that afflicted Europe in the mid-thirteenth century.

The attractive bushy nutmeg trees were for thousands of years found only on a collection of tiny volcanic islands adrift in the stunning reef-girt Banda Sea. Their peach-like fruit consisted of the outer flesh, good only for sour jam, the inner kernel or nutmeg itself, and the mace, a soft red skin with a milder flavour which encased the nut. Nutmeg has been renowned as a versatile condiment and preservative for millennia and was also used as a hallucinogen and aphrodisiac.

Cloves and nutmeg have been traded commodities for a very long time. They were readily available in the Roman Empire and early Han China at the time of Christ. Maritime trade between the Spice Islands, Java, Sumatra, the Malay peninsula, and thence to India and China was well established by this time. But the history of these spices goes back much, much further than that.

10. Nutmeg fruit, showing the outer fruit and the red mace coating the inner nut.

The spice journey

11. One of the very earliest surviving regional maps, this Babylonian tablet with cuneiform script dates from around a millennium after the Terqa cloves arrived in what is now Syria and was found just down the Euphrates from them. Some scholars argue that this is the earliest surviving map of our mystical world. The limitations of contemporary mapmaking in Babylon—one of the most advanced societies of its time—contrast with the astonishing maritime capacity to bring cloves all the way there from the Spice Islands nearly 4000 years ago. This amazing piece is in the British Museum.
Image credit: Shadsluiter CC BY-SA 4.0

The oldest claimed[2] evidence of Spice Islands spices goes back to clove remnants discovered in a 1970s archaeological dig of an ancient household in Syria and dated to 1721 BC. The enormity of the journey required for cloves to have arrived in a Syrian kitchen from the Moluccas 3700 years ago is scarcely conceivable. This is so far back through the sands of time that we stand in the Bronze Age at the dawn of humankind's earliest organised states in Egypt and Mesopotamia. It is the very first days of recorded history. For the majority of these cloves' amazing journey, we have no supporting historical evidence.

We can only speculate that to arrive in Syria they could have come either via the Mediterranean from Egypt and, to get there, via Punt (roughly modern Somalia), or alternately up the Euphrates from the Persian Gulf, and before that from present–day Pakistan or India.

Unfortunately, we have no hard evidence of how the cloves would have made it across the Indian Ocean to Punt nearly 4000 years ago, or to have arrived in the Indus region at the same time. And how they were shipped from the Moluccas to India is also a mystery.

It is estimated that annual trade between China and India via the Straits of Malacca began only around 200 BC,[3] with Chinese voyages directly to Java and Sumatra beginning only during the Western Han dynasty. To the west, Indian merchants may first have arrived directly in Alexandria about the same time.[4]

The Arabs, who later controlled much of the trade of the Indian Ocean, did not begin searching the East Indies islands for the precious spices until the early seventh century AD.[5] All these voyages are far, far too late for our cloves to be in Syria in 1721 BC. In terms of recorded, historical journeys, we are at a dead end. The overland Silk Route between China and the Roman Empire was pioneered only at the start of the Christian era. The other legendary spice routes—the Cinnamon Route and the Pepper Route— also date only from the Classical era.

To envisage the trip from the Moluccas to the Indus as an extended series of coasting voyages—where small craft exchanged the cargo from port to port across the Moluccan, Banda, Flores and Java Seas, the Malacca Strait, the Andaman Sea, the Bay of Bengal and then hopped up the entire west coast of the subcontinent—is scarcely

2   The authenticity of this clove find at Terqa has been challenged by academics.

3   *The Austronesians*, p. 146.

4   *Early Mapping of South-East Asia*, p. 61.

5   *Early Mapping of South-East Asia*, p. 50.

plausible at such an early period of feuding port cities, nascent maritime trade links and limited nautical technology.

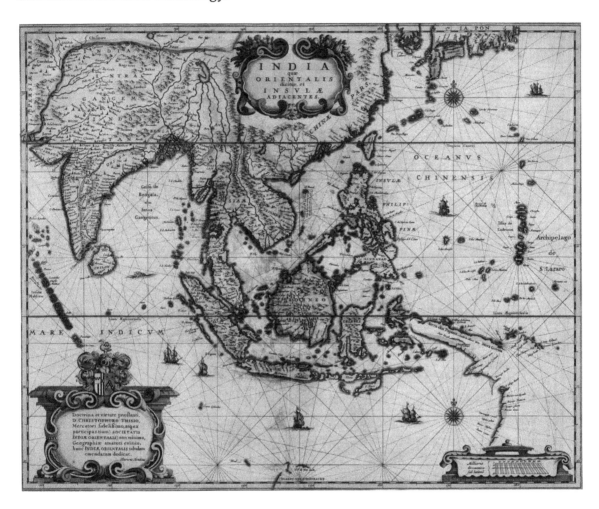

12. *India Quae Orientalis Dicitur, et Insulae Adiacentes*, a very comprehensive depiction of the archipelagos of the East, by Hondius in 1629. Visible is the eastern Indian Ocean and the western Pacific, the islands that make up modern Indonesia and the Philippines, Japan, China, Indochina, Malaya, Ceylon, India, and one of the very first glimpses of Australia, with western Cape York at far right. While the Dutch had only recently arrived in the Indies when this map was made, the Portuguese had already been sailing these waters for 130 years.

If we discard the overland route—which was not safely, securely and consistently traversable until Mongol times (after around 1250 AD)—and the voyage of interminable coasting, there remains just one alternative, and that is to cross the entire Indian Ocean from Java or Sumatra to the East African coast, perhaps stopping at Ceylon or Southern

India on the way. We know that Indonesian peoples took exactly this route from at least 2000 years ago on huge rafts, wafted not by the monsoon, but by the circular ocean currents, as the Roman naturalist and scholar Pliny the Elder, writing around the time of Christ says of cinnamon traders:

> 'These … carry it over vast tracts of sea, upon rafts, which are neither steered by rudder, nor drawn or impelled by oars or sails. Nor are they aided by any of the resources of art, man alone in his daring boldness, standing in place of all these; in addition to which, they choose the winter season, about the time of the equinox, for their voyage, for then a south easterly wind is blowing …'.[6]

What we do know is that the Pharaohs did have maritime trade with Punt at around this time, and that later at least, Punt enjoyed trade with both the African coast further south, and India. Madagascar was populated with raft or outrigger sailors from the Indonesian islands by about 800 AD. Until further evidence on this theme is found, we can only speculate as to how spices crossed 6000 nautical miles of unforgiving ocean and a small stretch of desert to arrive in the eastern Mediterranean region.

Despite the uncertainty over the journey of our oldest cloves, we do know more about how the spice trade worked in more recent times, immediately before European ships arrived in the Spice Islands. Cloves from the Moluccas and nutmeg from the Bandas mostly ended up in Malacca, on the Malay peninsula. The clove islanders were never long-distance sailors and always relied on others to collect their produce from Ternate, Tidore or Makian.

At various times, the traders picking up the cloves hailed from Banda, Makassar, Java, India, China or the Malay peninsula and perhaps even Arabia and Japan. Unlike the Moluccans, the Bandanese did ferry their nutmeg in junks to Malacca, often carrying cloves as well, but it was a tiny part of the overall clove and nutmeg carry trade.

The schedule for this trade between the remote Spiceries and Malacca 2000 nautical miles to the west was dictated by the seasonal rhythm of the monsoons. Malacca was perfectly located between the Indian Ocean and the China seas, where India-bound traders pivoted west, and China-bound ones turned north. It also lay at the junction of the Asian wind system, where the south-west monsoon of the Indian Ocean that blew from May to October met the north-east monsoon blowing south from China in the northern winter. Further to the east, around Banda and Ambon, the south-easterly trade winds dominated from June to October, making it a quick passage north to Ternate or west to Java, but impossible in the other direction.

---

[6] Pliny's *Natural History*, c. 77 AD.

13. Cloves and nutmeg were transported from the Moluccas and Bandas across the Indian Ocean and through the Middle East for thousands of years, with the overwhelming part of the journey across seas not always this placid. Here, a Bandanese longboat glides through crystal clear tropical waters to approach the ruins of Fort Colombo nestled under Gunung Api volcano, in the Banda Islands.

In December and January, the Chinese junks hove into Malacca, while the Indian traders arrived a few months later. The Indians had to complete their business quickly and beat the south-westerlies—which started in May or June—back to the subcontinent or wait another half year. Merchants seeking the Spice Islands could leave Malacca with the northerlies, sail east to Java in January, make Banda a month later, then load and wait for the trade winds to bring them back in July and August.

Often merchants making their way to Banda also sailed north to load cloves at Ternate in July and August, but were then stuck there until the next January, waited at Banda again for the trades in July, and finally returned to Malacca one and a half years after leaving. In Portuguese times, for the galleon that left Goa and stopped at both Ternate and Banda and returned to Goa after a stop at Malacca, the journey could take just short of three years. From Goa back to Lisbon then took another half a year. All these voyages, however, were dependant on the benevolence of the winds, which were in any case generally light and not always seasonally consistent.

At the bustling entrepot of Malacca, traders from China hawking porcelain mixed with Arabians seeking cloves, Guajarati cloth merchants, and miners from Sumatra selling artisanal gold. Luzonites loaded pepper for Canton, Bengali fishermen offered their catch grilled in banana leaves under shady coconut palms, Malabar Jews rented stores to arriving traders, Persians, Armenians and Somalis crowded around Sinhalese selling rubies and Siamese peddling ivory; all thronging the narrow streets and crowded bazaars.[7]

The river was too shallow for most ocean-going ships, and so three-masted junks from Fukien, prahus from Java and dhows from India and Arabia all anchored along the beach that fronted the city. The sultan provided a local administration, space for warehouses, a reliable legal system and a standard scheme of coins and weights, and for all that took about five percent duty from every shipload, which made his sultanate—only established in around 1400—ridiculously wealthy.

At first, around 1500, the Portuguese purchased all these spices in India, but they followed the scent further and further east, their caravels[8] wafting on the south-westerly monsoons. By 1509 they had located Malacca, spice emporium of the East, and finally they arrived at the source itself in the Spice Islands, becoming the first Europeans to locate these legendary, mystical lands.

The Portuguese arrival in Malacca quickly upset the delicate balance that had facilitated smooth operation of trade between a myriad of nationalities for a century or so. A number of their traders were lynched or imprisoned, and in response Afonso Albuquerque stormed the city and deposed the sultan in a hard-fought battle. Portugal had won sovereignty over Asia's fantastically valuable spice emporium before any other nations had even rounded the Cape. Learned Europeans at this time were still debating whether the Indian Ocean was a closed sea, and here, the Portuguese had sailed right through it from the Atlantic.

However, despite their impressive efforts to dominate the Indian Ocean and the seas of South-East Asia in the early sixteenth century, Portuguese control over the clove and nutmeg trade was always incomplete and only fleeting. The rulers of the Spice Islands were happy to sell spices to anyone, including the Portuguese, but never seriously complied with their demands for a monopoly. Even with a fort at Ternate,

---

[7]   See *Early Portuguese Malacca*.

[8]   Caravels were light Iberian exploration sailing vessels developed during the 15th century, generally lateen rigged with three masts. They became larger with time, but were always low draft, manoeuvrable and good at sailing upwind.

Malacca in their hands and more forts scattered around India and the Persian Gulf, the Portuguese lacked the ships and men to close all the sea routes to the west from Asia.

From Makassar and the islands that would soon become the Philippines, spices went north to China and Indochina in local craft. From Java, and especially Aceh on the northern tip of Sumatra, ships avoided Portuguese-controlled Indian Ocean ports and sailed direct to the emerging Ottoman Empire's new bases in the Red Sea. While Portugal controlled the oceanic passage around the Cape and in the Persian Gulf, there were many leakages in their system. The northern European nations of the Netherlands and England soon exploited the fragility of their under-manned, under-resourced and under-capitalised empire. By 1650, they had lost nearly all their hard-won forts in the East, including Malacca and the Spice Islands, and had bowed out of the spice trade.

Upon their arrival in the Spice Islands in the early 1500s, the Portuguese estimated the annual clove crop at about 1600 tonnes.[9] And this had to supply the entire global demand, including loss from wastage, shipwreck and spoilage over intercontinental distances. In the even more remote Banda Islands to the south, total annual output of nutmeg in 1515 was assessed at about 1800 tonnes, along with just 270 tonnes of mace—worth about seven times as much as nutmeg.[10]

Extrapolating yields and prices, this made all the clove Moluccas about five times more valuable than the nutmeg Bandas; indeed, given their tiny land area, it made them the most valuable real estate on earth.

Down the jungle-wrapped hillside in 1522 from old Ardi, our clove picker, at the new fort soldiers sweated and lazed in the shade of palms, playing games of dice to while away the long, steaming hours of the day and cursing the local labourers who did the same when they should have been raising the ramparts. Other local men came and went from the trade stalls roughly built outside the fort, each with their basket of clove buds, weighing and haggling with the Portuguese factors. No coins changed hands; the trade was all about barter. Most popular among the Moluccans was the soft white cloth from Gujarat,[11] and foodstuffs, because on Ternate they grew nothing but cloves and depended totally on imports.

---

9   *Suma Oriental*, p. 213. The original figure is 6000 *bahars* at approximately 270 kg each. The bahar was a confusing weight that varied from time to time, place to place and even commodity to commodity. Pires (p. 277), Galvao (p. 369) and Keay (p. 277) all rate it at this time on Ternate at around 270 kg.

10   *Suma Oriental*, p. 206.

11   Gujarat, on the north-west coast of India, at the time famed for its cloth/linen exports throughout Asia.

There was a Portuguese royal monopoly on cloves, but of course the king's officials skimmed what lay in the scales to hoard a portion and sell to Malay traders when they arrived with the winds of the monsoon in June or July. The king's product was gathered for the annual galleon which sailed west, south then north on the longest trading voyage in history, across 15,000 sea miles, stopping first at Malacca, then at Goa, and onwards around the perilous Cape, up the length of the Atlantic, to finally unload up the Tagus River at Lisbon late in the European summer, up to two years after leaving the Spice Islands.

At Lisbon, the spices' journey was not yet over. The Portuguese sold them off for distribution to northern Europe and Dutch coasters sailed them north to the markets of Amsterdam and Hamburg. The kilogram of cloves that Ardi had swapped on Ternate for cloth and rice bought in Malacca for about two *reals*[12] were worth around 700 reals in Lisbon, representing a royal margin of 35,000%.[13]

Every year of the sixteenth century, Portugal shipped home 3000 tonnes of spices from Asia.[14] The bulk of these spices were not nutmeg and cloves, but pepper from Coromandel in India and Sumatra, and cinnamon from Ceylon, but the product of the Spice Islands made up a significant portion of the overall volume, and an even greater portion of the value.

Pound for pound, pepper was worth about half as much as cloves, cinnamon fell in between the two, mace (the skin of the nutmeg kernel) was equal to cloves, though nutmeg itself was just one-seventh of the value of cloves. By comparison sugar, grown mostly in the Caribbean at the time, was worth a little less than pepper, and ginger from India about a third of a like weight of cloves.[15]

When the Spanish made the Spice Islands a decade after their Iberian neighbours, they too quickly realised the incredible profits involved. Magellan's Moluccan Fleet of five small ships carrying 250 men turned a modest profit on their epic circumnavigation when they brought back 25 tonnes of cloves, despite losing Magellan himself, four ships and all but 18 men during their three-year ordeal. The Spanish dispatched more fleets, but for years without success. The Portuguese, with a closer jumping-off point to the Spice Islands from their new bases in India and Malacca, were able to corner the market, but not for long.

---

[12] A Portuguese copper coin of the time, 400 of which equalled a silver *cruzado.*

[13] *The Spice Route,* pp. 217–8.

[14] *The Portuguese Seaborne Empire,* p. 59.

[15] economics.utoronto.ca/wwwfiles/archives/munro5/SPICES1

Still, their short interruption of the centuries-old coasting trade from the Moluccas to Malacca to India to the Levant to Venice rang the bell on two empires; the Mamelukes in Egypt, and mighty Venice itself. Both relied on taxes from the spice carry-trade to fill their treasuries.

14. A modern nutmeg plantation on Banda Besar, largest of the Bandas, with towering kenari trees behind. The kenaris provide shade from the afternoon sun for the nutmeg trees.

Other European nations also began to target the spices at their source, starting with the English. Following in Magellan's path, Francis Drake in 1580 became the first captain to command a complete circumnavigation of the globe, stopping at Ternate to pick up six tonnes of cloves which, along with several tonnes of looted Spanish silver, much more than repaid the expedition costs.

A few years later, the 1600-tonne Portuguese galleon *Madre de Deus*, returning to Lisbon, its holds bulging with the wares of the East, was captured by the English off the Azores. This solitary ship was carrying 45 tonnes of cloves, three each of nutmeg and mace, over 400 of pepper and 35 of cinnamon, as well as silk, ebony, precious stones and other exotic goods of Asia. The total value of this single galleon's cargo equalled half Queen Elizabeth's coffers at the time and opened English eyes to the riches that they were missing out on.

The Dutch also smelt the enticing flavours and profits of the Indies. Their first trade fleet arrived back from Java in 1597, less one of their four ships and two-thirds of their men, but with enough Sumatran pepper and Bandanese mace to turn a profit overall. The lure of the East sent five expeditions totalling 22 ships the next year from the Netherlands, the best of which repaid their shareholders with a 400% return.

By the mid seventeenth century, the spice trade was in the hands of the Dutch, who adopted a brutal commercial approach, exploiting the Spice Islands for several centuries, before they and the entire Dutch East Indies were taken from them in 1942, by Imperial Japan. Long before this though, intrepid French and English naturalist-adventurers had finally managed to steal seedlings and cultivate cloves and nutmeg in new tropical locations, stripping the monopoly the Spice Islands had enjoyed for millennia.

Today, Indonesia is still the world's largest producer of cloves, harvesting over 100,000 tonnes per year, but it is grown on Java, Sulawesi, Bali and Sumatra as well as in the Moluccas. The bulk of the crop is used in production of the wildly popular local *kretek* cigarettes. Other producers include Madagascar, Zanzibar (Tanzania) and Sri Lanka. Nutmeg is still grown in the Bandas, but also in other parts of Indonesia, which still produces three-quarters of the global annual crop of 10,000 tonnes.

2. The search for the Spice Islands

15. From Ternate, looking south to Tidore, with Ngade Lake in the foreground and tiny Maitara offshore. Mare, Motir and Makian are in the distance to the right of Tidore. The equator lies just south of Makian. The first Spanish ships anchored just to the left of Maitara.

As the sun dipped towards the tropical sea on Friday 8 November 1521, two worn carracks[16] dropped anchor under the towering volcano of Tidore Island, one of the Spice Islands in the far east of what is today Indonesia.

Just a cannon shot away on neighbouring Ternate Island, a lone Portuguese trader named Pedro Lorosa watched their arrival with great interest. Lorosa had sailed to India from Portugal around 1505 and had spent the last decade as a trader on Timor and around the Spice Islands. Timor was home to sandalwood, an aromatic timber highly valued in India and China, already traded for centuries, and Lorosa was the first European to source it to Timor. He had married a local woman and settled on Ternate to trade spices, but was dismayed by the lack of support the Portuguese crown applied to this potentially most bountiful of trading posts. By the time the Spanish arrived, he was the only Christian in a shifting, tribal, threatening Muslim world.

As we have seen, long before Lorosa's arrival, Malay, Chinese, Javanese and Arab mariners had been sailing to the Spice Islands for centuries, driven by the seasonal monsoons. However, as no pre–European maps of the Spice Islands have survived, to follow the documentary search for the Spiceries, we must follow the path from a European perspective. And while the incredible endeavours of the Portuguese and Spanish navigators defined the modern world in their quest for the Spice Islands, they were not the first Europeans to seek them out.

The first explorers known to have sailed from European seas towards the Indies were the Genoese Vivaldi brothers, who left the Mediterranean in 1291 in two galleys, turned south, and were never heard of again. A sea voyage to the Indies was regarded as completely absurd by Europe's men of science in medieval times, who brandished Ptolemy's newly found world map showing a landlocked Indian Ocean. Apart from the Vivaldis, no–one was brave enough to challenge that mindset until the Portuguese started south along the African coast in the early fifteenth century.

The land journey across Eurasia was considered much more geographically feasible, though in itself an incredible ordeal of desert, steppe and mountains, plagued by bandits and hostile tribes. There was a window of time of around one hundred years from the mid–thirteenth century when the extension of the Mongol Empire allowed adventurous travellers and traders to cross through one stable sovereign entity on the long traverse from west to east. This window shut down with the descent into chaos of the Mongols and the rise of the Ottomans but, by this time, John of Carpini, William of Rubrick, the Polos of Venice and Oderic of Pordenone had all crossed to the East, and left accounts which were closely studied by European mapmakers.

---

16 A three-masted, square-rigged, cannon-armed, long-distance sailing ship able to carry bulk trade goods, but slower than the caravel. Also known as a *nao*.

Marco Polo's *Travels*, published around 1300, was wildly popular and gave Europeans their first extensive account of the mysterious East. Polo lived in China for 16 years, was engaged as a minor official for Kublai Khan, and travelled extensively through his domains. While he did not venture there himself, he wrote about Java, and noted that spices, among them nutmeg and cloves, could be found in its ports. Slowly, the Ptolemaic concept of a closed Indian Ocean started to be challenged, hinting that a sea route to the East may be possible.

It was another Venetian trader, Nicolo de Conti, who, with considerable difficulty, journeyed across the Muslim world from 1419, spending 25 years in Asia, and gave us the first European account of the Spice Islands, although it's unlikely he actually visited them personally. An anonymous map from 1457, the *Mappamundi*, based on his account includes the island of *Bandam* (Banda), the first of the Spice Islands ever to appear on a European map.[17] The Portuguese took notice, and continued their exploration down the African coast, seeking out and finding their way into the Indian Ocean in 1488.

16. An anonymous Genoese world map from 1457, the first European map to identify one of the Spice Islands. 'Bandam' (Banda) is the red island speculatively placed in the extreme south east of the map. Image credit: US Library of Congress.

---

[17]   *The Cartography of the East Indian Islands,* p. 48.

Yet another Italian, Ludovico Vartherma of Bologna, writing in his *Itinerario* regarding his travels in the East, claims to have visited the Bandas in 1505, which would make this the first recorded European visit to the Spice Islands. However, his description is unconvincing: '*... said island (Banda) is about one hundred miles (or 161 km) in circumference and is very low and flat country*'.

17. The sun sets behind Gunung Api volcano and the island of Bandaneira. Bandaneira, or just Banda, holds the main township of the Bandas and is separated from the volcano by a narrow channel. It is difficult to reconcile Vatherma's description of them as 'low and flat' when approaching from the sea.

The circumference of Banda Besar, the largest of the Banda Islands, is around 32 kilometres, and its central range reaches over 400 metres high. A musket shot away is the island Gunung Api with its active volcano reaching up 666 metres. The hills on the main island of Banda are over 200 metres high in places. Vartherma also claims to have visited the islands where cloves grow (the Moluccas) and found this line of towering volcanos also 'low'. It is hard to envisage an arriving sailor referring to any of the main Spice Islands as low and flat, so it is likely Vatherma's information was second-hand, perhaps gleaned from a sailors' bar in a Sumatran or Malabar port. And by this time the intrepid Portuguese, and Lorosa, were already in India and on the trail to the Spice Islands themselves.

Portugal's journey to the Spice Islands had been a long one, and for its determination, it deserved to win the race. Its tentative explorations down the African coast started with the capture of Ceuta, Morocco, in 1415 and continued slowly south, overcoming the challenges of adverse winds, hostile tribes, lack of water and provisioning stops, and their own superstitions, until they finally rounded the 'fairest Cape of them all' past Africa's southern tip in 1488. The aim of all these journeys was to locate a route into the Indian Ocean that gave access to the spices of the Indies. Ten years later, Vasco da Gama used the seasonal breezes of the monsoon and a local pilot to cross the Indian Ocean, the first captain to sail to India via the Cape of Good Hope.

Here, in the advanced, bustling, cosmopolitan port cities of the subcontinent, the Portuguese found their spices, but these had arrived from much further east. And it was there that they were headed. In 1509 they reached Malacca, South-East Asia's great spice capital, capturing the port sultanate two years later. While the city still smouldered from the battle, an expedition was dispatched with local charts and pilots to find the Spice Islands far to the east, indicating the importance that the Portuguese applied to this task. Both the Bandas and Moluccas were reached by parts of this expedition in 1512.

The Spanish were also after the spices of the Indies, but they took a different route to their Iberian neighbours. Christopher Columbus sailed west in 1492 and reached the Bahamas, and in later voyages Central and South America, but remained convinced they were the Indies, though he was puzzled not to find any spices. A look at two spectacular sixteenth century maps illustrates the comparative Portuguese and Spanish methodologies to reach the Spiceries.

The *Cantino Planisphere*, a mariner's sea chart dating from 1502, is the earliest existing representation of the first Portuguese discoveries. They were extremely guarded with their maritime 'portolan'[18] maps, so terrified of allowing competitors into their spice ports that they levied the death penalty on navigators and mapmakers who leaked 'trade secrets' to foreigners.

Despite this, an Italian spy named Alberto Cantino purchased the chart from an unknown but well-informed source in Lisbon for 12 gold ducats,[19] and delivered it to his boss, the Duke of Ferrara, not far from where it can be seen today in the Biblioteca Estense in Modena, Italy.

---

[18] Portolan charts were charts specifically developed for maritime navigation. Most prominently, they are criss-crossed by rhumb lines emanating from compass roses. In Portuguese service, they were used in conjunction with *Roiteros* (sailing directions) and *Regimentos* (rules and regulations) to define the standard routes to be taken across the world's oceans and seas.

[19] A solid gold coin of around 3.5 grams, widely minted and used throughout Europe in medieval times.

The Italians were astonished, and rightly so, for the chart was not only a 'road map' to the Indies, but also showed in amazing detail the east coast of north America up to modern New York, Brazil, the Caribbean, all of Africa, the Persian Gulf and the Indian Ocean, much of which were largely unknown to contemporary Europe. The implications of the discoveries shown on this chart heralded the demise of the Venetian Empire, at the time one of Europe's most powerful, and the major supplier of spices to the continent.

While the Spice Islands aren't shown—they were yet to be found by the Portuguese navigators—the search for them is the purpose of the chart. Far out to the south-east of this attractive three-piece vellum map lies Malacca, the key to the Spiceries.

By comparison, Flemish cartographer Abraham Ortellius' 1589 *Maris Pacifici* illustrates the Spanish route to the same Spice Islands, by a different and even more arduous route. Columbus, a Genoese sailing for Spain in 1492, had found the Americas while seeking the Indies by heading west from Iberia. But to the Spanish, the Americas were not at this time a destination, they were simply a barrier on their road to the Indies and its spices. That the Americas were in fact separate continents to Asia took a long time to appreciate. What was needed was to find a route around them.

And so it was that Ferdinand Magellan, a Portuguese adventurer in the service of Spain, set out with a little fleet from Seville in 1519 on the most amazing journey in the history of maritime exploration—to reach the Spice Islands from the east, a feat that required traversing the immense Atlantic and a totally unknown Pacific; in total over 230 degrees of longitude.

Magellan, luckily, had what would today be called 'inside information'. He had already fought for the Portuguese at Malacca in 1511, alongside his friend Francisco Serrao. Magellan then returned to Europe, but Serrao had been part of the first Portuguese reconnaissance to the Spice Islands in 1512, and had jumped ship at Ternate, married a local princess and become military advisor to the island's sultan. He had written to Magellan, encouraging a voyage from the east so the two could link up as lords of the Spiceries, and Magellan had then convinced the Spanish king to sponsor the venture.

Magellan was just 1500 nautical miles away from being the world's first circumnavigator when he was cut down in a petty skirmish on Mactan in the Philippines, a couple of week's sailing from his furthest confirmed easterly bearing at Malacca.[20] In a touch of extreme irony, Serrao had died of poisoning at the Ternate

[20] Andre Rossfelder in *In Pursuit of Longitude* p. 81 argues—as have others—that Magellan was likely to have been dispatched on reconnaissance missions during the 18 undocumented months he spent in Malacca after the capture of that port city, and may have already explored west to the longitude

court around the same time, and only 700 sea miles from where his friend Magellan met his end. It is intriguing to imagine how Spice Islands history may have turned out had these two ambitious and battle-hardened warriors linked up on Ternate.

Ortellius' map, appearing 86 years after Cantino's *Planisphere*, was also revolutionary. The first to show the entire Pacific Ocean and large sections of the western coasts of the Americas, it also places several of the Spice Islands correctly astride the equator, including Ternate (*Terenate*), Tidore, Machian, Bachian and Banda (*Bandan*).

Again, they are the purpose of the map. What is intriguing is that while the tiny Spice Islands of the Moluccas and the Bandas are located with some accuracy, much more significant islands such as Japan, Taiwan, the principal Philippines, Java and New Guinea are misplaced and misshapen. It was clearly the Spice Islands the Spanish were focused on.

In the later 1520s and 1530s a number of maps came out in Europe reflecting the cartographic knowledge that had arisen from the Magellan voyage and subsequent Spanish expeditions which followed the same gruelling trans-Pacific route. Until the last quarter of the sixteenth century, the Iberian monopoly on Asian voyages would be interrupted only by the French Parmentier brothers making Sumatra in 1529. Both succumbed to disease there, but other returning survivors of that voyage provided much material for the famous Dieppe School of mapmakers in France.

Gradually, the tiny Spice Islands became a fixture on Asian and Pacific maps, even though much more prominent insular landmasses—for example, Ceylon, Sumatra, Borneo, Taiwan, Japan, New Guinea and Sulawesi—were misplaced, inaccurately detailed or missing altogether. With Munster's *Cosmographia* of 1540, we start to see the correct relationship between the Spice Islands, the Philippines and Asia. Gastaldi's *South-East Asia* in 1548 incorrectly shows Ternate on Halmahera, but also includes 'Anbon', 'Baca', 'Machian', 'Motil' and 'Tidora'.

By the time the first Dutch and English voyages arrived in the region from 1595, navigators knew where the Spice Islands could be found, and how incredibly remote they were. The general term 'Spice Islands' became subdivided into the Moluccas off Halmahera, which produced cloves, and the Banda nutmeg islands 400 sea[21] miles to the south.

---

of Mactan on voyages to the Philippines or the Spice Islands. This would make him the very first circumnavigator.

[21]   Sea miles and nautical miles are used interchangeably. Both equal 1.85 km or 1.15 imperial miles.

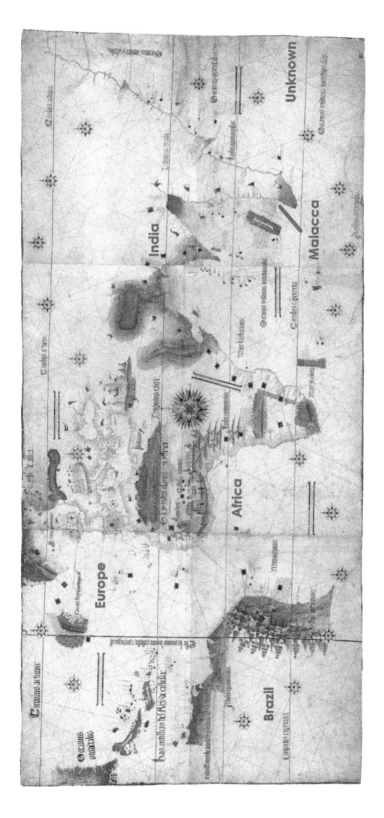

18. The stunning Cantino *Planisphere* created by an unknown Portuguese mapmaker in 1502 for an Italian spy, Alberto Cantino, and now held by the Biblioteca Estense Universitaria, Modena, Italy. It was stunning not just because of its beauty, but because the rest of Europe had no idea that the Portuguese had explored so widely. Image credit: Biblioteca Estense Universitaria.

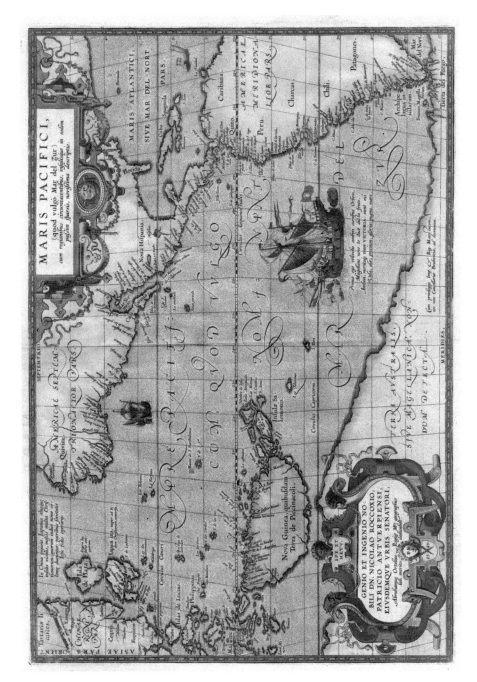

19. *Maris Pacifici*, engraved in 1589 and published the next year by Abraham Ortelius, was the first map focused on the Pacific Ocean and shows the *Victoria*, which went on after Magellan died to pick up a load of cloves at Tidore and circumnavigate the earth, the first to do so. The Spice Islands are at the extreme left of the chart, west of New Guinea.

Image credit: Paulus Swaen Old Maps

20. Ship-wrecking reefs, blazing heat and humidity, exploding volcanos and maddening seasonal winds made the spice-laden islands no sailors' paradise, but the early colonial adventurers must have been struck by the rugged beauty of these remote and mystical islands. This view looks from Run in the Bandas to the main islands of the group in the distance.

Plancius' *Insulae Moluccae* from 1595 is a spectacular example of the status of nautical charting at the time the first Dutch ships sailed to the Indies, and an indicator of the vital importance of nutmeg and cloves—illustrated along the base of the map— throughout the wider region. Continual improvements in navigation and science occurred during the seventeenth century, but it is interesting that even in the late part of that century, adjacent islands such as New Guinea were only marginally understood.

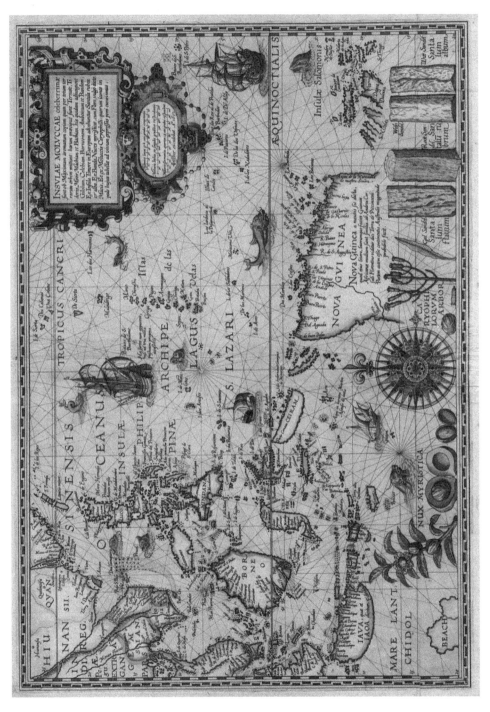

21. Petrus Plancius' *Insulae Moluccae*, first issued in 1592. This was the Dutch road map to the Spice Islands, and a few years after it was released the first fleet from the Netherlands found the islands. It is the most stunning of all Indies maps and only a few dozen copies exist; an uncoloured version recently sold for US$75,000.
Image credit: Helmink Antique Maps.

22. Part of the *Hondius* map of 1629, one of the first publicly available maps to include a stretch of Australian coastline—part of the western side of Cape York, shown on the lower right. VOC skipper Willem Janzoon did not recognise the gap in his chart as the strait between the 'Southland' and New Guinea in 1606, and after losing nearly half his crew in an attack by aboriginals, he turned back to the Indies. Later that same year in September, Spaniard Luis Torres arrived from Peru and became the first captain to thread his way through the reefs of the Strait later named after him.

And not only did the search for the Spice Islands lead directly to the discovery of the Americas, but they facilitated the world putting the great south land, the continent of Australia, on the map for the first time. The VOC ship *Duyfken*, under Willem Janzoon, departed the nutmeg capital, Banda—most easterly of the Dutch bases in the Indies—on a voyage of exploration to the south-east and provided the first known charts of the Australian coast, when it came upon the western side of Cape York in March 1606.

Janzoon failed to appreciate the strait between New Guinea and Australia and never considered them separate land masses. A few months later, Spaniard Luis Torres, after a long journey in the *San Pedro* from Peru via Vanuatu discovered the strait that now bears his name, separating New Guinea and Australia, sailed through it from east to west and then ran north with the trade winds to anchor off Kastella at Ternate.

23. The replica *Duyfken*, built at Fremantle, Australia, in 1999 under full sail in a light breeze. It carries around 2900 square metres of flax canvas with hemp running rigging on a keel of 17 metres and displaces 110 tonnes. Since completion, it has voyaged to the Spice Islands, the Netherlands and around Australia, including to Cape York, sighted by its namesake in 1606, 164 years before Cook's arrival. *Duyfken* is based in Perth and available for day sails on the Swan River, while the Duyfken 1606 Replica Foundation plans its next oceanic voyage. The original *Duyfken* lies off Ternate, crippled in a battle with Spanish galleys in 1608. See duyfken.com.
Image credit: Duyfken Foundation.

Returning to Pedro Lorosa on Ternate in 1521, the two ships he watched drop anchor were the last survivors of Magellan's Spanish squadron. They were the first to cross the Pacific, having left Spain just over two years before. Magellan himself had been killed a few weeks previously in a skirmish in the Philippines, and one of the ships, the *Victoria* under Juan Sebastian Elcano, would soon sail off to the west and immortality to complete the first circumnavigation of the earth.

What was momentous about this largely overlooked occasion was that the subsequent meeting between the Spaniards and Lorosa on Tidore represented the closing of the world for the very first time. For Lorosa had arrived from the west around

Africa, and Magellan's ships had reached the Spice Islands from the east, around the Americas. It was the first time humans had circled the globe.

The Portuguese had navigated 120 degrees of longitude, the Spanish much more at around 240 degrees, but both journeys were similar lengths at between 15,000 and 16,000 nautical miles. After a century of battling storms, contrary winds, reefs, adversaries and pirates across unknown oceans, Iberian sailors had finally defined the circumference of the earth and done so right at the equator. And they had also put the Spice Islands on the map. It was an incredible achievement.

3. Pre-colonial times to 1512

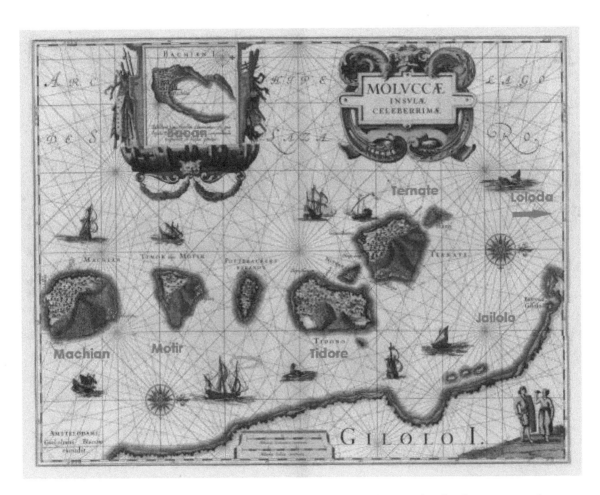

24. *Insulae Moluccae*, c. 1640. An engaging Spice Islands map by the famous Dutch cartographer Willem Blaeu. North is to the right. The original 'divine' kingdoms of the Moluccas were Loloda (off the map to the north), then Jailolo, Ternate, Tidore and Bacan (shown in insert; it was further to the south). The great island of Halmahera, shown along the bottom (east) side of this map was also called Gilolo. To give an idea of the scale of the map, from the north of Ternate to the south of Machian (Makian) is 66 kilometres.

25. A Hemisferium reproduction of an 'oriental' astrolabe from Lahore (in today's Pakistan) dating from 1647. Arab and Persian mariners traded from East Africa to China over a thousand years ago using similar equipment and were aware of the Spice Islands as early as 850 AD. Islamic scientists refined Classical Greek navigational techniques and instruments, some of which later found their way to the Iberian Peninsula and were then used by the Spanish following the Reconquest in 1492. The Portuguese relied on Arab navigators to show them the initial path across the Indian Ocean to Malacca around 1500. Astrolabes such as this were in use on dhows across the Indian Ocean into the 1800s. See hemisferium.net.

According to legends that were told as ballads and passed down through the mists of time, the rulers of the first five kingdoms of the northern Moluccas were divine. Original, and most powerful, was the kingdom of Loloda, on Halmahera, which was then followed by the kingdoms of Ternate, Tidore, Jailolo and Bacan. Jailolo's king, or *kolano*, was 'Ruler of the Bay'; Tidore's 'Ruler of the Mountain'; Bacan's was 'Ruler of the Far End'; and Ternate's, signifying his pre-eminence, was 'Ruler of Maluku'. By 1500 Ternate's sultanate was the most powerful of the four traditional kingdoms; the original Loloda by this time having declined to insignificance.[22]

As no pre-colonial written accounts of the Spice Islands have survived, we are dependent on the early Iberian chroniclers for descriptions of the cultural, economic and military affairs in the region prior to European arrival. Naturally, the Portuguese and Spanish were focused on the military capabilities and weaponry of the local kings and so Tome Pires' *Suma Oriental* of 1515, Governor Galvao's account from around 1544 and Bartholomew Argensola's *History of the Discovery and Conquest of the Molucco and Philippine Islands* from 1609, are very revealing on these matters.

When the Portuguese sailed into the waters of the Indies in the early years of the sixteenth century, the main regional influence was the extent of Islamisation of the archipelago. Islam had arrived only around half a century before the Portuguese caravels, brought by Arab and Malay traders out of Malacca, to where it had spread by 1414 from the port cities of India. By 1500, the rulers of Ternate, Tidore, Jailolo, Bacan and Banda were all Muslims, as were the elite of their societies, while the balance of the population continued with traditional forms of worship. The extension of Islam into the region and the development of Malacca as the regional trade hub coincided with the decline of Ming China's maritime influence in the area.

The Portuguese categorised the various kingdoms according to their available manpower, the size of their fleets of *korakora*,[23] and the wealth they derived from their spice crops: cloves in the Moluccas and nutmeg in the Bandas.

Ternate's principal rival and immediate neighbour was Tidore. Both islands contained around 2000 fighting men, but Ternate had a slightly larger fleet of around 100 korakora, as opposed to the 80 of Tidore.[24] Ternate's area of influence included parts of eastern Sulawesi, the Sula Islands, Bacan, most of northern and parts of south-

---

[22] See *The World of Maluku*, Chapter 2.

[23] *Korakora* were long, slim outrigger canoes used for raiding, the largest capable of carrying hundreds of men. They were paddled from the outriggers, capable of high sprint speeds, but unstable in other than calm conditions. A sultan's power in the Spice Islands was defined by how many korakora he could put to sea.

[24] *Suma Oriental,* p. 214.

western Halmahera and half of Motir, while Tidore's power base included Makian, the other half of Motir, and extended across southern Halmahera and throughout the islands to the Papuan mainland. Both Ternate and Tidore produced clove crops of around 400 tonnes[25] per year.

26. A Spice Islands korakora (or corcoa) with double outriggers, around 45 rowers, 50 soldiers and armed with a cannon and lighter guns. They were hazardous in any seaway and carried very limited water and food supplies, but they struck terror into anyone who saw them approaching.

Makian, favoured port of Javanese traders and vassal of Tidore, fielded around 3000 men, had 130 korakora and also produced about 400 tonnes of cloves. Motir, located between Tidore and Makian, held 600 men and grew around 320 tonnes of cloves.

---

[25] A *bahar* equalled around 270 kg at the time (*Suma Oriental*, p. 277), each island producing around 1500 bahars.

Bacan, further south, was aligned with Ternate and had the largest fleet and most manpower of all the islands, but only limited wild cloves.

The kingdom of Jailolo was the most powerful on Halmahera. It had a large force of warriors and many korakora but, like Bacan, only some wild cloves. Off the north of Halmahera, Morotai was controlled equally by Ternate and Tidore, and grew a large quantity of the local food staple, sago.[26]

27. Spice Islands scene: a coastal village ringed by coral reefs and steep jungle, clustered around a mosque and an anchorage. This is the main village on Run, outermost of the Bandas, and once the key English base of Nathaniel Courthope.

The Moluccas with their clove wealth, korakora fleets and concentrated manpower were the only regional powers capable of large-scale expeditionary warfare. To the south (refer to Introduction map), the larger islands of Ambon, Buru and Seram had dispersed populations and no spices. Because there was little trade, Islam did not yet

---

[26] *Suma Oriental,* pp. 214–8.

significantly penetrate them. Settlements there were based more on independent village communities, rather than aggregated into kingdoms as in the Moluccas, and because they had no nutmeg or cloves, they lacked wealth, had not formed into complex societies and lacked significant military capability. Any power they had was often dissipated in senseless ongoing warfare with neighbouring villages.

Further south again, the Bandas had wealth from nutmeg, contained a total of around 3000 people across the entire island group and were governed by local councils of elders, rather than a single ruler. In total, the islands produced about 135 tonnes of mace and 1600 of nutmeg each year. Mace was roughly equal in price to cloves for similar weights, and nutmeg around one-seventh the value of cloves. Hence, the annual wealth of all the Bandas in spice terms was around three-quarters of that of either Ternate or Tidore.

The Bandanese were the only maritime traders of the Spice Islands, maintaining a number of junks which brought in food and cloth from Java, but had few korakora. Because they were on the trade routes from Java, they often suffered from raids and pirates, and maintained mountain hideouts where the population could flee when attackers arrived.

Spice Islands warfare

Argensola describes the Moluccans as '... *strong, much addicted to warfare, but lazy in all other tasks*'. Tome Pires says, '*They are at war with one another most of the time*'.

Being blessed with the world's only bounty of clove trees meant, economically, they did not need to toil at agriculture; hence their time could be spent much more profitably raiding and pillaging. Because the dispersed island populations were relatively small, however, manpower was a crucial commodity. There was no desire to waste the limited resource of warriors in fruitless conflict against equally numerous adversaries, and so dramatically outnumbering an enemy seems to have been a favourite tactic.

Maritime raiding allowed a concentrated force to be deployed that would be superior in numbers to any single settlement. Inevitably, the defenders would take to the hills, abandoning their reed and timber houses, which could quickly be rebuilt in any case. Like the Bandanese, many communities would have fallen back to the safety of remote hideouts where their valuables were already stored.

Full-scale battles and sieges were unheard of; skirmishes and raiding were the norm. On Ternate and Tidore, each village was required to maintain a number of korakora commensurate with their population, with all their associated equipment and weaponry, and be ready to combine with others whenever the sultan decreed.

28. Anonymous Dutch watercolour from around 1700 of an Ambonese warrior. His personal arms are representative of the basic Spice Islands individual weapons for hundreds of years before this time.
Image credit: Rijksmuseum.

A typical raid might involve a few dozen korakora, led by the sultan's flagship, carrying altogether several hundred men. They might travel for several days or a few weeks, overnighting at friendly settlements or isolated coastal reaches along the way, then descend on their target, aiming to secure any valuables or food, and some captives who could be used as slaves or on-sold. The danger with raiding with too large a force was that the home island was vulnerable when they were away. For example, Ternate and Tidore are just two kilometres apart, so when one sultan was seen leaving to raid with his fleet and the pick of his warriors, it was something of an invitation to his rival to attack the island in his absence.

Argensola, describing maritime warfare at the start of the seventeenth century, writes that korakora had:

> '... about 100 men row in each of them, to the sound of a Tambour and a Bell. They carry twenty Soldiers, and six Musketiers. The rest are employed around four or five little Brass Guns. Both the Men that Row, and the Soldiers are armed with Cymiters, and Shields and an abundance of Calabays, and Sagus, being long Canes burnt in the Fire, to harden them; which they throw, without tacking, as the Moors do their Darts. Their way of fighting is to come within Gunshot and as soon as they have Fired, both sides fly with all speed, till they have Loaded again, and then return to the same Post.'

In Asia generally in pre-colonial times, the concept of state-funded standing naval forces was rare. It was the Portuguese arrival with powerful cannon-armed ships in the early 1500s that led to the formation of various Indian, Javanese and Chinese coastguard fleets to combat them. In view of this, the korakora fleets maintained by the Moluccan sultans were something of a novelty.

Fortifications were built at key points, but these differed from the later European forts of the area. Firstly, rather than being positioned on the coast to facilitate trade, resupply and naval support, they were often located up steep mountains inland, such as the Jailolo fortress that the Portuguese captured under Tristao de Altaide in 1533, or the royal fort at Gamafo on Tidore taken by Antonio Galvao in 1536. They relied more on their distance from the coast and a difficult ascent than strong walls. The danger of the attacker's vessels being destroyed by a force hidden in the jungle nearby while they were advancing inland to assault the fort was the nightmare of any such invader.

Secondly, the forts relied on earth walls and timber palisades, rather than stone, and so were less sturdy, and vulnerable to artillery.

Thirdly, they liked to have a secure retreat route into jungle if the besiegers were considered too strong, whereas European forts were designed to withstand sieges with no thought of leaving the safety of the walls.

29. When the Portuguese first arrived in Asia around 1500, cannon were already being produced in the region. Most of the weapons captured at Malacca were accredited to Indian founders from Burma and Chinese gunmakers from Siam, although other guns came from Calicut in India. China, which had pioneered gunpowder armed warships from the 1200s, had by 1500 fallen far behind in weapon technology and eagerly accepted modern Portuguese cannon as gifts. The Portuguese also introduced firearms to Japan from the 1540s. This is an example of a locally produced 'lantaka' type bronze swivel gun from the eighteenth century in the grounds of the Maulana Hotel, Banda.

Finally, they lacked modern firearms for defence. When Albuquerque's men stormed Malacca in 1511, they captured 3000 pieces of artillery; two-thirds of bronze and the remainder iron *berco*-size swivel guns able to fire a three-pound ball.[27] It is not clear however that such weapons had made it to the Spice Islands by this time in any quantity, if at all. In any case, competent use of such arms required training, discipline, reliable shot and gunpowder, knowledge of loading and aiming, and an understanding of the tactics associated with their use. Even at Malacca in 1511, this combination of

---

[27] *Albuquerque: Caesar of the East*, p. 89.

requirements was not present and the firearms used in its defence against the Portuguese attack were poorly served.

30. Local mosque seen through the ruins of the Portuguese tower at Kastella, on Ternate. The relationship between European forts and local Islamic communities was generally tense.

Sultan Abu Lais' interest in Serrao's small force of musketeers in 1512[28] and the Rajah of Jailolo's intense attention to Spanish weaponry in 1522[29] lend support to the assertion that firearms had not arrived in the Spice Islands to significantly change traditional warfare—if at all—by the time the Iberians arrived.

Galvao, Portuguese captain of Ternate writing around 1544, describes the Moluccan offensive arms as:

---

[28] *The Discovery and Conquest of the Molucco and Philippines Islands,* p. 5.

[29] *Magellan,* p. 216.

'... swords called pedang, with only one edge, very wide and of a fair length. The hilts are of wood and the guards of a tin alloyed with lead ... The swords are of dull iron and heavy. They are able to cut a person through the waist with one stroke.' ... 'They have Javanese krisses, which are like serpentine daggers. They use missiles resembling harpoons, which are called turana ... lances made from long cane sticks ... and canes like rods into which wooden barbed points have been placed ... they can certainly pierce a double coat of mail.'

For defensive arms, they wear *'... padded suits, like house coats, which reach halfway down the leg and cover neck and head to the ears; their name is* barut. *They use cuirasses made from coarse buffalo hide ... They make shields six or seven palms long and two palms wide'*. He also notes they have *'... lances, surcoats, coats of mail, bucklers, helmets, bombards and muskets'*, the latter imported from Malacca, Java and Banda, given by the Spanish or captured from the Portuguese.

Of battle, Galvao says:

'They are always waging war, they enjoy it; they live and support themselves by it. They kill and capture each other ... they never spare each other, and they immediately cut off the other's head ... They go in for tricks and traps, and they are men expert at arms.'

One of the rules of war among the Moluccans was never to wound or kill a royal—a rule which Governor Galvao broke when he slew Prince Bohejat, leading his counterattacking troops at Tidore in 1536, much to the astonishment of the Prince's men.

Regional snapshot

Around the compass from the Spice Islands, sultanates and small-scale societies were scattered, owing their existence to either trade, agriculture or raiding, or a combination of all three. To the east New Guinea was a wild land of dispersed tribes and head-hunters, its main article of value being the colourful feathers of the bird of paradise, much desired in Ottoman martial headgear.

To the north were the thousands of islands of what are now the Philippines, which would soon become the Spanish East Indies. Islam was established then as now in the southern islands around Jolo and Sulu, but otherwise large cities, extensive trade and standing military forces were lacking.

On Sulawesi (also Celebes) to the west was a multitude of small kingdoms, all either targets of Spice Islander raiding, or themselves occasional raiders of the Spiceries. The Bugis of Sulawesi were particularly renowned for maritime piracy and marauding and would eventually become a headache for the Dutch until the Sultanate of Makassar was destroyed in 1667. Further west again on enormous Borneo, small coastal communities were the norm, except for the sophisticated and powerful Sultanate of Brunei, which would be smashed by the Spanish in 1578.

31. Ternate city, dotted with mosques, faces the dawn over Halmahera. The colonial era dawned in the Spice Islands with the arrival of the Portuguese in 1512 and extended until 1949.

To the south-west the regional power was the Hindu Majapahit Empire, based on northern Java. By 1400 its golden age had passed and it was in decline—a decline accelerated by the emergence of nearby Malacca as the dominant regional trading centre. The Majapahits had been a trading empire based on distributing the valuable natural resources of the region to the Asian mainland empires in China, India and modern South-East Asia. Sandalwood from Timor, camphor from Sulawesi, pepper from Sumatra, rice from Java, gold from Sulawesi, Borneo and Sumatra and, of course, nutmeg and cloves from the Spice Islands were the principal exports. They practised large-scale maritime expeditionary warfare using a cousin of the korakora and exercised a loose authority over much of today's Indonesia. They had at the end of thirteenth century even defeated a Mongol invasion by Kublai Khan, but by the time of the European arrival two centuries later, were largely a spent force.

As the sixteenth century dawned across the region, no longer would the Spice Islanders and traders of South-East Asia have the lands of nutmeg and cloves to themselves—the Europeans were coming, lured by the intoxicating profits of these rare and precious spices.

4. The Portuguese period 1512–1575

32. Elmina fortress, built by the Portuguese in 1482 and held until taken by the Dutch in 1637, as seen today, on the coast of Ghana, west Africa. The modern fort was heavily modified by the Dutch and subsequently the British (from 1792), but the high round tower visible on the right formed part of the original Portuguese work.

Portugal's endeavours to establish an empire in the early colonial period are nothing short of astonishing. Despite being an insignificant, underpopulated, predominantly agricultural backwater on the periphery of Europe, not only did the country manage to navigate the Atlantic and Indian oceans as well as the seas of Asia to locate the Spiceries when much of Europe still envisaged the Indian Ocean as landlocked, but by hijacking the spice trade, Portugal dealt fatal blows to the Venetian and Marmeluke Empires, defeated a host of powerful Asian entities and followed this up by emerging the victor after a lengthy confrontation with Spain, Europe's pre-eminent military power of the time.

Much of the credit for the sophisticated strategy of creating the first global maritime empire should go to the House of Avis, Portugal's ruling dynasty since 1385. John I, head of the Avis line, embarked on Portugal's initial overseas venture in 1415 by storming the North African city of Ceuta, which itself had been the springboard for the Islamic invasion of Iberia 700 years earlier.

Destruction of Islam was one of the fundamentals of Portuguese strategy, but this crusading zeal had to coexist with more mundane commercial imperatives, like finding the source of the gold and spices that were so valuable in contemporary Europe.

Among the riches of Ceuta were considerable quantities of gold which had arrived from south of the Sahara. Illustrating their systematic approach to achieving their goals, the Portuguese decided to locate the source not by camel, but by caravel. Exploring slowly and fearfully down the African coast, by 1471 they found the gold in today's Ghana, and in 1482 built Elmina, first of a chain of forts that would soon stretch all the way to China.

Taking a ton of gold back to Europe from Elmina in the 70 years from 1490 — as well as slaves and ivory — the Portuguese financed their further efforts in the quest for the spices of the East. The Avis kings took this quest seriously and addressed the challenges with a vigorous and methodical approach. Spies were sent overland to India and Ethiopia to report back; the science of oceanic navigation was funded and promoted; new technology was applied to ship design; cartographers and their maps were gathered from across Europe and studied; new light but hard-hitting stone-firing *perrier* cannon were designed and built in quantity for the caravels; and a class of experienced mariners, navigators and ship masters began to form.

In 1498 Vasco da Gama was first to cross the Indian Ocean and reach the wealthy cosmopolitan trading ports of the subcontinent. Here he found the spices they were looking for: cinnamon, pepper, nutmeg and cloves.

When the next Portuguese fleet to the East under Cabral arrived on the Indian coast at Calicut in 1500, with the *zamorin's*[30] permission they set up a trading post to accumulate spices to fill the holds of future fleets. They were initially intent on trade not conflict. Relations with the local Arab merchants, who correctly recognised the newcomers as a real threat to their ongoing commerce, deteriorated however, and when the Portuguese factor and dozens of his staff were massacred by the Arabs, the Portuguese retaliated. They bombarded Calicut, sunk all the ships in the harbour, razed the town and set up a base in a rival port nearby, Cochin.

No maritime states in the Indian Ocean fielded blue water naval forces in these times, and so the superiority of the Portuguese ship technology, tactics and weaponry

---

[30]   A zamorin was a hereditary Hindu monarch.

was quickly demonstrated to all. Ships sailing in the Indian Ocean not carrying a Portuguese *cartaz*[31] were plundered and sunk by the wide-ranging caravels and carracks. In response, the Mamelukes in Egypt, with no ships available beyond the Mediterranean, ordered construction of a fleet to take on the Portuguese, and when it was ready 20 Red Sea–built dhows joined a force of around 60 smaller Malabar craft loaded with thousands of men.

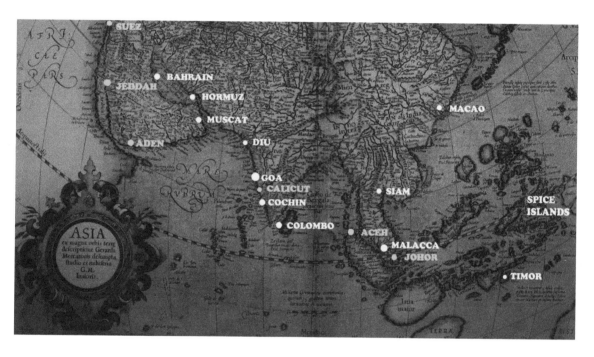

33. *Asia* by the legendary Flemish cartographer, Gerhard Mercator, first appeared in 1595. The Portuguese (selected forts or trade posts in yellow), with major bases at Goa and Malacca, had control over virtually the entire Indian Ocean, the Persian Gulf and the route around the Cape. Muslim strongholds are in green. The Ottomans had taken control of the Red Sea, to which Aceh was able to ship some spices, avoiding the Portuguese stranglehold. The Spanish at Manila faced the long haul east to Mexico for support.

The Portuguese fleet of six caravels and a dozen carracks under da Gama took them on, off Calicut in 1503. In the first major demonstration of how a fleet should use line-ahead stand-off gunfire, da Gama smashed the combined armada without his fleet sustaining serious damage. Again in 1508, the Egyptians tried to clear the western

---

[31]   A permit to trade in the Indian Ocean, issued-for a fee-by the Portuguese authorities.

Indian Ocean of Portuguese seapower, dispatching a fleet of new galleys—partially organised by Venice—that combined with local shipping. Although they managed to defeat a small Portuguese squadron at Chaul, they were destroyed by the main fleet at Diu in 1509.

34. Albuquerque, architect of the Estado da India (Portuguese India). He captured Malacca, established Goa, dispatched the first expedition to the Spice Islands and built forts across the littoral of the Indian Ocean.

Under the strategic genius of Albuquerque, Governor of India from 1509 to his death in 1515, Portugal's Estado da India rapidly took shape. His main achievements were capturing the western and eastern chokepoints of the Indian Ocean, Malacca (1511) and Hormuz (1515), and fortifying them, and in 1510 establishing Goa as the capital of the empire. It would remain in Portuguese hands until invaded by India in 1961. He also built forts on the African coast at Sofala (1505) and Mozambique (1507), and on the Arabian Peninsula at Muscat (1507) and Socotra (1507), along with others on the Indian west coast to support Goa.

Albuquerque's capture of Malacca was a crucial step on the road to the Spiceries—not only did the spices of Asia amass there, but local pilots knew where to find the Spice Islands, far to the east. Malacca became a strategic Portuguese base; the guardian of the Straits, the pivot between the Indian Ocean and the China seas. From here, Albuquerque launched the first expedition to the distant Spice Islands in late 1511.

Portugal finds the Spice Islands

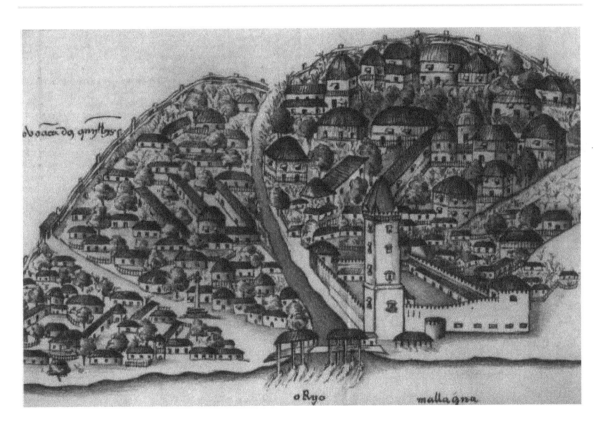

35. A view of Malacca by Gaspar Correia shortly after its capture, showing the new Portuguese fort and tower. The bridge across the river was the main battleground in the struggle for the city. After an initial repulse, Albuquerque rammed a junk loaded with soldiers and swivel guns into the bridge and fought off several counterattacks before the sultan fled and victory was achieved.

When this little three-ship fleet under de Abreu found the Bandas in 1512, they were concerned with securing the priceless spices that had been the purpose of Portuguese exploration strategy for a century, not colonisation. They loaded up with nutmeg and mace and returned to Malacca (losing one ship en route; more on this ship later), the round voyage taking a year.

Another small fleet visited Banda in 1513, again, filling with nutmeg and tracing the route back to Malacca with the trade winds. The Portuguese were content to send regular trading voyages to the remote Spiceries from Malacca rather than attempt colonisation, secure in the knowledge that no other European powers had the faintest idea where to find them. Fortress building this far east was not yet on their agenda.

In 1515, a third Portuguese fleet finally discovered Ternate, capital of the clove islands of the northern Moluccas, and was quite surprised to find some Portuguese from de Abreu's missing ship there.

That ship, captained by Francisco Serrao, had separated from the others in a storm after leaving Banda in 1512, and was then shipwrecked nearby. After some travails, Serrao finally ended up in Seram then Ambon, fully armed and with a dozen of his men. With their armour and uniforms, arquebuses, military bearing and battle experience, Serrao's small troop were clearly an asset for any warring prince of the Indies, of which there were many.

Indeed, when they landed at Rucutelo on the north coast of Seram, they assisted that settlement in battle, bringing victory against the neighbouring town of Veranula.[32] The local superpowers, the Sultan of Ternate and Rajah of Tidore, heard of these strange men and each vied for their favour, dispatching a squadron of korakora to pick them up. Ternate's Sultan Abu Lais (also Bayan Sirrullah or Bolief) won the race, and brought Serrao's group back to Ternate as his honoured guests, the first Europeans to set foot on these legendary islands of cloves.

Ternate and Tidore were in a state of almost constant warfare. It was low-key warfare, with enthusiasm tempered greatly by the tropical heat and the limitations of their weapons, but the implications of their conflict extended right across the Spice Islands. Both sultans eagerly sought the services of Serrao in 1512, not just because of his little troop of soldiers, but because he represented a new and powerful force that had just arrived in the region, a force that could be decisive in their ongoing conflict. These Moluccan rulers had heard of the fall of their co-religionists at Malacca, from where traders buying their cloves had always sailed, but in the interests of aligning themselves with Portuguese power, they competed to offer the newcomers a regional base.

Serrao had boarded the first korakora to arrive, those of Ternate, and so the Portuguese found themselves established there. While he was in no way an official ambassador of the governor at Goa or the court in Lisbon, Serrao developed a strong

---

[32] *The Discovery and Conquest of the Molucco and Philippines Islands*, p. 5.

relationship with the sultan, who retained him as a military advisor and sought enhanced Portuguese relations. This relationship with Portugal increased his prestige among the lesser kings of the region. He declared himself a vassal of King Manuel and asked for a fort to be built and his soldiers to be armed and trained in modern weapons.

The Portuguese authorities in Malacca were in a difficult position regarding Serrao. He refused to return to Malacca and was essentially a renegade, though with the ear of the most powerful ruler of the Spice Islands, a very influential one. And while he had 'gone native' and married a local princess, he was still favourably disposed to Portugal. While the spices kept coming, the Governor was not overly concerned.

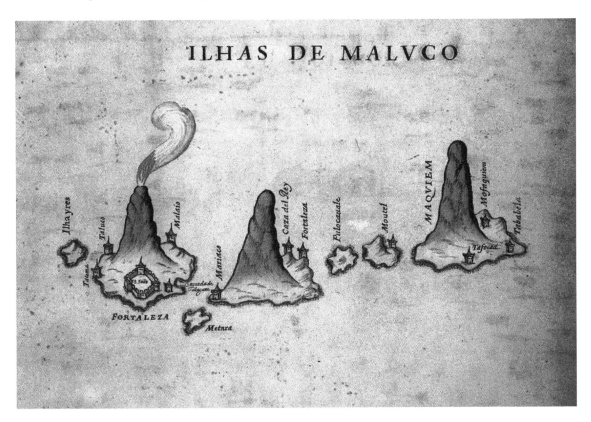

36. A fascinating image of the Moluccas showing the three major (Ternate is on the left, then Tidore, with Makian on the right) and four minor islands, some of the forts and an enhanced scale of the volcanos. The map was included in a survey of Portuguese forts across the empire by Antonio Bocarro from 1635, just as the colonial spice wars were winding down. North is at left.
Image credit: Biblioteca Publica de Evora.

Strategic direction for the Estado da India—which governed Portugal's possessions in the Indian Ocean and Asia—was provided by the royal court in Lisbon, but the communication difficulties associated with the length of the voyage from Europe meant that the king's representative in Goa had to exercise considerable autonomy.

Receiving an answer from the viceroy at Goa in response to a query sent by the king in Lisbon took a minimum of 18 months but could take as long as three years. And Goa was only half the voyage from Lisbon to Ternate. Before receiving orders from the king to fortify the Spice Islands, Governor Diogo de Sequeira at Goa had already appreciated the need, and dispatched an expedition commanded by Tristao de Meneses to do exactly that in late 1518.

37. Makian was a major clove producer with control often shared between Ternate and Tidore. The first Spice Islands fort was intended to be built here to avoid alienating either of those kingdoms, but ended up instead on Ternate. Note how the island has been nearly rent in two by volcanic activity associated with the 1357-metre Kie Besi. In the most recent major eruption in 1988, the island's entire 15,000 population needed to be evacuated.

The fort had been intended for the clove rich island of Makian, control of which was at the time shared by Ternate and Tidore and would therefore have been on 'neutral' ground, but Ternate's sultan with Serrao's backing argued with de Meneses for construction on Ternate.[33] Not wanting to defy them, de Meneses surveyed a location

---

[33] *A Man in the Shadow of Magellan,* p. 109.

on Ternate where Kastella would later be built, voyaged to Banda and Ambon while waiting for favourable easterlies, then took on a load of cloves and sailed back to Malacca, intending to allow the governor at Goa to make the final decision on the fort's location. By coincidence, at Malacca in 1521 he met the de Brito fleet with orders from King Manuel to build a fort on Ternate as a bulwark against Magellan.

Back in early 1519 in Lisbon, intelligence had arrived that a Portuguese adventurer (and good friend of Serrao), Ferdinand Magellan, was preparing a voyage in the service of arch-rival Spain to approach the Spice Islands from the east. Magellan knew the Indies well, had already fought for Portugal extensively, including at the destruction of the Egyptian fleet at Diu in 1509 and with Serrao at the capture of Malacca in 1511, but had recently fallen from favour with King Manuel.

Manuel was worried that the Spice Islands his fleets were already trading with may actually be in the agreed Spanish sphere of control, as defined by the 1494 Treaty of Tordesillas, which astonishingly divided the unknown world between the two Iberian nations. While nautical science of this era could reliably track the latitude element of a journey, the longitude could only be estimated, and so no one could say with certainty in which hemisphere the Spice Islands lay. The source of his newfound wealth might be taken away, and this Manuel would not stand for.

But when Magellan's plans became known to the king, the 1519 Portuguese fleet had already left Lisbon, under Jorge de Albuquerque. With 18 ships, it was stronger than in the previous several years, but had a long list of forts to build, tribute to collect, kingdoms to send embassies to, recalcitrant rulers to punish and trade factories to establish. Manuel's orders had to wait for the next Indian fleet.

Magellan arrives from the east

Meanwhile, Magellan's five-ship squadron set off from Sanlucar de Barrameda at the mouth of the Guadalquivir River near Seville in September 1519. News of his departure was carried from Lisbon in the ten-ship fleet of Jorge de Brito departing in early 1520. Among many other missions, de Brito was to intercept Magellan and to build then command a fort on Ternate. Other Portuguese squadrons were sent unsuccessfully to South America and the Cape of Good Hope to intercept Magellan's ships.[34]

The urgency for a Ternate fort may have been obvious in Lisbon, but the strategic situation in the Portuguese Indies at the time was precarious, and because of the long

---

34 *Magellan*, p. 214.

communications lag, not all of this was understood in the king's court. Extensive campaigns were constantly required from East Africa to the East Indies to maintain and expand the young empire in the face of determined resistance from powerful Muslim opponents, who naturally resented their lucrative spice trade being interrupted.

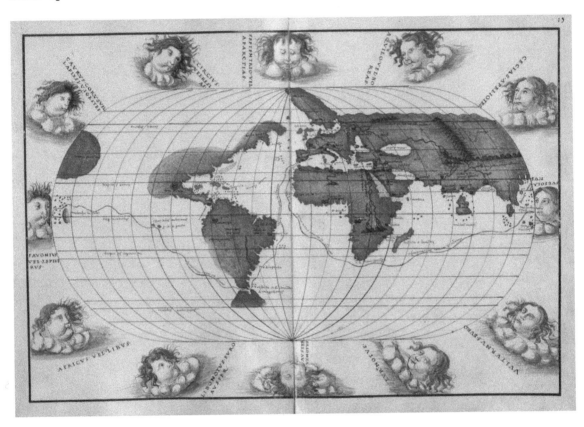

38. Produced around 1544 by Genoese mapmaker Battista Agnese in Venice, this impressive world map was part of an atlas of portolan charts produced multiple times for distinguished clients. The first circumnavigation by the *Victoria*, starting with Magellan and finishing with Elcano, is shown and is based on some accounts of that voyage decades before. Note that the charting of the Far East and, in particular, the Spice Islands is rudimentary, considering the knowledge the Portuguese then possessed.
Image credit: Library of Congress.

A bright spot in 1518 had been a trade treaty with Buddhist Siam, the first friendly (and non-Muslim) nation the Portuguese had encountered since arriving in Asia in 1498. However, the need to defend their hazardous positions in the Persian Gulf, rectify reverses in East Africa, campaign against the Ottomans in the Red Sea, maintain their widespread positions in India, establish new bases in Ceylon, Martaban, Burma, the Maldives, Sumatra and Indochina and commence trade with China all required enormous resources from an undermanned empire.

Additionally, the two main bases at Goa and Malacca were under sustained attack from the previous owners, and there were shortages of shipping, manpower, silver and artillery throughout the whole of the Indies.

As an example, in early 1521 Governor de Sequeira, having just dropped an embassy to Prester John[35] on the Somali coast, first raided the Red Sea, then campaigned unsuccessfully against Diu 1300 nautical miles away on the upper Indian west coast with 48 ships, 3000 Portuguese soldiers and 800 Malabar troops. A thousand sea miles to the south, one of de Sequeria's captains, Lopo de Brito, broke the siege of the new fort at Colombo on Ceylon and routed the local king's armies. Another 2000 sea miles east, another commander, Jorge de Albuquerque, later that year attacked Pacem in Aceh on Sumatra where Manuel had decreed a fort to protect the pepper trade—a trade as lucrative as the cloves and nutmeg of the Spice Islands. After hard fighting against over 3000 Aceh warriors supported by elephants, the Portuguese prevailed, but Jorge de Brito—tasked with building the Ternate fort—died in the battle.

His responsibilities for the Ternate mission passed to his brother, Antonio, carried in the same fleet, who with six ships and 300 men then sailed off to the Spice Islands, meeting de Meneses at Malacca on the way. De Albuquerque headed south with 18 ships from Aceh to Bintang, where the Malaccan sultan had fled and was marshalling forces, and after a strenuous series of engagements routed him and burnt the town. Such was the intensity of an average year of the Estado da India operations, an empire that at no time could field over 10,000 Portuguese fighting men.[36]

On 8 November 1521, the survivors of Magellan's fleet arrived off Tidore and, as we have seen, Pedro Lorosa on Ternate watched them drop anchor. The 25-month journey from Spain had been one of incredible hardship; navigating the South Atlantic, transiting the freezing Magellan Strait and then crossing the immense and unknown Pacific. Magellan had defeated a mutiny among his crews in South America and lost one ship in a storm, with another deserting him and returning to Spain.

He arrived in the Philippines in March 1521 but was killed at Mactan the next month in a minor skirmish with King Lapu-lapu. It was an ignominious and tragic end to a bold man of incredible vision and determination. His was unquestionably the greatest voyage of the entire Age of Discovery. The worn out *Concepcion* was abandoned and

---

35   Prester John was a legendary ruler of a Christian empire somewhere on the flank of the Muslim world. The kingdom was eventually located by the Portuguese in Ethiopia.

36   *Asian Trade and European Influence*, p. 130.

burned by the survivors, and the other two ships, *Trinidad* and *Victoria*, with 100 men between them, headed south, eventually finding the Moluccas, avoiding Ternate which they suspected to be a Portuguese base, and anchoring off Tidore, home of Rajah Almansor.[37]

39. A memorial to the first circumnavigation of the earth, located near the old royal fort of Rum on Tidore, looks out at tiny Maitara island. The memorial was completed in 1993 by the Spanish Embassy in Indonesia for the visit of the Spanish Navy sail training ship *Juan Sebastian de Elcano*, named for the Basque skipper who captained the *Victoria*, and anchored right here in 1521. The crews of the *Trinidad* and *Victoria* built the very first Spice Islands fortlet, a small structure to hold supplies as the *Trinidad* was careened, close to this spot.

Despite their battered condition, the rajah received them with great pomp, eager to create an alliance with Spain, to counteract Ternate's relationship with Portugal. The

---

[37] *Magellan*, p. 212.

wars between the two Iberian nations—officially at peace in Europe—in the forts and seas of the Spice Islands half a world away were about to begin.

Apart from Magellan, a round of deaths punctuated the narrative in 1521. Serrao died on Ternate of poisoning—probably by Sultan Almansor—around the same time as his friend Magellan was killed, in early 1521. Sultan Abu Lais of Ternate also died of poisoning not long after Serrao, his throne taken by his seven-year-old son, with the sultan's brother Darwis acting as regent. King Manuel of Portugal died in December, being succeeded by his 19-year-old son, who became John III. Into this whirlpool of intrigue and unpredictable politics the Spanish sailors dropped anchor.

Apprehension about the Portuguese forces arrayed against them on Ternate disappeared when the Spanish found just one Portuguese trader stationed there, Pedro Lorosa. Unbelievably, there were no Portuguese soldiers, no fort, no galleons. Lorosa, alone in a menacing world, felt deserted by Portugal, and he joined the Spaniards, showing them how to trade spices. Loaded with 25 tonnes of cloves, *Victoria* under Elcano left for Spain via Ambon and Timor in December 1521, arriving back at Sanlucar in September 1522, completing the very first circumnavigation of the globe. Despite losing their admiral, four ships and over 200 men, *Victoria's* load of spices turned a profit for the voyage as a whole, highlighting to the Spanish the immense rewards that the Spice Islands offered.

Back at Tidore, *Trinidad* required further repairs to make it seaworthy. While the ship was unburdened and caulked, its trade goods were unloaded and a small fortified trade-post built to house the crew on Tidore. It was a mud-brick walled structure reinforced with timber beams on which were mounted light cannon from the *Concepcion*.[38] It seems likely that this fortlet was on the north-west of Tidore, where the later fort at Rum was built. This was close to the rajah's court at Marieco (or Mareku), while the waters between tiny Maitara and Rum provided the best shelter to careen a ship during the north-westerlies of the winter monsoon. This simple structure was, in a way, the very first of the colonial Spice Islands forts. *Trinidad* was repaired as well as possible and sailed north in April 1522, hoping to cross the Pacific back to Mexico. It left behind four men with Lorosa on Tidore to maintain the trade post and await the next Spanish fleets.

Just a few weeks later, on 13 May, Portugal's long delayed counterattack finally arrived. De Brito's fleet anchored off Ternate, having picked up a caravel and some more men at Banda and stopping for a punitive raid against Bacan. Faced with seven ships and hundreds of Portuguese, Sultan Almansor quickly switched sides, swearing eternal allegiance to Portugal, and denouncing Spain.

---

[38] *Magellan*, p. 220.

Prima ego velivolis ambivi cursibus Orbem,
Magellane novo te duce ducta freto.
Ambivi, meritoq; vocor VICTORIA: sunt mi
Vela, alæ; precium, gloria; pugna, mare.

40. The Spanish carrack *Victoria*, named after the church in Seville where Portuguese Ferdinand Magellan swore an oath to the king of Spain, was the first ship to sail around the globe, taking just over three years to do so. It was built in Basque country in northern Spain, and captained back to Spain by a Basque mariner, Juan Sebastian Elcano. Elcano had participated in the mutiny against Magellan in South America and was chained below for much of the subsequent Pacific crossing, but moved into command with Magellan's death. After returning to Spain, he set out again for the Spice Islands, but perished crossing the Pacific the second time. The *Victoria* was lost in an Atlantic storm in 1570, an incredibly long life for a ship of that era.

De Brito sent a force to Tidore to destroy the little Spanish trade fort and arrest the two Spaniards that remained. The unfortunate Pedro Lorosa was dragged back and beheaded for treason.

The luckless *Trinidad* then appeared back on the scene, unsuccessful in its attempt to sail east across the Pacific, its crew half dead. It was captured by de Brito and the men incarcerated ashore. Soon after, the *Trinidad* was swept aground and wrecked on the reefs of Ternate, laid to rest among the scent of cloves it had long laboured across the oceans to find.

41. The catalogue of the Portuguese Armadas shows Jorge de Brito's carrack leading the fleet dispatched from Lisbon in early 1520 to build the first Spice Islands fort. Jorge died fighting on Sumatra, and it fell to his brother Antonio to make it to Ternate, hunt Magellan and construct Kastella.

The first Spice Islands fort

On 24 June 1522, de Brito set the first stone of the new fort, christened John the Baptist (today known locally as Kastella), as it was commenced on that saint's feast day. The 20-odd surviving Spaniards were put to work building the fort, using timber salvaged from the *Trinidad*, and some of its light cannon for armament.

The location of the Portuguese fort had been chosen by de Meneses back in 1519 and lay adjacent to the residence and royal town of the sultan at Gammalamma on the south-west corner of Ternate, around six kilometres from the main anchorage at Talangame. Ternate and Tidore are surrounded for the most part by coral reefs which prevent larger vessels from approaching too close to the shore. Only in occasional places are there breaks in the reefs, notably at Talangame and Tolukko. Off Kastella there were three narrow passages that allowed small caravels or ship's boats to reach the shore, and it was the difficulties that these reefs presented to ships that sought to bombard the fort or launch a direct amphibious attack that presumably attracted de Meneses to the site.

42. Some of the remains of Portuguese Kastella can still be seen today, most notably foundations and some wall structure of the two-storey tower that stood centrally in the fort. Nearby are some sections of wall and part of a bastion, as well as foundations of the jetty and sea tower. In 2022 these stones will celebrate their 500th birthday.

Early reports describe a very modest fort, around 60 square metres, surrounded by a two-metre wall with an 11-metre tower. Ruins of this tower and some walls can still be seen today. Despite de Brito having brought some masons and materials from Portugal however, progress of the construction was slow.

The fort concept had been a favourite of the deceased sultan, who had promised labour to assist. His successor, just a youth, and his regent, were distracted by power struggles with the widow of the sultan, who was opposed to the fort and conspired against the Portuguese. No doubt the 120 Portuguese soldiers who remained on Ternate were not overjoyed having to carry out hard labour in the tropical sun building ramparts and bastions, as clove pickers like old Ardi bartered spices for linen with the merchants.

Matters were further complicated when a patrol galley of de Brito's ran aground on a reef at Tidore with most of the two-dozen crew being beheaded by the Tidorese. Portugal had now been sucked into the vortex of poisoned relations between Ternate and Tidore, on the side of the former, and hence it too fell into a state of ongoing conflict with the latter.

43. A speculative view of the Portuguese fort St John the Baptist around the 1530s, after it had been under development for several years. Like most fortifications, it was continually modified, neglected, improved, expanded and upgraded. Accounts from the 1520s and 1530s referred unflatteringly to its defensibility and habitability, and it was only as the relationship with the locals deteriorated that the fort captains began to take its defences more seriously.

De Brito was not up to the challenges facing him, and in September 1524 was replaced by a new captain, Garcia Henriques, sent from Goa. Henriques quickly combined his troops with Ternate allies and attacked Tidore's capital at Marieco. Though repulsed three times they eventually succeeded in capturing a local fort armed with some Spanish cannon and defended by at least some Spaniards (survivors of Magellan's fleet), and then putting the enemy to flight.

The royal settlement was destroyed and Sultan Almansor sought peace shortly before he died, while the Spaniards were exiled to Halmahera. It was reported that the Ternateans presented Henriques with 600 severed Tidorean heads from this battle, claiming a bounty of Indian cloth he had previously offered for each.[39] The Portuguese had established an early supremacy, but how long could it last against the power of mighty Spain?

44. Some of Kastella's 500-year-old ruins. The Portuguese tower is on the left, the inland fort wall extends across the background and the inner building foundations are in the foreground. Much more is left of the Portuguese fort than the later Spanish fortress.

---

[39] *The World of Maluku*, p. 118.

The first follow-up to Magellan's fleet to the Spice Islands set off from Coruna, Spain in July 1525 under Garcia Loaisa. What started out as six ships and 450 men dwindled with the torturously long passage around South America, so that just one ship with 100-odd men arrived off Tidore in January 1527. Henriques quickly sunk it, but most of the crew escaped to Tidore.

Another expedition of four ships and 250 men left Spain in early 1526, but never even made it into the Pacific. This would be the last attempt by Spain to send reinforcements via the Straits of Magellan. Future fleets would sail from New Spain—the Pacific coast of Mexico. The first of these, under Alvaro Ceron—three ships and 100 men—sailed in November 1527, attrition reducing it to just one ship and 30 men by the time it finally arrived in the Moluccas. The ship dropped survivors at Tidore and set off back to the east trying to find the winds to return to Mexico, but after 18 months and two attempts, ended up back at Halmahera, where the Portuguese also sank it.

45. Looking north along the east coast of Tidore. Tohula fort is in the foreground, standing above the spread of modern Soa Siu town. The first Spanish defences of the 1520s as well as the later Portuguese Reis Magos fort of the 1580s are now lost without apparent trace in the urban sprawl of Soa Siu. Tidore's volcano towers up on the left.

To protect themselves from the more powerful Portuguese, and with the permission of the new king, Rajah Mir, the Spaniards on Tidore again constructed a small fort. This was now on the eastern side of the island, at the main town of Soa Siu overlooking the anchorage, and consisted of two bastions armed with light cannon and joined by a four-metre-high wall, with another bastion protecting the anchorage. It seems to have formed a citadel behind some other defensive walls that faced north.[40]

Despite these fortifications, the Spanish position on Tidore was perilous. They had no ships, and crucially had been unable to contact Spain or the colonies in the Americas, not finding the key to the winds for a passage back across the Pacific to Mexico. The last Spain had heard from the Moluccas was from the original circumnavigator, *Victoria*, back in 1522. Nothing was known of the fate of the ten ships and 800 men dispatched between 1525 and 1527, and it was assumed that all had been lost—not far from the truth.

From the Spanish perspective, King Charles (ruled 1516–1556) was preoccupied with ongoing conflict in Europe against France and in the Mediterranean against the rising might of the Ottomans, and his treasury was denuded. Portuguese and Spanish cosmographers and cartographers had been arguing where the Tordesillas antemeridian sat in relation to the Spice Islands since 1524 to establish ownership but had been unable to agree in which hemisphere they lay (they were actually in Portugal's).

It seemed clear to King Charles that while the Portuguese could reliably support and reinforce their Moluccan positions, his mariners could not. Additionally, he had just married the Portuguese king's sister. Preoccupied and short of funds, to settle the ownership issue he gave up his claim to the clove islands of the Molucca's, in favour of Portugal, in return for a staggering payment of 350,000 gold ducats (around 1.2 tonnes of gold[41]) at the Treaty of Saragossa in April 1529.

That should have meant an end to the conflict half a world away between the two Iberian neighbours, but this was not to be. A new Portuguese captain for Ternate, Jorge de Meneses, had arrived in May 1527. He was the worst so far, and probably ever, managing to alienate the Ternateans and facilitate the gradual combination of all of Portugal's Muslim enemies. Rather than concentrate on collecting spices, he became involved in local justice, crossing the line between trading and sovereignty. A Portuguese operation in 1529 ended in disaster when one of de Meneses' galliots accompanying a Ternatean squadron of korakora was caught by a combined Tidorean-

---

40   For more on the early Spanish fortifications on Tidore, see Marco Ramerini's excellent colonialvoyage.com website.

41   350,000 ducats @ 3.5 grams 99.5% pure gold.

Spanish fleet and destroyed. For revenge, he waited until the enemy fleet had left Tidore, and then sent his lieutenant, Vincent Fonseca, to attack in force. Naturally, they knew nothing of the Treaty of Saragossa signed in Europe the month before, nor, with momentum and numbers on their side, would they have cared.

46. Both the Portuguese and Spanish struggled with the epic interoceanic voyages to reach the Spice Islands. This rendering from the *Memorandum of the Armadas* shows the Portuguese fleet of 1500 which left Lisbon under Cabral with 13 ships, five of which were lost to storms, and two in a collision, with another two turning back. One of the captains lost was Bartholomew Dias, the first captain to sail into the Indian Ocean, in 1488.

As the Ottomans were retreating from their siege of Vienna back in Europe, once again the Spanish fort on Tidore was destroyed, its artillery taken to Kastella. The remaining Spaniards under Fernando de Torre were banished to Samafo[42] on northern Halmahera, an area under the vassalage of the Rajah of Tidore, where they were forbidden from trade or interference in local affairs.[43] Confrontations between the Spanish and Portuguese now died down for some time, and in 1533, after news of the Saragossa Treaty arrived, the Spaniards on Halmahera who were not inclined to join the Portuguese were repatriated to Goa and onward to home.

While the confrontation with the Spanish was resolved, Portuguese relations with their Ternatean hosts deteriorated. A new captain sent to relieve de Meneses was shipwrecked at Aceh and killed, and it was not until 1530 that a replacement, Gonzalo Pereira, arrived. He clapped his predecessor in irons and shipped him back to Goa but was himself assassinated by some of his subordinates in a complex coup in 1532. Yet another replacement was dispatched from Goa. The new captain, Tristao de Altaide, immediately tried to enforce the supposed royal monopoly on clove trading, to the astonishment of locals and Portuguese alike, who all made their fortunes trading on their private accounts.

Altaide attacked local kings at Jailolo on Halmahera and at Bacan, destroying both settlements in revenge for earlier raids. The campaign against Jailolo required a lengthy siege as the town's defences were sophisticated to a degree that clearly indicated Spanish engineering. Inevitably though, the simmering resentment against the heavy-handed actions of yet another Portuguese captain now exploded into open rebellion. The Ternateans, who had generally supported the Portuguese since their arrival 20 years before and provided most of the manpower for their warfare, could no longer be relied upon for assistance. Additionally, the accession of a new Ternate sultan to replace Abu Lais was still unresolved.

There were a number of possible young heirs to the vacant sultan's throne, and one of these, Bohejat, established himself at Jailolo, espousing jihad against the Portuguese, while his half-brother Hairun was groomed to rule in the fort at Kastella. Portuguese missionaries had by this time enjoyed quite a success in converting animist peoples of Halmahera to Christianity, and it was their settlements that became the target of increasing jihadi attacks. Some raids were even mounted against Ternate itself, inviting brutal Portuguese reprisals. Villages were destroyed, civilians slaughtered. Old Ardi was killed one day by marauders from one side or the other, his clove trees were hacked down, his village burnt and his kin enslaved.

---

42   *Turbulent Times Past in Ternate and Tidore,* p. 43.

43   *The Portuguese in India 1481–1571,* p. 389.

Captain Galvao

Into this chaos of warfare, deprivation and destruction in 1536 arrived undoubtedly Ternate's best Portuguese captain, Antonio Galvao, the first appointed by royal command from Lisbon. The fort was a ruin, the local town burnt out, the island depopulated, food scarce. The '... *artillery lacked cascabels, trunnions and carriages; and the fleet was in very bad repair. There was neither iron nor blacksmith and very little gunpowder'.*[44]

ANTONIO GALVÃO.

47. Antonio Galvao from a contemporary rendering. He wears a cuirass with spaulders and vambrace over a mail suit with his plumed burgonet beside him. He carries a cup-hilt rapier, albeit with a heavier military blade, indicating it was not just for show. It may have been the weapon he used to cut down Prince Bohejat at Gomafo in 1536. The exertion required to climb a tropical volcano in such armour can be imagined.

---

[44] *A Treatise on the Moluccas*, p .231.

An army under Bohejat of over 20,000 men[45] from Tidore, Makian, Bacan and Jailolo was gathered on Tidore to deal the death blow to Portugal and Kastella, which could muster not even a few hundred Portuguese troops in response. Against Galvao, all the kingdoms of the Moluccas—Ternate, Tidore, Bacan and Jailolo—were united for the first time in decades, if not ever. Galvao tried to talk peace, but his overtures were rejected and 300 enemy vessels stood off Talangame,[46] threatening attack. A captive revealed that Tidore's town had been fortified with '... *walls, bulwarks, ditches, stockades and caltrops, and could not be entered from any side'.*[47]

Bohejat's men fielded 500–600 firearms and were plentifully equipped with armour, lances, shields and swords, whereas Galvao mustered just 170 Portuguese including 150 musketeers, and 120 slaves. He took his small fleet—two galleons, a caravel and two korakora—and reconnoitred Soa Siu, bombarding the defences and observing the response. Though they lacked heavy guns, the huge concentration of warriors ashore precluded a daylight attack over the beach, which would in any case leave his undermanned ships vulnerable to the more numerous smaller craft of the enemy. Galvao quickly needed another plan.

Under further questioning the prisoner taken the previous day advised of a path leading across the north side of the mighty 1700-metre volcano that dominated Tidore to the hilltop fort of the rajah (today called Gomafo). This timber-palisaded fort was located about 300 metres above and around 1500 metres west of Soa Siu, no doubt situated there to be out of range of seaborne cannon fire and coastal raiders.

Just after midnight on 21 December 1536, Galvao, at the head of 120 Portuguese with accompanying slaves to carry weapons and equipment, boated silently across to Tidore. Contemporary accounts do not specify their route, but based on the descriptions, it seems clear that they landed on the island's west coast near Marieco and marched in darkness around eight kilometres, including crossing a saddle in Tidore's volcanic spine at 700 metres, then arrived at dawn near the hilltop fort. Sentries eventually spotted them and sent for help from the warriors clustered below at Soa Siu. Hundreds made the steep climb up to counter the Portuguese.

As the two groups clashed, Prince Bohejat, leading from the front, died in single combat under Galvao's sword,[48] and his forces consequently crumbled, fleeing in disorder back to Soa Siu. Galvao burnt the royal fort high on its hill and swept down

---

[45]   *Turbulent Times Past in Ternate and Tidore,* p. 60.

[46]   Ternate's harbour.

[47]   *A Treatise on the Moluccas,* p. 241.

[48]   The local warriors were stunned, as it was forbidden to strike a man of royal blood in their society.

with his small force of musketeers, fended off feeble attacks from ten times his number, torched the town and tore down its defences. It was an incredibly successful outcome to an audacious operation, and one of the most brilliant Portuguese campaigns in their Indies history. The combined army and their fleet skirmished with Galvao over the next days, but were continually bested, and presently sued for peace.

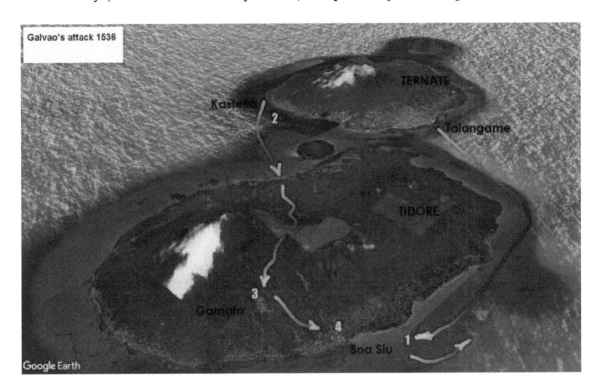

48. On arrival as captain of Kastella in 1536, Antonio Galvao was immediately faced with an alliance of all the kingdoms of the Moluccas, gathered on Tidore in overwhelming numbers, intent on destruction of the Portuguese. His first move was to take his small fleet to assess the enemy at Soa Siu (1). A landing against the force arrayed was out of the question, so he next set out from Kastella by boat at night and landed near the ruins of Marieco with around 200 men (2). They climbed all night, skirting the 1700-metre volcano, attacked the sultan's fort at Gamafo at dawn (3), defeated a strong counterattack, and then advanced down to Soa Siu, fighting off huge numbers of enemy warriors before burning the township (4). Image Credit: Google Earth 2020

Displaying wisdom and diplomacy unseen in his predecessors, Galvao was magnanimous in victory, restored all the rebellious rulers to their thrones and had Hairun crowned as Ternate's new sultan. He treated the Moluccans fairly, and gained their respect. With commendable energy, he organised repopulating the islands, encouraged agriculture, rebuilt the city around Kastella in stone and mortar and enclosed it with a masonry wall, established gardens to provision the fortress, built bulwarks and generally improved the defences, repaired the fort's weaponry, constructed workshops, storerooms and a hospital, improved the channel through the reefs off the fort and built several cannon-armed galleys for naval warfare.

49. While the Portuguese maintained small naval units—mostly galleys—at Ternate, they were never available in sufficient numbers to counter the massed local korakora fleets, which meant it was essential to have some of the local sultanates on their side. Forts without supporting seapower were very vulnerable in the Spice Islands—as the Portuguese found when they lost their forts on Ternate, Ambon and Tidore. This is Fort Duurstede, near Ambon, looking powerful, but in reality, isolated and vulnerable.

Widespread peace allowed the Portuguese to comprehensively explore the region, and expeditions were sent to Sulawesi, Mindanao, Halmahera, Seram and New Guinea, charting coastlines, checking resources and allowing Jesuit monks to spread Christianity among the animist peoples of the scattered islands. An attempt to establish a fort on Banda in 1529 had been abandoned due to local hostility, but other small forts and trading posts were now established on Ambon, Bacan and Halmahera. Occasionally, battles still had to be fought. In 1538 a combined Ternate / Tidore /

Portuguese fleet of 25 korakora with 440 men clashed with a Javanese force of 200 *paraos*[49] intent on colonising Ambon and surrounding islands, and drove them off.

50. German cartographer Sebastian Munster's 1552 *India Extrema* was one of the first European maps to display just Asia. Considering the extensive Portuguese knowledge of Asia at the time, it appears clear that they provided absolutely no input to this map. Image credit: Barry Lawrence Ruderman Rare Maps.

On another occasion, Galvao dispatched a strong Ternatean force to subdue a recalcitrant tribe on Seram, which it did, taking 1000 prisoners. But Galvao's tenure was unfortunately limited, and in October 1539, he handed over the keys of Kastella to Jorge de Castro and returned to Portugal, not only leaving the Moluccas and the

---

49   A small junk-like local vessel.

Portuguese position there immeasurably better than when he found it, but also leaving us with an excellent account of his time there.[50]

51. The spice wars soon extended beyond Ternate and Tidore and across neighbouring islands, including Halmahera. The Spanish and their Tidorean allies battled unsuccessfully against the Portuguese–Ternatean forces until abandoning the islands in 1533. The Spanish would, however, return after they established the beginnings of their Philippine Empire to the north in 1571.

---

[50]   *A Treatise on the Moluccas* from 1544 is thought to be a summary written by Governor Galvao himself, and gives a brilliant contemporary account of the early Portuguese Spice Islands.

The rise of Ternate

Another Spanish fleet of six galleons and 400 men left Mexico in November 1542 under Ruy Villalobos, intent on colonising the Philippines, rather than challenging the Portuguese in the Moluccas, even though the Philippine archipelago was further into the Portuguese hemisphere than the Spice Islands. As no spices were known to exist in the Philippines, the impetus for this colonial zeal was to spread Christianity among the local peoples. The travails of this fleet matched those of previous Spanish expeditions. Ships were lost to storms, or became separated, settlements established in the archipelago had to be abandoned, crops failed, hunger and disease took a toll.

Eventually, the remnants arrived at Jailolo on Halmahera, where some survivors of previous expeditions remained. The Sultan of Jailolo, empowered and armed by the Spanish, built impressive fortifications with Spanish advice, and began raiding through the islands. When de Castro threatened Villalobos with a battle the outnumbered Spaniards could not hope to win, they submitted and they too were packed off to Goa, most—including Villalobos—dying en route. Meanwhile the Portuguese and Ternateans reduced Jailolo after a lengthy siege, greatly assisted by a brace of earthquakes from the volcano above the town striking the defences. Three hundred defenders and 18 Portuguese were killed during the siege.[51]

The later years of the 1540s through to the 1560s in the Moluccas were characterised by two main themes: widespread missionary work (including St Francis Xavier, who was based in the Spice Islands for two years from 1545) converting animist peoples, and sometimes Muslims; and the emergence of Ternate as the regional superpower, with a concomitant weakening of the Portuguese position.

The one constant seemed to be incompetent Portuguese captains. At one point the Portuguese had to seek the Sultan of Jailolo's help when Ternate and Tidore combined against them.[52] The new Christian communities on Halmahera and Ambon came under increasing persecution from forces operating in concert with Sultan Hairun. The incensed Jesuits complained to Malacca, then Goa, and finally in person to Portugal's new young king, Sebastian, in Lisbon in 1565.

In response, he ordered Sultan Hairun deposed and a new Spice Islands headquarters established at Ambon, where the local population appeared much more receptive to Christianity than those of Ternate. Located between the clove islands and the nutmeg islands, possessing a fine harbour, plentiful agricultural land, and a large and dispersed

---

[51]   *The Portuguese in India 1481–1571*, p. 494.

[52]   *The World of Maluku*, p. 131.

population at least partly receptive to Christianity, Ambon was a much more strategic location for the Portuguese regional hub. A dozen galleons and 1000 men were dispatched from Lisbon to this end, but as usual, many were lost or side-tracked. Ternate's new captain, Diego Mesquita, and his admiral, Pereira Marramaque, first skirmished with the Spaniards at Cebu under Legazpi, before eventually arrived at Ternate with much less of a force than had set out.[53]

52. A depiction of the killing of Sultan Hairun by a Portuguese officer on Captain Mesquita's orders in 1570, on a memorial in the grounds of Kastella, where it occurred. The five-year siege then began.

Mesquita was to be the last formally appointed Portuguese captain of Ternate. Initially, he worked with Hairun, campaigning north to Mindanao against the Spanish while sending Marramaque to build the fort at Ambon. When he arrived there, Marramaque was surprised by a Javanese force much superior to his own and endured

[53] *The Moluccan Archipelago and Eastern Indonesia in the Second Half of the Sixteenth century in Light of Portuguese and Spanish Accounts*, p. 3.

his careened warships being burnt and his unfinished fort attacked before he led a counterattack, repulsed the enemy and captured a number of korakora to replace his own ships.

He then had to make haste back to Ternate to relieve Kastella, under siege by Hairun, beating off an attack on his 14 vessels by a local fleet of 50 korakora. Word soon came that Ambon was under attack yet again, and the unfortunate Marramaque sailed back there, dying in the harbour of illness and exhaustion. He was succeeded by Sancho de Vasconcelos, who abandoned the ruins of the original fort on the north side of Ambon bay, and rebuilt it on the Leitimur peninsula among Christian communities on the south of the harbour. Much expanded and rebuilt over the centuries, Fort Victoria, as it is now generally known, can still be seen today, almost lost amid the bustle of Kota Ambon.

Back at Ternate, relations between Mesquita and Hairun had reached an epic low. Like most of the previous Portuguese captains of Ternate, Mesquita harboured a deep hatred of Muslims—a product of the age-old confrontation between cross and crescent, and decades of combat across North Africa, the Persian Gulf, India and South-East Asia against Islamic forces. He despised Hairun and all his people, felt obliged to protect the recently Christianised peoples that Hairun's forces were crushing and, reminded of his original orders from King Sebastian, he had the sultan assassinated in Kastella on 28 February 1570.

Immediately, locals crowned Hairun's son Babullah as sultan and, gathering support from far and wide, he laid siege to Kastella yet again. It should be appreciated here that to lay siege according to local understanding was not an overly aggressive course of action. In practise it meant to stop supplying provisions and to assail any Europeans caught beyond the walls of the fortress. There were no breeching batteries, no trench systems dug, no mining of ramparts and bastions, no mass assaults on the walls with scaling ladders. All these scientific components of European siege warfare were extremely exhausting in the relentless sun, which beat down at an average maximum of over 30 degrees every day of the year.

The sultan intended to starve out the garrison, be rid of the Portuguese forever, and to do it with minimum loss and effort. He concentrated on cementing his control over the entire region, sending expeditions against Christian settlements at Halmahera, Bacan and Ambon, wiping out most of the Jesuits converts, though his forces were unable to take Fort Victoria at Ambon.

Like all of the clove islands of the Moluccas, Ternate grew no crops other than cloves. All foodstuffs were imported, the principal staple being sago grown on Halmahera and Morotai. In 1570 there were nearly 1000 Portuguese and dependents within the walls of the Kastella complex,[54] and that they were able to survive through the five-year siege indicates intermittent resupply. Some sources of supply were from remaining Christian communities located on Tidore, Halmahera and, before they were destroyed by Hairun in 1571, Bacan.[55] It also seems likely that despite the now overwhelming size of the sultan's fleet, the Portuguese maintained some of their own small craft with which to break the blockade. But certainly, the siege took a toll of the defenders, hunger and privation adding to the standard killers of sickness and malaria.

While Goa and Malacca were aware of the perilous position on Ternate, they both had significant problems. The latest Viceroy of India, Luis de Aitade, relieved his predecessor at Goa in late 1568. He immediately was beset by crises around the compass, needing to dispatch squadrons to Malacca, Diu, Aden and Cambay, and to clear pirates along the Malabar Coast. Early in 1569, the viceroy sent 130 ships and 3400 men to the south of Goa, to Onor (today Honnavar), to subdue resistance there. The local town and fort were plundered and burnt, and the army moved onto nearby Barcelor, carrying out a similar mission.

Building a fort at Barcelor and leaving 600 men and a small naval squadron for its defence, and another 500 at Onor, the viceroy had to return to Goa, which came under attack from a confederation of Muslim kings of the area. Dispatching a relief force of 600 men and four galleys to Chaul, Aitade then withstood the most determined siege yet of Goa—lasting ten months—supposedly by 100,000 men, 35,000 cavalry, 2000 elephants and 350 cannon. Contemporary Portuguese accounts, aimed at impressing their king, often exaggerated, so it may be more accurate to divide these enemy numbers by five or even ten, but still with only 700 Portuguese troops and 1500 local troops, the threat of annihilation was very real.[56]

While withstanding the siege at Goa, the viceroy was still able to dispatch reinforcements to Mozambique and send a fleet to Malacca to intercept yet another attack by Aceh. After destroying an Acehnese fleet four times the size of his own apparently without loss, Luis de Mello had to then take most of his force back to help the viceroy at Goa.

Also of great significance at this time was the success of the new settlement at Macau on the south China coast. Grudgingly given a small island base by the regional mandarins in 1557 as reward for clearing out local pirates, the Portuguese reached not only the long sought-after China market of silk and porcelain, but also acted as the

---

[54]   *The World of Maluku*, p. 133.

[55]   *The World of Maluku*, p. 132.

[56]   Description of these campaigns comes from *The Portuguese in India 1481–1571*, Chapter XX.

only intermediary between China and Japan. This was an immensely lucrative trade, and of course, required ships, men and other resources. On top of this, the Portuguese bases in the Persian Gulf and along the East African coast always needed assistance, the annual trade fleet needed to be sent back to Portugal, and the usual problems of lack of men, ships, money and weapons never went away.

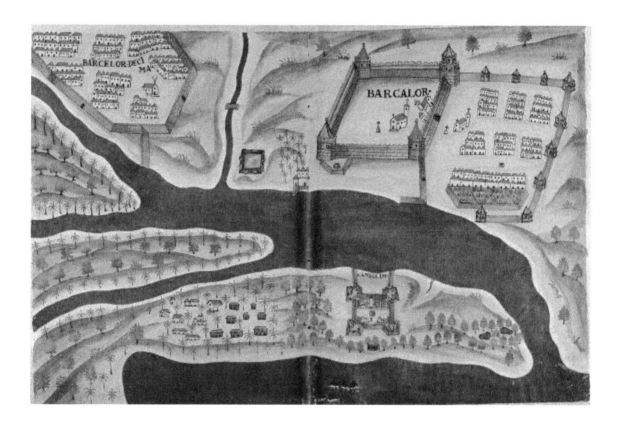

53. The fortifications at Barcelor, on the coast of Karnataka, near Mangalore, India. The Portuguese attacked the local ruler in 1569, destroyed his fort and built their own over its ruins. For a while it was an important outpost, but it was demolished in 1705. At the time it was built, the Portuguese were fighting large and small wars along the East African coast, the Persian Gulf, all over India, in Ceylon and throughout South-East Asia. The Spice Islands were just another of their battlegrounds.
Image credit: From the *Livro das Fortalezas* .

During Kastella's five-year siege, only four Portuguese ships reached Ternate. For three consecutive years no ships at all arrived, as they had left Malacca too late and ran head-on into the trade winds. Over half the garrison, their dependents and the

Christian families of the Portuguese township died during the siege, leaving just 400 alive in 1575.[57]

54. A Ternatean depiction of the handover of Kastella, at a memorial in the grounds of the fortress. The Portuguese are evicted by angry holy warriors. Considering the outrageous actions of some of Kastella's Portuguese captains over the years, the sultan's forces acted with considerable restraint in allowing those remaining in the fortress free passage to Ambon.

While the firepower and defences of the fort had been sufficient to prevent being stormed, the morale of the remaining inhabitants was naturally extremely low. When the sultan offered them their lives and free passage to Ambon, the exhausted garrison

---

[57] *The World of Maluku,* p. 133.

accepted, and on the day after Christmas 1575, the fort's last commander, Nuno Pereira, surrendered Kastella and sailed for Ambon with the survivors, watching in disgust as a galleon from Malacca dropped anchor on the 28th, just too late to save them.

And so, Sultan Babullah took possession of the fortress where his father and grandfather had been imprisoned and his father murdered. He was now the pre-eminent ruler of all the islands from Sulawesi east to Papua and from Mindanao south to Banda. He was widely respected for defeating the Portuguese, and now controlled virtually the entire global clove trade. This trade was opened up to all—Arabs, Malays, Javanese and Indians were all welcome to come and buy cloves, the sultan taking a ten percent clip of all sales. It was Ternate's golden age, an era of tremendous wealth and power. Babullah's sun was rising just as that of the Portuguese was setting.

55. The royal residence, the Kedaton, of the Sultan of Ternate today. The lineage of the Ternate sultans can be traced back to the thirteenth century. Sultan Mudaffar Syah, who as a boy in World War II was rescued along with his extended family from the Japanese by Australian commandos, died in 2015 aged 79. At the time of writing, several claimants jostle for the largely ceremonial throne.

Astonishing developments, however, were on the horizon, and Babullah would not last even a decade. Within a generation the Iberians would be back, and a new player in the spice game would also arrive on the scene.

5. The era of conflict 1575–1663

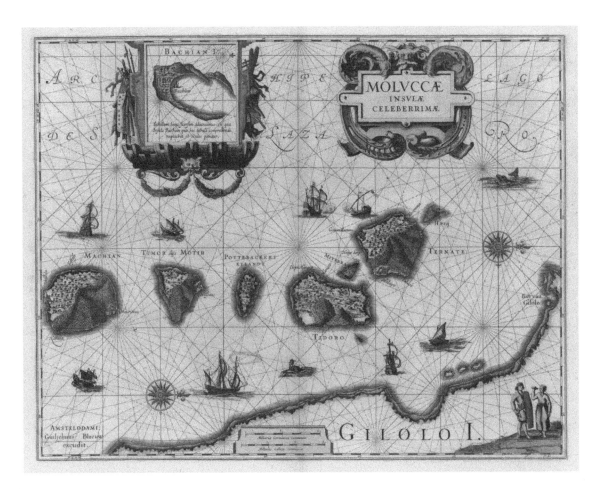

56. *Insulae Moluccae*, c. 1640. An engaging Spice Islands map by the famous Dutch cartographer Willem Blaeu. At this time the tussle for the clove islands between Spain and the Dutch was in full swing; for example, both had forts on Ternate, just a few kilometres apart. The four major islands—Ternate, Tidore, Motir and Makian—were all volcanic cones, as were the three smaller islands, Hiri, Maitara and Mare (shown here as Pottebackers). Bacan (Bachian), further south, is shown in the inset. The large island labelled Gilolo is now known as Halmahera. Many but not all of the contemporary forts are depicted on the map. North is to the right.

Kastella and Malacca

The Kastella complex in early 1576 was—quite naturally after a five-year siege—dilapidated. Frustratingly, we have no accounts of its layout or form at the end of the Portuguese period, but we can make some assumptions, based on previous observations by chroniclers. We know that the complex consisted of several parts—the citadel (the small original fort); the walled Portuguese town partially enclosing the citadel; and areas outside this combined space including the Jesuit quarters, provisioning gardens, small farms, factories and workshops.

The citadel and township sprawled along the coast, the farms and gardens spread inland up the gradual slopes towards the volcano, the peak of which was six kilometres north-east and towered 1700 metres over Kastella. Just past the eastern walls of the fortress was a narrow but rugged creek (still extant), generally dry, but coming alive with tremendous runoff from the mountain during monsoonal downpours. This formed a natural eastern boundary, but it was not a significant obstacle to attackers.

Based on contemporary Portuguese forts in Asia,[58] the layout would have the military citadel enclosed by its own crenelated walls on the waterfront, containing the tower, captain's residence, armoury, barracks and clove storerooms, with bastions at each seaside corner; the Portuguese township spread along the coast to the south-east of this, extending to the bastion Nuestra Senora on the coast and north to a bastion later rebuilt as Cachil Tulo, and enclosed by ramparts on the eastern and northern (towards the volcano) sides; the 'royal' township of Gamalama (or Gamlamo) located to the north-west of the citadel; and the sprawl of the local town, Limatahu/Baturadja, also along the shore and north of Gamalama.

On the ground today, the distance from Nuestra Senora to the remains of the jetty and its tower (north-western corner of the citadel) is approximately 350 metres, and bastion Kachil Tulo is about 250 metres inland from the sixteenth century shoreline (it has silted around 100 metres seawards since), so the whole area of the fortress was only around 87,500 square metres, including the citadel of about 3600 square metres.[59]

The fact that Kastella was neither breached nor stormed over a five-year siege (albeit not a vigorous one) by an attacker with massive numerical superiority when the able-bodied garrison numbered in the dozens rather than hundreds prompts a number of suppositions.

---

[58] Refer to *O Livro das Fortalezas.*

[59] So, the entire fortress was roughly the size of ten football fields, while the citadel was around half such a field.

Firstly, the fortress must have been enclosed by a wall system that was sufficiently high, solid and strong to confound escalade or breech. Secondly, the walls must have been properly configured, with access ramps, a patrol path along the top and sturdy parapets for protection (the sultan's forces had many muskets available) to allow rapid movement of troops to threatened sections, and the ability to direct firepower from a height. Thirdly, the garrison must have maintained some functional artillery deployed on the bastions that outranged or disrupted any cannon of the besiegers. Finally, it is known that dozens of quick reloading swivel guns armed the battlements, as they were captured when the fortress fell, so these would have made approaching the outside of the walls a risky venture.

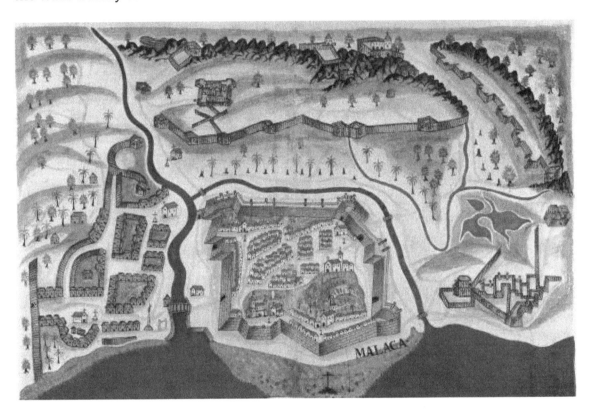

57. A view of the fortress at Malacca by Antonio Bocarro in 1635, as it appeared in his *Livro das Fortalezas* . The bridge to the left of the fortress that Albuquerque's men stormed in 1511 has been fortified, and substantial walls extend for the full perimeter. The Santiago Gate, the only part of the Portuguese fortress remaining above ground today, is on the lower right behind the Santiago Bastion. It is often incorrectly referred to as 'a Famosa', which was the name for the entire early citadel. Parts of the Santiago Bastion, long believed to have been destroyed with the rest of the Dutch fortress by the British around 1800, have recently been unearthed. Image credit: Biblioteca Evora.

While we don't have contemporary visual representations of Kastella at the close of the Portuguese period, we do have images of some of their regional forts of a similar vintage, and of these, Malacca is probably most instructive in gaining an understanding of what the fortifications on Ternate looked like.

Malacca was the regional capital of the Estado da India and had a Christian population of 7400 in 1613, so it was much larger than Kastella, which contained just 1000 inhabitants in 1570. Despite this, the two walled footprints were approximately equivalent, as Malacca's central area incorporated just the administrative and military functions, most of the residential areas being located outside the inner walls. The central walled city contained the residences and offices of the governor and bishop, convents, five churches, two hospitals, various ancillary buildings, and accommodation for the garrison, their dependants and 300 families, which would equate to an approximately similar number of inhabitants as Kastella.

Looking at the artwork of Malacca from a 1635 publication, we can note the waterfront location with high encircling walls punctuated with protruding bastions, 24 cannon mounted on the bastions and ramparts, a wet moat surrounding the walls, and clusters of civic buildings, churches and housing inside the walls. Kastella was certainly less sophisticated than Malacca; it was at the very edge of the empire, but in terms of defences, the style would have been similar.

When the Ternateans entered Kastella in triumph in December 1575, Sultan Babullah had shrewdly advised the surrendering Portuguese that he was merely holding the fort in trust until their return, but he was perceptive enough to appreciate that when they did reappear, they would likely be back in force. He wasted no time in readying for that eventuality.

Babullah focused on two themes: he fortified Ternate; and he continued a regional engagement program, where his korakora fleets spread across the archipelago collecting tribute, recruiting, showing the flag and solidifying support. Of the other traditional kingdoms of the Moluccas, Tidore and Jailolo had bet on the Spanish, while Bacan had wagered on the Portuguese, and none of these bets had come off. By 1575 Ternate was supreme.

The sultan astutely recognised that a network of strong forts combined with massed korakora fleets represented the best way to defend his enlarged kingdom. He established his palace within Kastella and had engineers from Johore and Java rebuild and rearm the battered walls, bastions and ramparts. Some detached outworks were constructed nearby, for example at Limatahu[60] and in front of the Nuestra Senora bastion. Cachil Tulo, the sultan's brother, rebuilt the eastern inland bastion, which was

---

60   *Sucesos de la Islas Filipinas*, p. 236.

subsequently named after him. In 1603 it formed a crucial part of Kastella's defences, being described as:

> '... a bastion of stone which had been reinforced by external wooden beams, mounted on the ramparts were three very large pieces of artillery, while two other pieces of artillery were mounted on the wall which connected it with the rampart of Nuestra Senora'.[61]

New forts were constructed at Tacome,[62] in the north of Ternate Island, and at Kota Janji,[63] commanding the steep approach up from Talangame harbour. The local fort at Malayo, which overlooked Talangame and later became Fort Orange, was either built or improved at this time, and was described by Argensola as:

> 'The king [i.e. sultan] has in the same island of Ternate half a league towards the East side another port, called Malayu surrounded by walls with many bastions and pieces of artillery of small and medium calibre; in this fort there are 500 warriors.'[64]

The Portuguese meanwhile were still able to secure cloves from Makassar, and Malay traders in Malacca and clung to their remaining regional forts at Ambon, Solor and on Timor. The Sultan of Tidore, as always intimidated by Ternate's overwhelming power, then invited the Portuguese back to the Moluccas to establish a base on his island, and so Fort Reis Magos (fort of the Three Kings) was constructed just north of the settlement of Soa Siu. It was started in January 1578 by Vasconcelos (who also built the Ambon fort) and described in one account as '... the fort was loose stone, square, thirty fathoms per side with two bastions at two corners, a much weaker work, which could easily be conquered'.[65]

While Vasconcelos' men worked on the little fort, back in Portugal, the new king, 24-year-old Sebastian, was planning another glorious crusade against the Moroccan infidels in the spirit of his ancestors. Portugal maintained a number of precariously

---

[61] colonialvoyage.com. *The Spanish Town of Ternate.*

[62] *The Discovery and Conquest of the Molucco and Philippines Islands*, p. 245.

[63] *The Discovery and Conquest of the Molucco and Philippines Islands*, p. 57.

[64] *From European–Asian conflict to Cultural Heritage: Identification of Portuguese and Spanish Forts in the Northern Maluku Islands*, p. 192.

[65] *From European–Asian conflict to Cultural Heritage: Identification of Portuguese and Spanish Forts in the Northern Maluku Islands* p. 192; 30 fathoms is about 55 metres.

held coastal forts in Morocco, including at Ceuta, Tangier, Mazagan and Asilah, and it was at the latter that Sebastian's invasion force arrived in August 1578.

58. Looking down from Fort Torre to the township of Soa Siu, capital of Tidore, and across to Halmahera. Fort Tohula is on the small hill above and to the right of the blue roof (today's sultan's residence); Makian is above it. The battle-scarred stones of little Reis Magos lie somewhere along the coast, directly above Fort Torre's entry tower.

For little Portugal it was an enormous army, totalling 18,000 men carried in 500 ships and including mercenaries from Spain, Germany and Italy, as well as all the nobles of Portugal. To mount it cost most of the wealth of the land; no doubt a fair portion of it the proceeds from nutmeg and cloves of the Spice Islands. Against all advice, the foolhardy Sebastian marched into the interior and was annihilated by a much larger Moroccan army at the battle of Alcazar. The last of the House of Avis perished in the dusty chaos of the clash, leaving no heir, and two years later the unthinkable happened. King Phillip of Spain—as a grandson of King Manuel I—combined the crowns of Spain and Portugal.

While it no doubt irked the Portuguese in the Indies to be subject to Spain, their help was somewhat welcomed as little seemed forthcoming from Lisbon, Goa or Malacca. The destruction of Sebastian's army had impoverished Portugal and withheld resources of men, ships and funding that were needed to maintain the Estado da India. For three years from 1579, no Portuguese ships made it to the Moluccas. To compound the global Portuguese problems, ten of their finest galleons, including the brand-new *St Martin*, a number of lesser ships and galleys, 1300 of its best seamen and 3000 soldiers were purloined by King Phillip II for his ill-fated Armada against England, from which adventure few returned.

59. When Drake made it to the Spice Islands in 1579, the Portuguese had already been there for 67 years. Three years before his arrival they built a fort at Ambon, which after four centuries of modifications, earthquakes, battles, sieges and accumulated damage can still be seen today, by the great harbour which it commanded for so long. It is now known as Fort Victoria; shown here, one of its battered bastions.

Coming just a decade after the disaster in Morocco, the losses in the Armada debacle made it impossible for the Estado da India to defend against the blows that were raining in from all sides in Asia.

The Spanish had finally found the way back across the Pacific to Mexico in 1565, which allowed them to reinforce their new position in the Philippines, just north of the Spice Islands. Manila was established as the capital of the new colony of the Spanish East Indies in 1571 and the Manila galleons, which would trade the silver of Bolivia for the long-sought treasures of the Indies and Cathay, made the first of the famous voyages to Acapulco that would run annually for another 250 years. In contrast to Portugal, Spain poured resources into the Philippines, building cities, forts and galleons and sending expeditions to China, Japan, Indochina, Taiwan, and even to New Guinea and the Solomon Islands.

By 1579, only one non-Iberian expedition had found the East Indies; that of the French Parmentier brothers, who both died of disease in Sumatra in 1529. But the Iberian powers, particularly the Portuguese, employed sailors, gunners and even navigators from many other nations in their efforts to man their endless fleets. Eventually, northern Europeans began to understand where to find the Indies and their treasures, and inevitably the Spanish and Portuguese found themselves no longer alone in the tropical waters of the East.

First to make it from the east by following in Magellan's track was the English privateer Francis Drake, his hold full of pillaged treasure looted from the undefended Pacific coasts of New Spain. Groping without charts for the Spiceries after crossing the Pacific, he was driven off by an Iberian galleon in Philippine waters[66] before dropping anchor at Ternate in November 1579. Sultan Babullah welcomed him in magnificent style, flaunting his immense wealth and entertaining the Englishman in the grounds of Kastella, hoping Drake's queen might be a counter to the Portuguese.

After a short stay, Drake loaded six tonnes of cloves and sailed off, south of Java to avoid a clash with the Portuguese in the Malacca Straits, arriving home back in England a year later. The Portuguese on Tidore and the Spanish at Manila took note.

---

66 *The World Encompassed,* p. 171.

60. The *Golden Hind* became the first ship to finish a circumnavigation under one captain, leaving England in 1577 and returning just under three years later. Along with looted Spanish silver, a load of cloves picked up at Ternate provided a return of nearly 5000% to the voyage financiers, which included Queen Elizabeth I. *Golden Hind* was a mid-size galleon, displacing about 300 tonnes, armed with 14 demi-cannon and half a dozen swivel guns.

Spanish attempts to defeat Ternate

When King Phillip II heard of Drake's voyage, he ordered the recapture of the Moluccas and their incorporation into the new colony of the Spanish East Indies. Prior to the royal directive, the Philippine governor had first dispatched a spy, Francis de Duenas, in 1582 to contact the Portuguese traders still in the Moluccas and to survey the strength and defences of what was now the Ternate Empire. The enterprising Duenas spoke Malay, dressed as a Chinese trader and spent several months in the islands. He reported back details of Ternate's fortifications, estimating Sultan Babullah's regional available manpower at over 120,000 and his fleet at 2000 korakora. The governor wrote to Phillip:

> *'If Maluco [i.e. Ternate] should be considered in England as of great value, and as a stronghold which can be taken and held with a few men, then they would feel bound to place a large force in it. Your Majesty should do much for its defence. These considerations impress me so strongly that, if I were supplied with more troops and artillery, I could by no means imagine a more necessary task. I will do what I can, however, in your royal service, although it is not under my charge.'*[67]

Just after this, Sultan Babullah died, probably of poison, which was the natural way for kings of the Indies to pass on. In 1583, his successor, Sultan Said, invited all the regional kings for his coronation, and had Tidore's sultan and his entourage garrotted after the feast, reigniting the fury of his island neighbours. Such were the ways of the rulers of the Moluccas.

Now came a quarter-century of unsuccessful Spanish expeditions from Manila to recover Kastella on Ternate.[68] The first, led by Captain Ronquillo in 1582, suffered an outbreak of beriberi and was abandoned. The next by Pedro Sarmiento in 1584 consisted of 300 Spaniards and 1500 native warriors in three galleons and a flotilla of small craft. It won an engagement with some of the sultan's fleet off Motir, and then took that island before landing a force some days later just east of Kastella. They dragged some cannon ashore and proceeded to batter Kastella's walls between the Cachil Tulo and Nuestra Senora bastions, but were hotly engaged in return. Again, sickness broke out and, unable to gain a quick breach, Sarmiento withdrew back to Manila.

---

[67] *The Philippines Islands*, Volume IV, p. 314.

[68] These attacks are listed in *The Discovery and Conquest of the Molucco and Philippines Islands*, Book V.

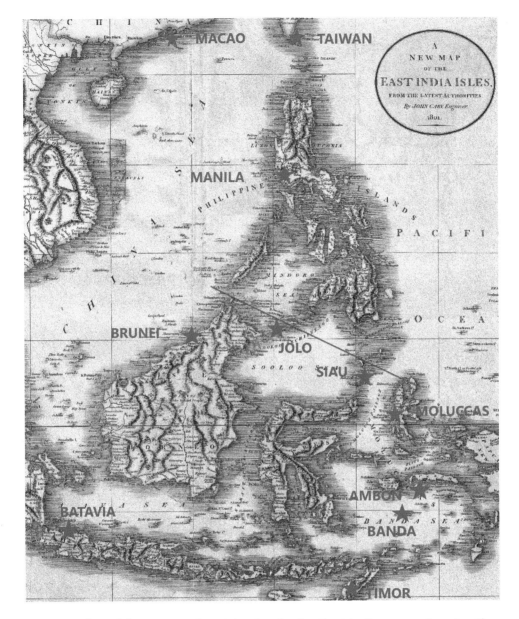

61. Part of English cartographer John Cary's 1801 East Indies map, showing the relationship of the Eastern empires of the Iberians and the Netherlands. The red line shows the approximate border between the VOC in the Indies and the Spanish Empire in the Philippines. Java, holding the VOC headquarters at Batavia, is at bottom left. Manila, capital of the Philippines, is above and right. Portugal maintained control over Macao and part of Timor. In this era of conflict, the three clashed at Macao, Taiwan, on Timor, at Manila, along the frontier and, of course, in the Spice Islands of the Moluccas, Ambon and the Bandas. The Spanish also campaigned against the Brunei sultanate on Borneo and the Sulu sultanate at Jolo.

The next year, an attempt by Juan de Morones started disastrously when the galleon carrying his heavy breaching cannon was lost with all hands just after leaving Manila. In the Moluccas he was joined by some Portuguese from Malacca and the kings of Bacan and Tidore, but rejected their advice to attack Kastella from the weaker western side. Instead he attacked from the east, but without his big guns he could make no impact on the walls, and with Kastella holding 3000 warriors, 1000 of them with muskets, he was vulnerable to sallies by the defenders. He gave up on Kastella, turned around and attacked newly built Fort Kota Janji, but failed in this as well so he too returned to Manila.

A fourth attempt ended in farce in 1593 when Governor Desmarinas assembled a mighty force of 1000 Spanish troops and 500 local musketeers, loaded them in galleons, galleys, frigates and korakora, but was himself killed a few days out from Manila when his Chinese rowers mutinied and took his galley off to Cambodia. The remainder of the disconsolate fleet returned to the capital.

62. Looking almost due east at the modern city of Ternate sprawled around Talangame harbour in the distance. Tidore is on the right and Halmahera a smudge in the background. In the left foreground, tiny Fort Kota Janji lies in sunshine, crowning a razorback ridge. It was built by Sultan Babullah around 1580 to guard the coast route to Kastella, as it climbs up from the port.

Distractions in Europe, including the death of King Phillip II and accession of his son Phillip III, the growing rebellion in the provinces of the Netherlands against Spanish rule, as well as threats to Manila by the Chinese, halted subsequent attempts to defeat Ternate until a combined Portuguese–Spanish attack in 1602–3.

Admiral Furtado left Goa with six galleons and 19 smaller craft, campaigned successfully against Ternatean–Javanese forces at Ambon, then took Makian, where he built a fort (which later became Fort Mauritius),[69] and sailed on to Talangame, arriving in October 1602. He waited there, inactive for nearly four months until the Spanish component under Captain Gallinato arrived from Manila with 200 soldiers in February 1603. They landed around 600 men, fought off a counterattack at Kota Janji and then emplaced their guns just 200 paces out from Nuestra Senora.

The guns the Portuguese had brought—two 13-pounders and two short stone-firing 16-pounders—were insufficient for the work required of them, and they were heavily engaged from the defences of Kastella, which mounted 36 heavy cannon. Bastion Cachil Tulo mounted three large guns, there were two more on the wall between it and Nuestra Senora, and seven heavy pieces in a ravelin in front of the latter. The ramparts were well equipped with a large number of swivel guns, and the walls sufficiently solid not to be troubled by the Iberian cannon. The Iberians had been outgunned.

A determined sally by over a thousand local troops was only just defeated, causing many Spanish and Portuguese casualties; powder and supplies were running low, and they expected enemy reinforcements at any time. Yet another attempt was unsuccessful.

The continued failure of the Spanish and Portuguese to defeat Ternate naturally enhanced the regard with which Sultan Said was held throughout the region. For his part, he had nearly succeeded in wiping out all the larger Christian settlements throughout the Spice Islands; a community surrounding Fort Victoria at Ambon was all that remained.

By the turn of the century though, the Iberians had a much larger problem; the Dutch had arrived. Ironically, it was the Spanish ban on selling spices to Amsterdam— then northern Europe's spice distribution capital—following the union with Portugal that forced the Dutch to seek the cloves and nutmeg at their source in the Spice Islands. The first Dutch fleet sailed to Java in 1595, and by 1601 some 14 fleets totalling 65 ships had sailed to Asia. Their appearance in East Indies waters led to the first major naval clash between the Dutch and the Portuguese in 1601. A Dutch squadron defeated a larger Portuguese force of galleons and galleys at Bantam Bay off Java and set the scene for future engagements.

---

[69] hpip.org/en/heritage/details/1532

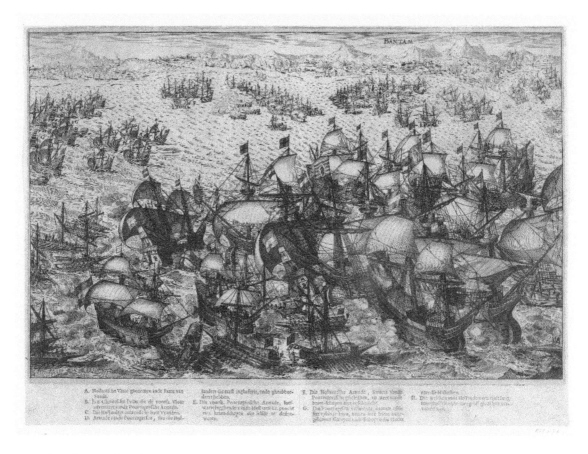

63. The Battle of Bantam, 27 December 1601, where a superior Portuguese fleet was bested by a squadron of Dutch trading galleons at Java. Eight Portuguese galleons supported by two dozen galleys were driven off by three Dutch galleons and two smaller ships; a fine achievement for the Dutch, a disaster for the Portuguese. It is probable that the Portuguese, armed for defeating lightly gunned Asian vessels, were at a disadvantage against the modern firepower of the Dutch. The depiction shows a number of different views of the action simultaneously.
Image credit: Bartele Gallery.

64. A bronze 24-pounder showing the VOC logo, under an 'H', signifying the Hoorn chamber of the company. The other chambers were the Dutch port cities of Amsterdam, Middleburg, Enkhuizen, Delft and Rotterdam.

In 1602, the *States General* (Dutch Parliament), recognising that a single corporate entity would not only facilitate more profitable trade with the Indies but also put pressure on Spain—with which the Netherlands was in the midst of an 80-year war—established the *Vereenigde Oostindische Compagnie* (VOC). As a harbinger of the modern age, it was the world's first global corporation, the first company to issue equity stock, and possessed the first widely recognised corporate logo. The Dutch capture of the Portuguese carrack *Santa Catarina* off Singapore in 1603 with its priceless cargo of Chinese silk, musk and porcelain highlighted the rewards on offer. The proceeds from this *single* cargo brought in over six million guilders,[70] instantly doubling the capital of the fledgling VOC.

The VOC was chartered to wage war, make treaties, mint currency, maintain armies and forts, and establish colonies, but unlike the Spanish and Portuguese trading systems, it remained a commercial entity, separate from the state. The early Dutch voyages had shown the incredible profits available from shipping spices back to Europe, and they had a competent and rapidly expanding merchant fleet of well-armed trading ships capable of transoceanic voyages. It was the VOC that made the next move.

The Dutch attack Ambon and Tidore

The first Admiral of the VOC, Steven van der Hagen, stood into Ambon harbour with nine East Indiamen in February 1605, and anchored under Fort Victoria,[71] whose guns stayed silent. The Portuguese fort was no stranger to attacks, having beaten off Ternate in 1591 and 1593, Java in 1598, and the Dutch once before in 1600. Perhaps overawed by the size of the enemy armada—such a powerful fleet had never been seen in local waters—or perhaps incentivised by bribery, Fort Victoria surrendered with no resistance. The VOC now had their very first Spice Islands fort and the perfect base to control the nutmeg isles of Banda to the south and the clove volcanos to the north.

Part of der Hagen's force then moved onto Tidore. An English ship, the *Red Dragon*, under Henry Middleton, was trading cloves there, and observed the subsequent battle. We also have an excellent contemporary engraving of the course of the action (see Image 67). The Portuguese defences consisted of Fort Reis Magos with 11 guns and 70 men, and a battery to the south at the base of the hill on which later would be built Fort Tohula, with three or four cannon. Two galleons were moored near this battery,

---

[70] Approximately US$100 million today.

[71] Known then by the Portuguese as *Forte de Nossa Senhora da Anunciada*.

but these were the first targets of the Dutch, and both—probably outgunned, and undermanned—were quickly destroyed.

65. The Dutch squadron stands off the rather rudimentary Fort Victoria at Ambon in 1605. Despite previously holding off several other attacks, the fort surrendered without a fight on this occasion, giving the VOC the first of their Spice Islands forts.
Image credit: Rijksmuseum, Netherlands.

Next the Dutch stood off and bombarded Reis Magos for two days, not causing much damage, but neither troubled by the defenders' guns, indicating that the Portuguese cannon were quite small (probably only nine-pounders).

The Dutch had convinced a reluctant Sultan Said of Ternate to provide some troops for the attack, and these landed from korakora to the north of the fort along with some Dutch soldiers and their breaching cannon. The importance of the supportive local forces was as clear as it always had been to opposing Europeans. Local warriors, though ill-equipped and often difficult to control, were available in the hundreds, while Europeans were in much less numbers. If the native forces were allowed to close for hand-to-hand fighting, there was always the danger that their numbers would prevail.

Not waiting for a breach, the Dutch escaladed the walls with ladders and gained the ramparts, but were repulsed by a spirited Portuguese counterattack where the defenders used hand grenades to clear the enemy from the battlements. The attackers were thrown back in confusion. Just then, a flank attack by another Portuguese–Tidorean column completed the rout and came close to taking the Dutch guns. Right when defeat loomed for the Dutch, a lucky shot from the ships—they fired 1500 at Reis Magos that day—scored a direct hit on the powder magazine in the fort, the resulting explosion killing half the garrison and destroying the defences.

66. Looking west from the town of Ambon across the broad reach of Ambon bay. It extends around 25 kilometres north-east from its mouth and is up to 400 metres deep. The ranges in the background stand over 700 metres high, dwarfing a fish factory ship heading out into the Banda Sea. Der Hagen's fleet sailed in from the left to take on the Portuguese fort further up the bay.

The remaining Portuguese surrendered and Tidore's main town was torched. The Dutch established trading posts on both Ternate and Tidore, but with their eyes on a spice monopoly, they prevented the English in the *Red Dragon* from doing the same. The Dutch neither fortified nor garrisoned either place, leaving them exposed for the riposte that arrived from the Philippines the next year.

Portugal had now lost all its Spice Islands possessions; after more than 80 years, its last strongholds had fallen. The Dutch however were unrelenting in their pressure, and not just in this theatre, but across the entire Portuguese empire. In the 50 years after

1600, at various times the Dutch attacked Portuguese settlements in Brazil, the Gold Coast (today's Ghana), Macau in China, India, Ceylon, Malacca, Mozambique and across the Indonesian archipelago. Particularly crippling was their extended blockade of Goa, capital of the Estado da India, which the VOC maintained on a semi-permanent basis. The Dutch were also adept at exploiting local grievances against the Portuguese, supporting the Ternateans in the Spice Islands, and the Acehnese against Malacca.

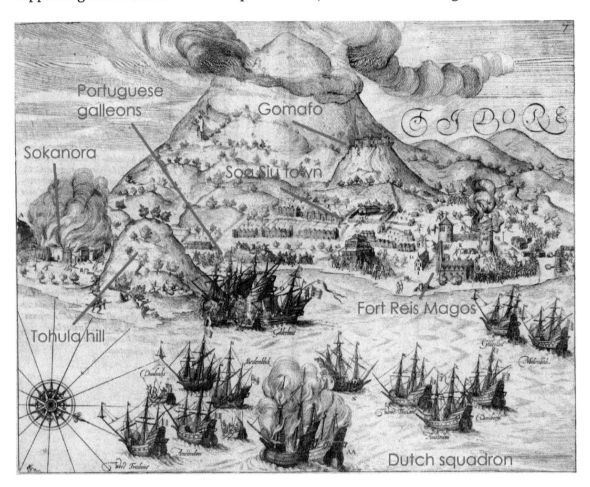

67. A much-copied engraving showing the 1605 Dutch attack on Fort Reis Magos at Tidore. On the far left, Sokanora burns during a Dutch assault; to its right is the hill on which Fort Tohula was later built; off the Tohula hill, two Portuguese galleons are destroyed by bombardment; behind the galleons is the local township of Soa Siu; high above the town is the sultan's fort-palace at Gomafo; and on the right, the battle rages around Fort Reis Magos.

Portugal's leadership was unable to respond with decisive effect and remained perpetually on the defensive, reacting lethargically and ineffectively to the continued

VOC blows. When they tried to concentrate resources, the rewards were generally fleeting, as in 1606 when Goa dispatched their largest force ever to the East Indies. Totalling 18 galleons and a host of smaller vessels carrying 3000 Portuguese soldiers, the fleet sailed to relieve a combined Acehnese–Dutch siege of Malacca.

68. Monte Fort in Macao, built by the Jesuits from 1617, was the key to the Portuguese defences during a major Dutch assault in 1622. The attackers put 1300 men ashore, who were advancing towards the town when a round fired by a Jesuit monk from Monte's ramparts exploded a powder barrel in the midst of the attacking troops, causing great casualties and disorder. A Portuguese counterattack threw the Dutch back with hundreds of losses and they withdrew, losing a ship to cannon fire from the forts as well. Much modified over the years, today Monte Fort holds the Macao Museum, with its battlements offering a fine view over the former Portuguese colony.

In the naval clash that followed, called the Battle of Cape Rachado, both sides lost a couple of ships and the Dutch under Admiral Matelief were driven off. But after refitting at Johore, Matelief returned a few months later, found only five galleons on guard off Malacca, and sunk them all. The remaining Portuguese ships then returned but lost three more galleons in the ensuing battle. As they were always short of galleons and mariners, outcomes like this spelled eventual doom for Portuguese seapower, and by extension, their empire.

The Spanish retake Ternate

69. Looking north-east from the ruins of Portuguese Kastella towards the battleground. On 1 April 1606, Acuna's Spanish troops formed up facing the sultan's outer defences, beyond where the stand of coconut palms is on the extreme right. Bastion Cachil Tulo stood around 200 metres beyond and in line with the mosque's dome. The high ground which was initially fought over is far left, behind the coconut trees. The mosque stands near the site of the former St Paul's Church.

The Spanish, however, were still determined to regain Ternate and with it, control over the Moluccas. They were also concerned that their China trade from Manila was threatened by the emergent VOC. And they appreciated that the Spice Islands, lying between the new VOC possessions on Java and the Philippines, represented a crucial strategic buffer. Governor Acuna set off from Manila in January 1606 with an enormous force. Five galleons, 13 frigates, four galleys and assorted smaller craft carried 1300 Spaniards and 400 local troops with all the necessary equipment and provisions for an extended expedition. Acuna did not intend to allow a sixth failure against Ternate.

Tidore's sultan, who was naturally keen to see the demise of his neighbour on Ternate, provided a squadron of korakora and 600 men for the attack. On the 1st of April, the Spanish landed between Talangame and Kastella, near Kaya Merah (Red Cape), and sent two columns towards Kastella: one along the narrow coast path, and one higher up through the hills. The higher route outflanked the sultan's fort at Kota Janji which guarded the narrow pass on the way to Kastella; this same fort had caused Morones and Gallinato so much trouble in previous attempts. Its defenders pulled back to Kastella, with the Spanish hot on their heels.

Acuna arrived, reconnoitred the defences, selected the site for his breaching cannon, positioned his troops and ordered the guns to be brought ashore. Kastella's defences were strong, well-armed and well-manned, and no doubt he considered that the path to victory would be long and difficult. We have a good contemporary account of the day's action, and it reveal much about Spice Islands warfare.

The Spanish were spread in companies facing the length of the wall between Nuestra Senora and Cachil Tulo bastions '... *within musket shot of the wall*'[72] (about 200 metres given the topography)[73] and taking fire from the cannon of the defences. Some tall trees nearby held enemy sentries who could survey the Spanish deployment and report this to those on the ramparts, so a force of musketeers deployed and eliminated these, and Spaniards were sent aloft in their place. This ability to observe and report on the moves of the sultan's forces was crucial to the subsequent victory.

Around noon, the hottest part of the equatorial day, one of Acuna's officers, Captain Cuevas, led a group of 25 musketeers to take a small rise that overlooked Cachil Tulo. This would be approximately the position where Fort Nova was later built. Not wanting to surrender the high ground, a force of Ternateans saw this move and left the fort to intercept, but after a brief skirmish, they retreated, and Cuevas established his force on the hill.

---

[72] *The Discovery and Conquest of the Molucco and Philippines Islands*, p. 244.

[73] allthingsliberty.com/2013/08/how-far-is-musket-shot-farther-than-you-think

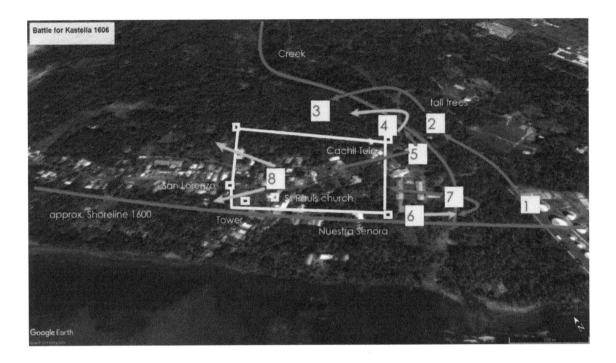

70. Pedro de Acuna, Spanish Governor of the Philippines, landed at Ternate and stormed Kastella on 1 April 1606. The battle is shown superimposed over a modern image. After advancing from his landing at Kayu Merah, Acuna deployed his companies to protect the position for his breaching cannon (1). Enemy observers in tall trees to the north were replaced with Spanish scouts (2), and a platoon of musketeers was sent to occupy higher ground looking down on the defences (3). A force of the enemy from bastion Cachil Tulo was sent to attack this group (4) but were themselves intercepted by Spanish pikemen (5). Another Ternatean force sallied out from bastion Nuestra Senora, but were repelled by companies from the main Spanish force, which then attacked the walls, and cleared the eastern ramparts (5 & 7). The Spaniards attacked fortified St Paul's inside the fortress, at which point the local forces fled (8).

Image credit: Google Earth/ Digital Globe.

More defenders led by the sultan himself emerged from Kastella to counter him, and pikemen had to be sent by the main force to assist. Again, the local forces retreated before the disciplined Spanish formations. They passed through a sally port into the fortress, with two groups of Spaniards following them through, and others mounting the walls. The first Spaniard atop the wall, Captain Cervantes, raised the colours, but was immediately run through the eye with a lance and thrown down, mortally wounded. Brutal hand-to-hand fighting along the wall ensued—Spanish rapier against Malay scimitar.

The scouts in the trees reported another counterattack, this time from Nuestra Senora, and Acuna deployed his own Halbardiers[74] and a company of musketeers to repel them. The Spaniards already inside the fortress by this stage had cleared both the bastions and the ramparts between them but were then halted at St Paul's, which had been converted to a strongpoint, armed with four cannon and defended by musketeers and arquebusiers.

Quickly it too was assaulted, and the defenders, including some Dutchmen, fled. That ended organised resistance. Luckily the old Portuguese fort inside the fortress was not defended:

> '... the attack was made so furiously, that the Spaniards gave not the King [sultan], nor his men Leisure enough to get into the old Portuguese Fort, which was within the Wall; for had they done so, they might have defended themselves some Time, and our men would have been oblig'd to batter the Walls with Cannon; and tho'the Fort is small, and built in more unskilful Times, it would have cost Trouble.'[75]

The sultan fled and his army disintegrated. His mistake was trying to fight in front of Kastella's walls rather than from behind them. The Spanish lost 15 dead and 20 wounded, which was a very light price to pay for what had been a frustrating quarter-century campaign. The Spaniards looted and pillaged the fortress and the royal city, while Acuna had St Paul's cleaned up so he could attend mass and give thanks. He had handled the campaign commendably and dealt with the peace with similar competence.

The sultan was enticed to return, then exiled to Manila, and a puppet installed on his throne. The sultans of Tidore and Bacan were rewarded with land and spoils from Ternate. Acuna had Kastella rebuilt in modern form, improving existing bastions and constructing new ones, as well as modifying the gates and building earthworks to protect the walls. Captured cannon—including many pre-1575 Portuguese guns—were supplemented with artillery from the fleet to arm the defences properly.

On a small rise that overlooked the fortress just to the north, and from where his musketeers had beaten the sultan's forces, Acuna gave orders for construction of a small new fort, to prevent attackers using its dominating position. This became Fort Nova.

On Tidore, Acuna also had the ruined Fort Reis Magos rebuilt and rearmed. A garrison of 500 soldiers was left at Kastella and another 100 on Tidore, all under the command of Lt Governor Esquivel. Both forts were left with ammunition and supplies

---

74   These troops were armed with a 1.5–2.0 metre lance-like weapon.

75   *The Discovery and Conquest of the Molucco and Philippines Islands*, p. 244.

for a year, and a small flotilla of armed galleys and brigantines based inside the reefs of Kastella. Small forts were established and manned (or existing lodges modified) at Jailolo, Makian, Motir and Bacan. In triumph, Acuna returned to Manila, but alas, he was poisoned and died soon after.

It was a year before another resupply arrived in the Spice Islands from Manila. Support for the garrison came from an unexpected quarter however, when Luis Torres arrived in January 1607 with two ships from Peru. One of the Manila galleons had been taken by the English privateer Thomas Cavendish off California in 1587 and, ever since, the Spanish had been actively exploring the Pacific to survey potential bases that could harbour pirates. In the process, they had discovered Vanuatu, the Solomons, Guam, the Carolines, Tuvalu, the Marquesas and probably Hawaii. Torres was on one of these voyages of exploration and after visiting Vanuatu and traversing the strait named for him between Australia and New Guinea, he sailed on to Ternate, staying there for five months waiting for the trade winds to take him north.

En route to Ternate, Torres had helped the allied Rajah of Bacan punish nearby rebels on Kayoa. Forty Spaniards supported 400 local warriors in four korakoras; their firepower helping to rout the enemy, with the combined force going on to destroy the fort and village. When he sailed for the Philippines, Torres left his smaller ship and 20 men at Ternate to bolster the garrison already much reduced by disease.[76]

New VOC headquarters

While Torres lay at anchor off Kastella, the next Dutch fleet arrived in the waters of the Indies. This was commanded by Admiral Matelief (who we have already met destroying two Portuguese squadrons off Malacca the year before). At Bantam he heard of the Spanish capture of Ternate and sailed there with eight ships and 500 men to re-establish control. When he viewed the new Spanish defences at Kastella, however, he realised his force was insufficient to overwhelm them, especially when the Ternateans offered him just 200 men rather than the 2000 he requested.

Matelief was an accomplished commander and a competent strategist. His young country had been at war with Spain—the most powerful nation in Europe—for over 20 years, and state-of-the-art fortifications in the Netherlands had played a crucial part in the Dutch success to date. The concept of a web of forts across the Indies commanding the spice plantations and bound together with superior VOC seapower

---

[76] *The Voyage of Torres*, Chapter 12.

represented an extension of the homeland strategy. It was now clear that the quick Dutch loss of Tidore and Ternate was the result of failure to organise and man proper defensive fortifications there, and so instead of attacking Kastella he decided to contain the Spanish by building a fortress on Ternate.

71. Fort Orange, Admiral Matelief's fortress built over an earlier local work, became the VOC headquarters of the Spice Islands from 1607. The sea used to lap at the bastions on the left.

He surveyed location alternatives and chose the existing local fort at Malayo as the optimum position. It was on the water's edge facing east, just north of the main harbour at Talangame, and looked across at Halmahera, from where much of Ternate's foodstuffs came. It was eight kilometres from Spanish Kastella, accessible to ships in all seasons and close to the main clove cultivation areas on the island. The local defensive engineering was improved, and a large irregular quadrilateral with four angled corner bastions emerged. It was 250 metres wide along the waterfront, reached inland 200 metres, sported a jetty, and had sufficient internal space to accommodate the regional administration, trade warehouses, magazines, barracks and workshops.

The new fort was commanded by Gerrit van der Buys and garrisoned with 40 men; three ships plus the yacht[77] *Duyfken* were left as the local naval squadron. Just after Matelief had departed for China, on 15 July, 250 Spanish soldiers from Kastella attacked the still incomplete fort but were repulsed with the help of Ternatean allies. It was a wasted opportunity for the Spanish. Never again would the Dutch position on Ternate be so vulnerable.

Matelief also recognised that the VOC needed a secure strategic base in the Indies to act as the anchor for the web of forts that were planned. Bantam had served as the main trade post to date but was not ideal as a permanent proposition. Ambon was too far east, Malacca remained in Portuguese hands; Singapore was even considered, but Matelief identified the village of Jacatra on the western end of Java as the most favourable candidate and reported this to the VOC command. Subsequently, Jacatra was acquired, became Batavia (now Jakarta) and served as the capital of the Dutch East Indies for over 300 years.[78]

Fort Malayo was followed by a flurry of Dutch fort building. New forts appeared at Tacome, Ternate (Fort Willemstadt, 1609), over an existing local fort and controlling the clove plantations in the north of Ternate, and on the island of Motir (Fort Nassau, 1609) between Tidore and Makian.[79] On Makian itself, the old Portuguese fort was captured and became Fort Mauritius (1612), and smaller redoubts at Tafasoho (c. 1615) and Tabelola (c. 1615) were established over previous trading posts. The Spanish fort— originally Portuguese—on Bacan was captured in November 1609, improved and renamed Fort Barneveld.[80]

Existing fortifications at Jailolo on Halmahera were also taken over by the Dutch and improved. In response to this construction campaign by the VOC, the Spanish could only manage a tiny fort today called Tolukko (1611), north of Malayo on Ternate; a fort on the west side of Tidore on the ruins of the old royal settlement of Marieco (1609); and a new and powerful fortress south of Soa Siu on the east coast of Tidore, Fort Tohula (1610–15). But it is away from the northern islands of cloves, and south to the

---

[77] Dutch term for a small warship; *Duyfken* had a crew of around 20 men, was armed with eight small guns and displaced around 100 tonnes. In 1606, the *Duyfken,* on a reconnaissance mission to the south, had been the first to map sections of the Australian coastline.

[78] Due to constant flooding and subsidence, Indonesian President Joko Widodo in September 2019 announced that Indonesia's capital would be moved from Jakarta to the island of Borneo.

[79] *The World of Maluku,* p. 153.

[80] colonialvoyage.com. *The Spanish Presence in the Moluccas: Ternate & Tidore.*

nutmeg-rich Bandas, that we must now turn, because this previously un-colonised area became a new battleground between the local people and the VOC, and between the English and the Dutch.

72. A watercolour published by Robert Sayer in London in 1754 showing the sophistication of Batavia, at the time the most European city of Asia. The citadel is visible on the left of the canal, with several other forts protecting the landward approaches.
Image credit: Rijksmuseum, Netherlands.

The battle for the Bandas

The Bandas had been 'found' by Portugal in 1511, but the islanders never allowed them any more than a trade post and paid no attention at all to Portuguese calls for a nutmeg monopoly. Bandanese and regional traders shipped the spices to Ternate and Malacca, and Portuguese galleons also called annually at the Bandas to purchase more. The system worked reasonably well without any military commitment, and in any case, the

Portuguese generally had their hands full in the Moluccas to the north. In 1529, they tried to build a fort on the main island, Banda (also Bandaneira), but when only the foundations were completed it was abandoned due to local hostility, and both sides reverted to the previous arrangements.

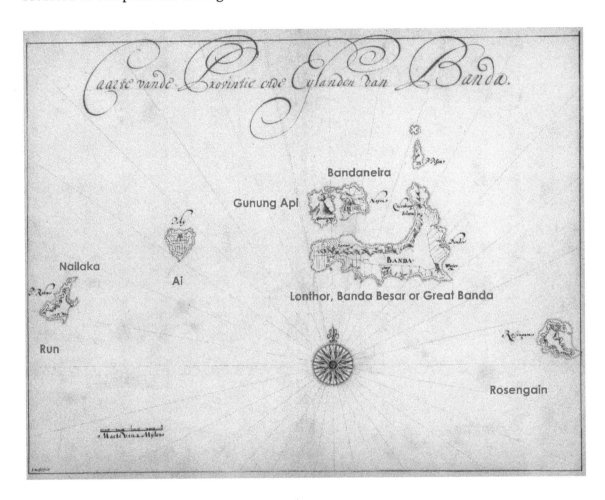

73. A nautical chart of the Banda group, by VOC surveyor Johannes Nessel from around 1650. Clustered in the centre is the largest island, known as Great Banda, with smaller Banda and Gunung Api just to the north-west. On the right is Rosengain, and to the west is first Ai, and then the legendary island of Run. From Run to Rozengain is around 22 nautical miles (41 km).

The first Dutch traders arrived in the Bandas in 1599 chasing nutmeg, and the first English ones in 1601. The Dutch left a trading lodge on Banda, and the English one on Run Island, eastern-most of the Bandas. This was England's very first overseas colonial outpost. Trading fleets from both nations continued to arrive annually, though the Dutch ones were much larger. They realised that nutmeg worth one *stuiver*[81] on Banda sold in the markets of Amsterdam for 320 *stuivers*,[82] and so quickly moved to establish a nutmeg monopoly.

The Banda *orang kaya*[83] were enticed by the Dutch to sign exclusive supply contracts in 1602—agreements the chiefs neither understood nor had any intention of complying with. Each subsequent fleet complained that the monopoly agreement was not being honoured by the Bandanese, and relations deteriorated.

Dutch Admiral Verhoeven sailed to Banda in April 1609 with a strong fleet and hundreds of men, charged by the VOC with gaining total control over the nutmeg industry. Naturally this meant getting rid of the English and all other traders and ensuring subservience from the locals. He entered drawn-out negotiations with the Bandanese, who struggled to understand why they should have their economy and future dictated to them by the Dutch. In frustration, on 25 April, Verhoeven put 750 men ashore on Banda to build a fort, without any sort of approval from the chiefs of the island. He initially rejected the site of the Portuguese fort—it was commanded by a nearby hill—but came back to it when the alternative was deemed unstable.

A few days later, he agreed to attend a meeting with some orang kaya in a remote spot on Banda and was ambushed and killed with 40 of his men. This 'vile treachery' (as the Dutch termed it) set the pattern for years of brutal warfare between the Dutch and Bandanese. The native population was almost wiped out, spice yields plummeted, and the VOC needed to plough more and more profits into maintaining garrisons, forts and fleets as well as importing slave labour to run the plantations.

In the immediate aftermath of the massacre, the remaining Dutch on Banda rushed to complete the new fort, christened Fort Nassau. It was a large quadrilateral with four corner bastions in the usual Dutch style of the Indies, around 100 metres from bastion point to point. Its guns could command the shipping channels from the west (Java) and from the north (Ambon) and the anchorage immediately to the south, as well as the main township nearby.

By July, the expected Bandanese attack had still not materialised and so the Dutch sent out a raid of their own against the township of Celamme on the large nearby island of Banda Besar. The locals had built what must have been a very effective defensive position, both well-armed and manned, and inflicted a stinging defeat on the

---

[81] A Dutch copper coin similar to a shilling, made up of 16 pennings. Forty-eight stuivers equalled a silver *rijksdaadler*.

[82] *Indonesian Banda*, p. 16.

[83] Village Councils of Elders.

attackers, causing 80 casualties. In response, the Dutch used their fleet to blockade the islands—which relied totally on external food supplies—and by August, in desperation, some of the Banda chiefs reluctantly signed another treaty of submission.

74. Dutch determination met Bandanese resistance head-on in the stunningly picturesque Banda Islands in the first decades of the seventeenth century, spiralling out of control into a cycle of violence and reprisals, with the Bandanese eventually losing not only their sovereignty, but also most of their population. This is coral-fringed Nailaka islet, near Run, with the cone of Gunung Api in the distance.

As previously, Dutch expectations and Bandanese compliance with the treaty provisions were wildly at variance. The English presence—they had by now established another trade lodge on Run's neighbour, Ai (also Ay)—prevented Dutch success in establishing a nutmeg monopoly, and neither the locals nor the English paid any attention to the VOC claim to sovereignty throughout the archipelago.

The VOC 'Gentlemen Seventeen'[84] back in Europe had appreciated the difficulties of communications with the distant Spiceries, and in 1610 appointed Peter Both as the first Governor General of the East Indies.

---

[84] The Heeren XVII were the governing council of the VOC, selected from the six founding chambers.

Both arrived with 11 East Indiamen and 500 soldiers at Ambon in March 1611 and sailed straight for Banda. He looked at Fort Nassau, recognised its vulnerability from the hill just to the north of it, and ordered construction to commence there of Fort Belgica. The possibility of the English acting in concert with the Bandanese and emplacing cannon above Nassau was too real to ignore. Fort Belgica started off as a smaller version of Fort Nassau, but after many modifications over the years its double pentagonal form emerged, and this is how it can be seen today, most magnificent of the Spice Islands forts, set amid the stunning scenery of the Bandas.

75. Unique among Spice Island Forts, Belgica (named after the Roman province that included the Netherlands) was rebuilt in 1673 with a high, round-towered, almost medieval pentagonal inner castle, surrounded by a low, outer, five-bastioned structure. It commands the main township of Banda, and the fortress of Nassau, below it.

Governor Both's next focus was on extending control over Ambon and evicting the Spanish from the Moluccas, and he sailed away to the north, believing the Bandanese, awed by his forts, would be suitably subservient. However, nutmeg continued to be sold outside Dutch control and the English remained on Run and Ai, encouraging rebellion among the locals. The Dutch tirelessly insisted that all nutmeg be handed over to them. The Bandanese in turn continued to demand the VOC remove their forts and their soldiers from the entire archipelago. In 1615 another powerful Dutch fleet arrived yet again, with strict orders to implement the monopoly on all nutmeg.

After preliminary negotiations failed to deliver the desired monopoly, General Reijnst sent Captain van der Dussen, commanding nearly a thousand men, ashore on Ai to establish VOC control. At the time, the island probably contained less than half that number of fighting-age local men, but they had some sophisticated defences, with strongpoints linked by trench systems covering the town beach and extending up to the island's high point in the east. The Javanese had some competent military engineers and had been allied with the Bandanese for decades in response to the Portuguese threat, and it is likely that they contributed to these defences. No doubt the English also provided some fortification expertise as well as weapons, and perhaps even training for the locals.

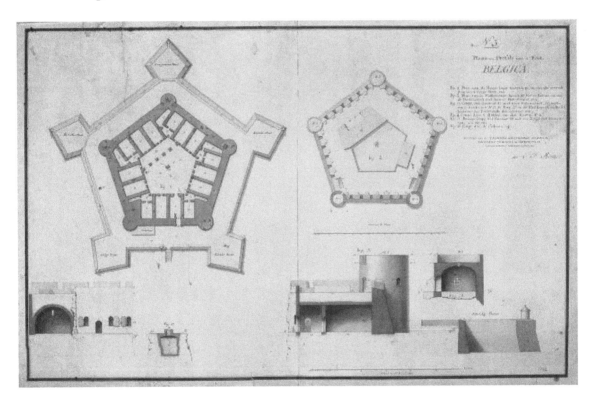

76. The fourth rebuild of Fort Belgica was designed by Dutch engineer Adriaan de Leeuw, who was also responsible for the improvements to the fortresses at Galle and Colombo in Ceylon (now Sri Lanka), and was completed in 1673. The sectional elevation in the bottom right shows the relationship between the inner and outer structures.
Image credit: Netherlands National Archives.

Nevertheless, the stronger Dutch numbers pushed the defenders back. Ai is tiny, at most just 2500 metres long, and as the sun dropped into the Banda Sea they had cleared all the defences except the final hilltop stronghold, suffering nine dead and 17 wounded to achieve this. They made camp, confidently expecting to confirm the victory next morning. During the night however, they were struck by a vicious counterattack and suffered heavy casualties—27 dead and 170 injured—and retreated to the ships. It was the heaviest defeat the VOC ever suffered in all the Spice Islands, and the third serious reverse the Bandanese had inflicted on the Dutch in four years.

77. Among the most tragic of all Spice Islands forts, Fort Revenge is a crumbling ruin—a reminder to the people of Ai of the carnage and destruction wrought on them by the VOC 400 years ago. Ai was totally surrounded by coral reefs and had no anchorage or fresh water, but it produced a decent nutmeg crop, and this proved its ruination.

Revenge drove the Dutch to return the next year in March. Van der Dussen was back with a land force 700 strong and a fleet under Admiral Jan Lam. After brushing aside an English squadron of four ships, the Dutch Indiamen were initially repulsed by shore-based cannon on Ai, but returned two weeks later. They landed, fought their way through the main defences, besieged the fort, stayed alert during the night, stormed the ramparts, then finished off the defenders over the next two days. At least half, and possibly most, of the 2000 inhabitants of Ai perished in the battle, its aftermath or in attempts to escape the island to Run. On the smoking ruins of the local fort, the Dutch built Fort Revenge.[85]

England versus the VOC

78. Tiny Nailaka (right) and larger Run (behind left) seem incongruous locations for a standoff between two of the great powers of the era, England and the Netherlands.

With victory at Ai, the Dutch became very aggressive defending what they regarded as 'their' East Indies from what they saw as other European interlopers. They had signed treaties with many local rulers throughout the Spice Islands which they considered gave them exclusive trade rights. No matter that the local rulers had signed these

---

[85]   atlasofmutualheritage.nl/en/fort-revenge

agreements under duress and failed to understand the language they were written in let alone their complex legalistic meaning. But, with many written accounts emerging in Europe about the Indies, the alluring profits from the spice trade were now apparent to all, and competitors began to accumulate.

Danish trading ships arrived in India in 1615, and a number of private French companies were formed at the same time for exploiting trade with Asia, many using ex-VOC officers as captains. One of the four ships of the French *Company of the Moluccas* sent to Java in 1616 was captured and impounded by the VOC at Bantam. A second fleet with three ships sent in 1619 from St Malo lost one vessel in a battle with Dutch ships off Sumatra, and the others had their Dutch officers arrested. Discouraged, from this point on, French efforts were focused on India, Persia and Siam.

But it was the English East India Company (EIC), established in 1600, that formed the biggest European threat to the VOC. In its early days it was never as well-resourced or funded in the Indies as was the VOC. Its fleets and manpower were always much more limited, its trading activities less disciplined. EIC maintained a trading lodge at Bantam on Java, and another on Run, and for a short time at Cambello on Seram, but while they exasperated the Dutch, they were not a serious threat to the activities of the VOC.

Arriving in 1613, the new factor of the EIC on Java, John Jourdain meant to change all that. In 1615 the English lodge at Cambello was attacked by the Dutch and abandoned.[86] Jourdain appreciated that Run was the last of the Spice Islands not in the hands of the Dutch or Spanish. The VOC forts of Nassau, Belgica and Revenge controlled all the other nutmeg islands, the Dutch commanded the coasts of Ambon and Seram, and the clove islands of the northern Moluccas were heavily contested between the Dutch and the Spanish. England had been too slow in planting its flag. Run was its last possible option.

In 1616 Jordain sent the aggressive and irrepressible Captain Courthope from Bantam with two Indiamen to Run, with orders to sign up the local orang kaya, challenge the Dutch domination of the islands, and secure more nutmeg. Courthope arrived in December with the winter monsoon, and quickly agreed a treaty with the chiefs, gaining sovereignty for England. Next, he modified the trading lodge on Run into the first English Spice Islands fort.[87]

On a small rise overlooking the main village and its tiny harbour, Fort Swan was constructed and armed with three guns from his ship of that name. On the adjacent

---

[86] *Annals of the Honourable East India Company*, p. 179.

[87] For more on Captain Courthope and the English Spice Islands forts, see *Nathaniel's Nutmeg*.

islet of Nailaka, Fort Defence was sited, also with three cannon. These defences covered the potential landing sites in an otherwise reef-ringed island, but the problem was Run had no water or food available, and so could be easily blockaded.

Today, dive tours from Banda often stop at Nailaka, and tourists snorkel along the great drop-off as huge manta rays and wrasse cruise by just offshore, oblivious to the tortured history of the island and its nutmeg just metres away. Four hundred years ago, the Bandanese traded nutmeg surreptitiously with the English on Run. They enjoyed evading Dutch overlordship, and anyway the English paid higher prices than the fixed VOC rates. The Dutch were aware of these leaks in their nutmeg monopoly and determined to stamp out the English presence in the islands.

79. While they look like torn down battlements, this rock shelf on Nailaka is part of the geological structure of the island, and not the remnants of Fort Defence, built in 1616 and destroyed by the Dutch in 1620. This had been one of Nathaniel Courthope's English forts.

In 1617, the VOC at Banda intercepted one of Courthope's ships, the *Swan*, chasing provisions, captured it after a short battle, and then bribed some aboard his other ship, the *Defence*, to surrender it at Banda. With no vessels left to obtain supplies, and the

Dutch blockading the island, time was running out for the English. An EIC supply ship was captured in sight of Run in 1618, leading to morale plummeting. Finally, an English fleet arrived at Bantam in early 1619, gaining a rare numerical superiority over the local VOC squadron. The two sides fired 3000 rounds at each other, leading the Dutch to withdraw to Banda, but the English failed to finish them off and then were repulsed in their attempt to capture the new VOC headquarters at Batavia. The English fleet withdrew to India, leaving the battered Dutch squadron still in command of the Indies.

The half-starved handful of English on Run survived until 1620, when the indefatigable Courthope was killed by a Dutch patrol while trying to run the blockade in a local vessel. His dispirited men, by then only a few dozen strong, long abandoned by their Company and country, were then faced with a Dutch assault by an overwhelming force. They surrendered, and were given passage to Ambon, while the Run islanders were enslaved and made to sign a treaty of submission. The Dutch destroyed the island's nutmeg trees, spiked the English cannon, and made the locals demolish the two little forts. Such a thorough job was done that not a trace of either can today be found.

The fourth Governor General of the VOC, Jan Pieterszoon Coen, was appointed in 1618. As a young trader he had been lucky to avoid death in the ambush that claimed Admiral Verhoeven and many of his staff, on Banda back in 1609. It was an event the Bandanese would now suffer even more for. Coen was young, energetic, ruthless and determined. Banda and Ai had been pacified, and the English driven from Run. Of the main islands, only Banda Besar, the largest island of the group, remained unsubdued. In March 1621 he invaded, putting in amphibious landings supported by his fleet at several points around the island. Gradually his forces established control, killing those who resisted, collecting and deporting the local population who would not submit and importing slaves from outside the region to tend the nutmeg groves.

As a finale, the last 44 of the orang kaya of all the Bandas were rounded up, tortured, tried and found guilty of rebellion, then beheaded and quartered in the grounds of Fort Nassau on 8 May 1621. Of the 15,000 Bandanese who are estimated to have inhabited the archipelago before the Dutch arrival, only about one thousand survived.[88]

By 1623, the VOC had unquestioned control over all the nutmeg islands, reinforced by their forts on all the major islands. To complement Nassau, Belgica and Revenge, new works were now built to maintain control over Banda Besar including a battery at Lakui (1620), Fort Hollandia (1624) and Fort Concordia (1630), as well as a number of smaller redoubts around the coast.

---

[88] *Indonesian Banda*, p. 55.

80. Views of the citadel and town of Batavia from around 1683. While it was a long way west of the Spice Islands, it was well positioned to access the Indian Ocean and the trade routes to China and Japan to the north.

The irony for the Dutch was that despite finally establishing control over the islands, nutmeg yields declined. They were delicate plants that needed to be harvested at exactly the right time by skilled labour, not slaves, and then preserved and stored in time-honoured methods, which no-one now knew.

In the end, the VOC's superior capital base allowed a combination of modern forts to spread throughout the Indies linked by strong naval squadrons, and this proved an insurmountable obstacle to the English. The few EIC ships were at the mercy of larger

Dutch fleets, and the trade was no longer profitable. The Ambon Massacre of 1623, where 17 English traders were tortured and executed by VOC courts for rebellion, brought the formal English presence in the Indies to an end, at least until 1796. Apart from the occasional local rebellion, the Banda Sea became a VOC lake.

The contest for Tidore

81. A VOC galleon battles a Spanish galley off Kastella on Ternate. Mediterranean-style oared galleys were very useful in the often-windless archipelagic waters of the Indies, and the Portuguese began building them at Malacca as early as 1512. Local potentates followed suit; the Acehnese had a number in their fleet which laid siege to Malacca in 1568. The largest of these mounted 12 camelos (18-pounders), 12 falcons and 40 swivel guns. The Spanish galley here probably mounted a single 12-pounder flanked by two nines in the bow, with a number of smaller swivels fore and aft, and would have been considerably outgunned by the galleon.

We can now return north to the Spanish–Dutch conflict, centred on the Moluccas. At the beginning of 1608, a stalemate had developed across the clove islands, though it was not to last long. The Spanish had a somewhat tenuous hold over the islands today known as the Philippines, to the north of the Moluccas, while the Dutch were working hard to cement their control over the islands to the south, now generally Indonesia. The flashpoint in the middle was the Moluccas. Here, each side had their local allies— the Spanish with Tidore, and the Dutch with Ternate—and both relied on local manpower to support their campaigning.

Ternate Island was divided between the two sides, while the Spanish held all of Tidore, and most of Makian and Bacan. The great swathe of nearby Halmahera contained settlements from both sides; extensions of the age–old conflict between the two principal sultanates, Ternate and Tidore.

A Dutch squadron under Admiral van Carden kicked off the next decade of conflict and fort building in June 1608 by bombarding Reis Magos on Tidore. Surprisingly, he found it too hard to crack, and so went on to capture Tafassoho fort on Makian to the south. Three Spanish galleys contested the attack and crippled one of the Dutch vessels, the little *Duyfken,* but were driven off.[89] Two VOC galleons, the *China* and the *Walcheren,* were sunk with all hands by a tsunami associated with a 'seaquake' during this operation; a reminder of the ever–present threat to ships and forts that natural forces posed in this geologically unstable region.

The Spanish, augmented by a fleet of Tidorean korakora, countered this by capturing Jailolo and raiding Gamkanora and Sahu, all on Halmahera. Van Carden then took a small force north and captured the remote Spanish fort on Siau Island, halfway between Ternate and Mindanao, and a prime location to intercept Spanish convoys between Manila and Ternate. Stopping near Gamkanora on Halmahera on the return voyage, his frigate ran aground; he was captured by the Spanish and ignominiously imprisoned in Kastella—a fortress which he declared the Spanish had by now made invulnerable to attack.[90]

Concerned about the undefended west coast of Tidore, in 1609 the Spanish quickly built a small two–bastion stone fort, Fort Marieco, to prevent the Dutch doing likewise. It was close to the ruins of the old sultan's capital, which had been overrun by the Portuguese back in 1524. At the same time, they rebuilt the damaged Reis Magos yet again. A few months later the next in an endless series of VOC fleets arrived in the Moluccas, under Admiral Wittert.

---

89   The *Duyfken* made it back to Ternate, but sunk as repairs were being made.

90   colonialvoyage.com/verrichtingen-van-de-admiraals-cornelis-Matelief-de-jonge-en-paulus-van-caerden-de-aanval-van-de-hollanders-op-de-estado-da-india

To illustrate the ambitions and resources of the VOC, which that year paid its shareholders a dividend of 325%, this fleet consisted of 13 ships, 2800 men and carried over 400 guns. Wittert considered the best way to punish the Spanish was to attack their base at Manila, and so led some of his ships there for the first Battle of Playa Honda in 1609, but was killed and his four ships destroyed by a scratch squadron commanded by the plucky Philippines Governor, Juan de Silva.

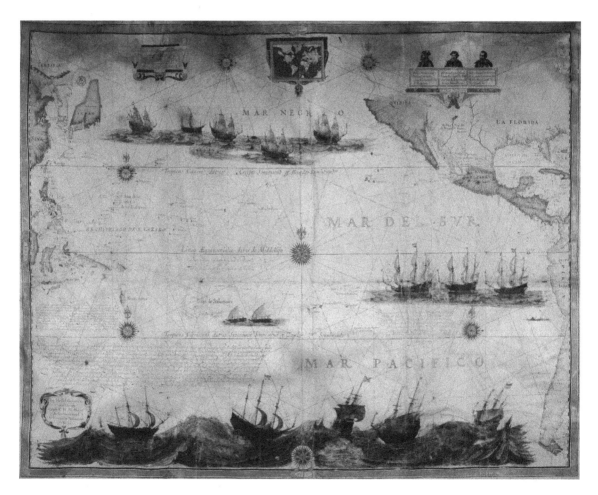

82. A captivating map of the Pacific Ocean, by Hessel Gerritsz from 1622. Gerritsz was a cartographer for the VOC, so the depiction is a good representation of contemporary knowledge, including a very early part of Australia's Cape York from the Janzoon *Duyfken* visit in 1606 (just above the lower left wind rose). Centred on the equator, the map shows the Spice Islands at far left, including the principal Moluccas, Ambon and Banda Islands. Out of deference to his pioneering voyage, Magellan is shown in the centre of the busts at right. The upper and lower ship images include Dutch Indiamen and Spanish galleons. The enormity of the Pacific is clearly apparent.

Van Carden was ransomed for 6000 ducats and released, then appointed Governor of Malucco, but incredibly, soon after was captured again by Spanish forces at sea near Makian and imprisoned until he died at Manila in 1615. After his Manila victory, de Silva spent the next five years coordinating a combined Spanish–Portuguese offensive to clear the Dutch from the Indies once and for all. Back in Europe in 1609, the Twelve Year Truce had begun between the Dutch and Spain—a break in their Eighty Years War—though it was to have only minimal effect on the ground in the Indies.

In 1610 a VOC fleet blockaded Tidore, bombarded Reis Magos, landed troops and guns to take the fort, but then suffered the misadventure of their admiral dying, and so packed it all up and sailed off to invade Bacan instead. After the loss of remote Bacan, Spanish Governor of the Moluccas Jeronimo de Silva recognised that with great fleets of the VOC arriving each year, his somewhat dispersed forces needed to be concentrated. In 1613 he abandoned some of his bases on Halmahera and reinforced his positions on Ternate and Tidore, including building a new fort in the south-east of the island, known as Sokanora. It protected the 'back door' of Fort Tohula and Soa Siu. Luckily, because it was there that the next Dutch fleet was headed.

With a fort at Marieco on the west coast of Tidore, the main town on the east coast bracketed by Reis Magos to the north and another more substantial fortress—Fort Tohula—under construction just to the south, with a fourth fort further to the south again, the Spanish position on the island was becoming impregnable. The few reef-free stretches of coast were all guarded by Spanish forts. Perhaps the VOC understood what a powerful fortress Tohula would become when completed, and therefore decided to act before it was.

Marieco linked closely with Kastella, and was well placed to intercept Dutch shipping heading from Fort Orange south to Makian, Bacan and Ambon. The VOC saw the expanding chain of Spanish forts as a real threat to their holdings. Galleys based at Tohula and Marieco could cut their Moluccan empire in half. In February 1613, Admiral Peter Both with five galleons and seven korakora carrying 800 Dutch soldiers and allied local warriors, crossed at night from Talangame to Marieco. The Spanish fort was defended by just two cannon and a dozen men. The simple defences could not make up for such a disparity in numbers, but the Spanish defended to the end, only one of them surviving the clash. Fort Marieco emerged much more powerful, with the Dutch swiftly giving it their standard four corner-bastion layout, arming it with 17 guns and stationing two companies as its garrison.

Now they held the key stronghold on the west of Tidore, the Dutch were after the east. In July 1613, Admiral Both with a dozen galleons, 700 men and assisted by 40 korakora with over a thousand Ternateans set out for Tidore. First target on the list was poor little Reis Magos, northern guardian of Soa Siu town. Always a weak and ineffective fort, it had been the focus of some heavy VOC attention. It was blown apart by the Dutch in 1605 and then abandoned, rebuilt by Acuna in 1606, bombarded by Matelief in 1608, attacked in 1610 and now in 1613 it faced yet another assault. It was never a strong work or provided with an adequate garrison, and it appears it was detached from the main town defences and hence difficult to reinforce. The Dutch ships bombarded it for three hours, firing 200 shots, and then eight companies landed and stormed the fort, the 50 or so Spanish soldiers dying to a man at their posts.

83. Looking south from above Soa Siu on Tidore, with the ruins of Fort Tohula in the centre. The fortifications at Sokanora were sited at the village in the middle distance, but no trace remains. Motir Island is in the background. The Dutch unsuccessfully attacked Sokanora from korakora in 1613 when Tohula was still under construction, but they were beaten off.

The Dutch then attacked the town defences of Soa Siu, just to the south. We have little knowledge of the Spanish–Tidore defences here in 1613, but they turned back 800 soldiers flushed with victory over Reis Magos and bent on looting Tidore's capital, so they must have been designed, constructed, armed and manned in a competent manner. It is likely they extended from the coast some distance inland to prevent outflanking, consisted of a series of palisades, ramparts, ditches and bastions, and were held by hundreds of the sultan's men, backed by Spaniards with swivel guns and muskets.

Repulsed at these walls, the Dutch then sent part of their force by korakora to attack from south of the town, landing at the village of Sokanora, which was defended by a small new Spanish fort. Three attacks against it were beaten back, and the Dutch had no alternative but to withdraw. They left a small force at Reis Magos, but this was untenable so close to hundreds of Tidore warriors and Spanish cannons, and they were withdrawn within months, no doubt to the relief of those posted there.

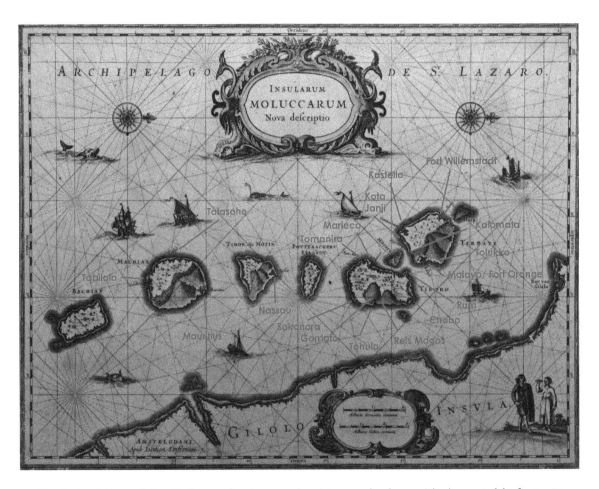

84. A depiction of the Moluccas by Jansson in 1645, marked up with the notable forts. It was one of the densest concentrations of colonial forts anywhere in the world. This distinctive map was originally produced by Jodocus Hondius in 1620, but the engraving was later purchased by Willem Blaeu, who engraved himself as the mapmaker. Such copying of other mapmakers' works was common in the era, and many other marginally different versions of this attractive map by many different producers have survived to this day. North is at right.

It was the last of the open battles between the Dutch and the Spanish in the Spiceries. Perhaps the peace from Europe was filtering through at last, although the Philippine Governor, Juan de Silva, had other ideas. He had been trying to combine with Portuguese forces from Malacca to clear the VOC from the entire East Indies since 1610. Finally, in 1616, he set out from Manila with a formidable force of ten galleons, 5000 men—including 2000 Spaniards—and 400 guns and sailed to Malacca to rendezvous with the Portuguese squadron. Unfortunately for the Iberians, they had already been destroyed by a Dutch fleet.

85. A jumble of volcanic rock is all that remains of the Spanish fort of Tomanira, built to outflank and keep an eye on Dutch Marieco in 1613. Though only slightly inland, the climb up is hard going; it must have been a challenge to bring the materials for a gun platform and its cannon up there. The defences were simply rolled down the hill when the Spanish departed in 1663.

De Silva died of sickness at Malacca soon after, as had many of his men through months of aimless cruising, and his fleet returned to Manila, never getting close to the Spice Islands. It was latest in a long list of Iberian naval disasters in East Indian waters, though had the intended blow connected it could well have spelled ruin, at least in the

Moluccas, for the VOC. Another combined Iberian fleet consisting of 732 seamen and 1700 soldiers in six galleons and some smaller ships left Cadiz for Manila in December 1619, but all except one were wrecked in a storm near Gibraltar with appalling loss of life.

The storm subsides

86. Often erroneously attributed to the Portuguese, Tolukko was Spanish built in 1611, abandoned to the Dutch soon after, and then given by them to the sultan who rebuilt it as his residence. It played a part in repelling a British attack in 1801. It remains the best example of local fortification engineering throughout the Spice Islands. The peak of Tidore's volcano is in the background.

Instead of open conflict, perhaps in light of peace in the homelands, after the 1613 battles the protagonists reverted to fort building. On Tidore, the VOC held onto Fort Marieco until June 1621, when they dismantled and abandoned it. It was little use to them as a lonely bastion on Tidore, and was very exposed. The Spanish had built two forts to contain it, Tomanira (1613) on a steep hill by a small cove 2400 metres south of Fort Marieco, and Run (1618), four kilometres to the north facing Tidore and Maitara. Tomanira held around 40 men and three guns while Run consisted of a waterside gun platform with five cannon to deter landings at the adjacent beach, and a higher observation tower set within a walled enclosure mounting four guns.

There was also an energetic burst of fort building on Ternate. The last fort built, back in 1611, had been tiny Tolukko. It was constructed by the Spanish to contain the Dutch at Malayo, but was too small to accomplish that and its position far too exposed to fulfil any meaningful role, and so it was abandoned by them soon after. The Dutch quickly took possession of it, then gave it to Sultan Modafar as his private palace, and he had it modified to suit his entourage. His engineers gave it the distinctive 'local' flavour we can still see today.

Further west on Ternate, two new forts also sprung up to define the 'frontline' between the Dutch and Spanish camps. Some 1600 metres separated the existing Spanish fort at Kota Janji (known then as Fort Don Gil or St Peter and Paul) and the Dutch fort on Kaya Merah (known now as Kalomata). In this space, two 'star' forts emerged in 1618, one Dutch and one Spanish. The exact location of these two works today is unknown; they are buried somewhere under the urban sprawl of Ternate city. But it would make tactical sense for the new forts to be supportive of the old ones. Furthermore, as both Kota Janji and Kayu Merah are waterfront structures, they were vulnerable to artillery emplaced inland of them on rising ground. Forts hate being overlooked, and so it is probable that the new forts were positioned inland and above the existing ones to prevent the opposition dragging guns up there.

First, the Dutch built their Fort Kalomata. Contemporary artwork shows a dry moat, an outer timber palisade with barracks inside for a company of troops, and then a stone-walled fort big enough to hold half a dozen guns. If we recall Acuna's attack on Kastella in 1606, he used pioneers to build a path around and above the sultan's defences at Kota Janji, outflanking it. Once the Dutch had built Fort Kalomata, the Spanish were no doubt concerned that history may repeat, and so they built their Fort St Lucia on higher ground, looking down at Kota Janji, to block this route. As the status quo settled down on Ternate, and skirmishes diminished, the Dutch abandoned their Fort Kalomata in 1625, and the Spanish moved into it, vacating their own Fort St Lucia the next year.

By the mid 1620s, the conflict between Spain and the Netherlands in the Moluccas had calmed down, although the war continued strongly in other areas. Formosa (now Taiwan) was a particular battleground from 1626 until the Spanish were evicted in 1642, and the VOC always coveted the Spanish Philippines. One last Moluccan fort was built, Fort Chobo, in the north of Tidore, by Spain in 1643, looking across to Malayo. The Eighty Years War finally came to an end with the Peace of Munster in 1648, and generations of conflict faded slowly away.

For the Portuguese, independence was finally achieved from Spain in 1640 but, unfortunately for them, this did not help in their struggle against the Dutch. On the contrary, after peace between the Netherlands and Spain in 1648, the Dutch became even more focused on dismantling the profitable parts of the Portuguese Empire. And they had the resources to do so. While the Dutch West Indian Company was defeated in its lengthy attempt to gain control of Portuguese Brazil, and Macau famously held off several attacks, the list of other Portuguese possessions built up at great cost in the heady early days of empire and now lost was extensive.

87. Once the period of conflict calmed, the scattered garrisons spread across the islands still had to contend with isolation, boredom, disease, harsh discipline, and a hard climate with the ever-changing monsoons. This is a crumbling, earthquake-shattered bastion of Fort Concordia, one of the most remote Spice Islands forts.

Hormuz fell to the Persians in 1622; the three forts on the Gold Coast were lost to the Dutch in 1637, 1640 and 1642; the Portuguese were evicted from Japan in 1639; on Ceylon, the Dutch took impregnable Galle in 1640, Colombo in 1656 and the last Portuguese stronghold, at Jaffna, in 1658; Luanda and Sao Tome were captured in 1641; Kupang on Timor fell to the VOC the same year; and finally, also in 1641, the greatest loss of all in South-East Asia, the spice hub of Malacca fell to the Dutch after a long siege and a sea blockade that had started back in 1634.

By 1650 the Portuguese were ejected from Muscat, last of their Persian Gulf bases, and by 1700 they had lost most of their remaining possessions in India. Apart from Macao, they were able to retain only Solor, Flores, part of Timor, and Goa, Diu and Daman in India. The incredible Portuguese had burst into the Asian world in 1500 like a howling typhoon, but now faded away like a soft tropical breeze at sunset. With determination, capital, ruthlessness and vision, the VOC had built an empire across the Indies in just 25 years, destroying Portugal's century-old version in the process.

In the Spice Islands, by the 1630s, imperceptibly at first, the importance of the Moluccas was beginning to decline. The twilight years of Ternate and Tidore were just beginning. Most significantly, cloves were now grown in plantations in other regions, and the plants in the Moluccas were no longer the only source. The Portuguese had started planting cloves in the Ambon area after they were ejected from Ternate in the mid-1570s, and the VOC continued and expanded this practise to include other parts of Ambon, and Seram. In addition, the powerful kingdom of Makassar on Sulawesi had developed into a major entrepot for spices—smuggled out of VOC-controlled lands—and attracted traders from all over Asia, as well as the English, Spanish and Portuguese. The incessant decades of warfare across the Moluccas had also taken their toll. Depopulation and destruction of the wild clove trees had dramatically decreased the annual crop.

Perhaps inevitably, the Spanish lost interest in their possessions on Ternate and Tidore. Rather than being the flashpoint between two warring empires, they were now a backwater in a changed world. The expense of maintaining the forts and garrisons was no longer worth the trade in spices, which were now in any case widely available. At Manila, the governor was perpetually anxious about threats to the Philippines from China and Japan.

In 1662, the decision was made to recall the Spanish troops stationed in the Moluccas and to demolish the forts. Kastella, Kota Janji, Kalomata, Chobo, Rum, Tohula, Tomanira and Sokanora were all wrecked with varying degrees of efficiency. On 2 May 1663, the last 'Captain of the Castle', Don Francisco de Attleinso, boarded a junk off Kastella, other junks taking his troops, guns, townspeople and spices, leaving the once-legendary isles of cloves to the Dutch. Of course, they maintained to the Dutch that their forts remained sovereign Spanish territory, but everyone knew that was a charade and that they were never coming back.

88. The sun set on the Iberian Spice Islands empires in 1663. The Portuguese had arrived in 1512, and the Spanish in 1522. Spain would retain control over the Philippines until lost to the US in 1898, while Portugal held on to part of Timor until abandoning it in 1975 but, after 1663, it was the Dutch who held all the Spice Islands.

6. The Dutch supremacy 1663–1942

89. Fort Amsterdam on the northern coast of Ambon Island was an example of the post-conflict period of Dutch fort style. Originally built in 1633, it was rebuilt several times after earthquake and tsunami damage, and periods of disrepair. Although retaining waterfront-angled bastions for mounting anti-ship cannon, the large central blockhouse became the fort's focal point, more suitable for dealing with local rebellion than attacks from other European powers, and reminiscent of the medieval 'keep' of times long past. A small garrison could withstand a local siege inside until help arrived, safe behind metre-thick walls.

With Spain's unilateral abandonment of Ternate and Tidore in 1663 and the departure of the English East India Company from their long-standing trading lodge at Bantam in 1683, the seas of the East Indies became unequivocally Dutch. Peripheral Portuguese bases remained on Timor, Flores and Solor, and there was an English fort at Bencoolen in Sumatra, but otherwise from Malacca to New Guinea and north to the Sulu Sea, the VOC ruled supreme.

Any celebrations at finally achieving sole control over the major nodes of the archipelago were tempered by some sobering realisations. As the Spanish had recognised before their withdrawal, the cost of maintaining the numerous forts and garrisons across the far-flung islands was ruinously expensive, but they needed to be kept up-to-date to deal with both external threats and internal security. Secondly, in reality, the VOC had no monopoly, for either cloves or nutmeg. A huge proportion of the crop was smuggled in local shipping to markets like Makassar, and soon the Spice Islands were no longer the world's only sources of these once-rare plants.

90. *De Ambonische Hingi of de Coracora Vloot*, an engraving from Francois Valentijn of 1726, depicting a *hongi* fleet of 66 korakora on a pacification/punishment deployment in 1702. Local rulers were required to provide the warcraft, manpower and supplies for these extended operations, which sailed under Dutch command.
Image credit: Rijksmuseum, Netherlands.

Another issue was that in the mid seventeenth century only a fraction of what now makes up modern Indonesia was under the control of the VOC. Even on the main island of Java, the Dutch were not masters until 1684 when their client sultanate, Bantam, destroyed Mataram in the Java Civil War. Pacifying and extending control over some of the outer islands like Borneo, Sumatra and Sulawesi took literally centuries. Aceh on Sumatra, which had fought the Portuguese almost non-stop since they first took Malacca in 1511, did not fully submit to the Dutch until 1912, and fought on against the Indonesian state until 2005. Bali surrendered, after decades of pacification campaigns, only in 1908. And authority over the wild valleys and mountains of western New Guinea (now Indonesian Irian Jaya) was only tentatively achieved in 1920. Western adventurers were still being consumed by local head-hunters there as late as the 1960s.[91]

There was an endless list of petty sultans, princes, merchants, holy men and pirates to negotiate with, cajole, bribe, subdue and destroy, and every operation required men and ships and guns and money and allied levies. In 1618 the VOC had started the *hongi-tochten* or 'duty-rounds' where administrators and soldiers would direct local militias and cruise on extended missions in huge fleets of korakora, demanding tribute and submission, rewarding and punishing. Destroying illegal spice trees was one of the prime functions. These visually spectacular operations would continue for more than two centuries and were the predominant method of the Dutch to maintain control over the widely spread outer islands.

The Anglo–Dutch Wars

In the period between the Spanish withdrawal in 1663 and the Japanese invasion in 1942, there were only two significant external interventions in the Spice Islands; these were during the French Revolutionary and Napoleonic wars, and both by Britain. A complex series of stop-start wars between England (Great Britain from 1707) and the Netherlands ran for over 150 years from the mid seventeenth century, some with just the two nations as protagonists, the latter ones involving much of Europe during the Coalition Wars against Republican France.

The First Anglo–Dutch War began in 1652 soon after the end of the English Civil War, when the English Navigation Acts—requiring trade to English colonies to be carried in English ships—threatened the very existence of the Dutch mercantilist model. There was also still residual anger about the Dutch eviction of the English from

---

91 nydailynews.com/entertainment/music-arts/michael-rockefeller-killed-eaten-headhunters-claim-article

the Spice Islands, and particularly the treatment of traders during the Amboyna Massacre of 1623. Naval battles in the Channel and the Mediterranean led to mutual exhaustion and peace in 1654.

The Second Anglo–Dutch War broke out just the next year, the English taking Manhattan Island in the Americas, but in the end being defeated by much stronger Dutch naval power. The raid by Admiral de Ruyter up the Thames, which signalled the end of the war, remains one of the most humiliating episodes in all of British naval history. Peace came with the 1667 Treaty of Breda, where the formal exchange of ownership of Manhattan to the English and Run Island to the Dutch was agreed as part of the broader settlement. A tiny nutmeg island was swapped for Manhattan!

Just five years later, there was war yet again between the two Protestant trading neighbours. This time a recently restored English King Charles was supporting the French invasion of the Netherlands. Dutch naval power defeated repeated Anglo–French attacks, the Netherlands emerging the victor at the end of hostilities in 1674. At this point, the Dutch were at the very peak of their global power, and England was recovering from a debilitating civil war. Yet another conflict broke out from 1781 to 1784 but, as with the previous three wars, it had little effect in the Spice Islands, apart from encouraging the VOC to ensure their fortifications were up-to-date.

In 1795, however, the fifth in the series of Anglo–Dutch wars commenced when the Republic of the Seven United Netherlands became the Batavian Republic, allied with Revolutionary France against the monarchist forces of the First Coalition. This struggle brought war straight to the Spice Islands.

Firstly, a British squadron took the crucial interoceanic base at Cape Town. This was followed up with operations out of India to seize Batticloa, Jaffnapatam, Trincomalee and Colombo in Ceylon (Sri Lanka), Cochin and all the other Dutch possessions in India, and the now sleepy Malacca, which the Dutch had taken from the Portuguese in 1641. Virtually all the way points between the East Indies and the Netherlands had been lost. Worse was to follow for the Dutch in the Spice Islands.

In February 1796, British Admiral Rainier sailed from newly captured Malacca and arrived off Ambon with the *Suffolk* 74, *Centurion* 50, *Resistance* 44, *Orpheus* 32 and other vessels including three troopships. The Dutch governor immediately surrendered Fort Victoria with its 164 cannon, 1118 muskets and all the islands under his control. Part of the spoils was 226,000 kg of cloves and 81,000 rixdollars.[92] [93] Leaving two companies

---

[92]   *Indonesian Banda*, p. 91.

[93]   A rixdollar, or *rijksdaadler*, was a Dutch one-ounce silver coin, roughly equal to a ducat. Some 81,000 today would be approximately US$1.5 million.

of Europeans and three of Indian infantry as a garrison at Ambon, Rainier sailed south to the Bandas where the garrison at least opened fire on the attackers.

91. Run Island, conquered by the VOC in 1620. Similarly, Manhattan Island, centrepiece of today's New York but then a swampy Dutch fur-trading station beset by Indian tribes, had been conquered by the English in 1664. The Treaty of Breda of 1667 formalised the status quo, with England conceding Run to the Netherlands, and in return taking sovereignty over what was then New Amsterdam on Manhattan. Contemporary observers looking at the deal and recognising the respective values of fur and nutmeg saw the Dutch as having got the edge in the negotiations.

Standing off the northern tip of Banda Island on 8 March, Rainier sent two frigates in to cover a landing by marines and sailors, the two ships engaging and silencing two small batteries, those of Balavier and Costricum east of the Pappenberg. Later that evening the governor surrendered the fortresses of Belgica and Nassau, their 367 guns, all the other defences throughout the Bandas, 67,000 rixdollars and around 100,000 kg of nutmeg and mace.

The expensively maintained forts, their hundreds of cannon and the garrison (over 500 men in 1756) were all vanquished in the light of a tropical day, the five British captains taking £15,000 (about US$125 million today[94]) *each* as prize money.

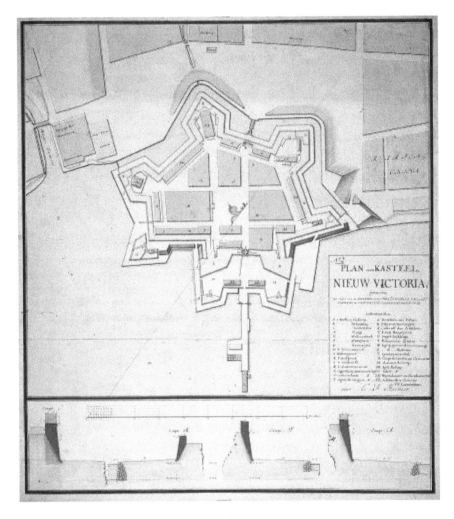

92. A surveyor's detail of Fort Nieuw Victoria just after a major rebuild, and just before it surrendered to the British without firing a shot in 1795.
Image credit: Netherlands National Archives.

A separate force was detached from Ambon in January 1801 to subdue Ternate. While it was supported by a frigate and a sloop of the Royal Navy, this operation was carried out by the East India Company (EIC), whose troops had formed the new garrison at

---

94   measuringworth.com

Ambon. It consisted of 40 gunners of the Madras Artillery, a company of the Madras Regiment, 40 marines of the Indian Navy, 36 men of a Wurttemberg Company, a platoon of pioneers, and some other volunteers, altogether around 350 men, half European.[95]

Perhaps inevitably, the British were also supported by a substantial force of local warriors from Ternate's arch rival, Tidore, under Prince Nuku. The Dutch were estimated at 50 Europeans with several hundred local troops assisting. Perhaps some of the EIC men were aware that 178 years before, their countrymen had been chased from these tropical isles by the very people they were just going to visit.

Upon arrival off Ternate, there was friction between the Royal Navy commander of the squadron, Captain Astle, and the EIC commander, Colonel Burr. Astle insisted the attack be directed initially at Fort Tolukko (then Fort Hollandia) prior to attacking Fort Orange, the key Dutch stronghold. On 11 January Astle's ships took the forts under fire, but the effectiveness of this was limited by the distance between the ships—sailing outside the reefs—and the range of the 18-pounders which formed the main armament of Aster's *La Virginie.* The force was then landed by boats to the north of Tolukko and marched along difficult coastal paths to form up for the assault. When they went in, the defensive fire from the small fort itself—it held one 12-pounder, five eight-pounders and three two-pounders—and flanking fire from two Dutch field guns on their right inflicted considerable losses on the British, and they were forced to retreat, abandoning two guns. Burr and Astle disagreed about the next course of action, and so the task force withdrew to Ambon.

In April, the EIC force returned to Ternate, without the Royal Navy but with some Company sloops for fire support, determined on conquest. This time, at the end of April, they landed south of Fort Orange and took a week to force the surrender of the fort at Kayu Merah (today known as Fort Kalomata). They then came under fire from the guns of a fort inland and above them, which would seem to be the old Dutch Kalomata fort. It then took nine days to establish a battery to subdue this Dutch work, during which time they suffered losses from sallies by the Dutch.

Finally, a month after landing, the Dutch abandoned their upper fort, the British troops occupied it, and then turned north to attack Fort Orange. It was a slow process, as they were frustrated by outlying batteries and the limited men available to them. The largest sloop, the *Swift,* had a couple of attempts to take on Fort Orange, but came off second best; hardly surprising when its largest guns were probably six-pounders and Orange's weaponry at this time included 18-pounders.

---

[95]   For more on these British operations against the Dutch East Indies, see *Frontier and Overseas Expeditions from India,* Chapter XXI.

93. Guns on the bastions of quaint little Fort Tolukko helped repel an attack by the East India Company in 1801.

Eventually the EIC blockade proved decisive and, short of provisions after 52 days of siege, Governor Cranssen surrendered Fort Orange and the Moluccas to the EIC on 21 June. The British officers inspecting Fort Orange found it to be a strong and well-armed work and, if properly manned and provisioned, victory would not have been achieved by the small British attacking force. In all, the defences on Ternate consisted of 120 guns in the works at Orange, Tolukko, Kayu Merah, and the four batteries between Orange and Kayu Merah.[96] This just proved once again, as always, that forts without adequate, motivated garrisons were a waste of the resources that had gone into building and maintaining the structures.

The British stayed on in Ternate, Ambon and the Bandas until restoring them to Dutch control in 1803 under the provisions of the Treaty of Amiens. The long series of wars had bankrupted the Netherlands, destroyed their merchant fleet and caused revolution and political chaos at home. The insolvent VOC was nationalised, with the Dutch state retaining its former possessions in the Spice Islands. The roles were now reversed; the Netherlands was at its nadir, and the British at the peak of their power. Unfortunately for the Dutch, the next war was not far away.

During one of the endless and complex Second, Third, Fourth and Fifth Coalitions against Republican France, the Netherlands was first ruled by Napoleon's brother, Louis, and then following the British invasion of Walcheren in 1809, annexed by France. As such, its colonies were once again fair game for the Royal Navy. In the space of six months in 1810, Ambon, Banda and Ternate all fell once again to the British.

An expedition was dispatched from India aimed at the Spice Islands in October 1809 consisting of the frigates *Dover* 38, and *Cornwallis* 44, and the sloop *Samarang* 18. Aboard were some troops and artillery of the Madras Regiment. Ambon's defences at the time were centred on Fort Victoria but included a battery to its north and a cluster of three batteries to its south. After an unsuccessful first attempt by the British lost its way in the darkness, on 16 February 1810, 400 men were put ashore to take the southern batteries.

In a textbook assault, troops captured first the elevated Wanetto battery, then turned its guns on the Wayoo battery below it, forcing its capitulation, while another force reached a hill above the Batto-Gantong redoubt, holding four 12-pounders, and forced its abandonment. This unit then turned the 12-pounders onto the Water battery built on piles over the bay in front of it, causing its gunners to flee, and finally, onto Fort Victoria itself, which quickly surrendered. The garrison's commander, Colonel Filz, was later executed in Batavia for surrendering the fortress with insufficient resistance.

---

96 *The Naval Chronicle,* Volume 26.

94. Looking south-west at Kota Ambon today, with the mouth of Ambon Bay in the background. Fort Victoria is out of view to the right. In 1809, the Water Battery was in the bay at left, while the batteries of Wayoo and Wanetto sat above the bay. Batto-Gantong with its 12-pounders was out of view to the left.

Captain Cole storms Fort Belgica

Another squadron, under Captain Cole, left Madras in May 1810, consisting of the frigates *Caroline* 36, *Piemontaise* 38, the brig *Barracouta* 18, and a transport. They were heading to take Banda. With just a company of the Madras Regiment, Cole set off to take on one of the most powerful forts of the Indies.[97]

The little fleet proceeded down past Malacca to Singapore and from here it would have been typical to approach the Bandas by maintaining an easterly heading through the Java Sea, leave Bali, Sumbawa and Flores to starboard, and come upon the islands

---

[97] See *Illustrative Account of Captain Cole's Splendid Achievement in the Capture of the Island of Banda* and *The Late Sir Christopher Cole.*

from the west. But this course would have taken Cole past the Indies capital at Batavia and risked an engagement with Dutch patrol forces based there.

Instead, daringly, he turned north, pushed along by the breezes of the south-west monsoon, taking a much longer passage (which the Portuguese had pioneered back in 1530) around the north of Borneo through the reef-studded Sulu Sea, across to the western tip of New Guinea and then south to the island of Gorom (today Gorong), which they made on 7 August, just two days sail east from Banda. It was an audacious route and much could have gone wrong, but the squadron arrived in good order and undetected at the lightly defended 'back door' of the Bandas after three months at sea.

The defences of the nutmeg islands faced mostly west and north. The only artillery facing Cole's squadron was the Voorzightigheid Battery on Banda, and the small de Lage Battery on tiny Rosengain. The northern tip of Banda Besar was unfortified, and though a gun fired a couple of shots from Rozengain when Cole sought to acquire it as a base, the ships were able to get away around 200 marines, sailors and soldiers into the boats at 11 pm on the 8th, just off the north-eastern point of Banda Besar, intent on taking Fort Belgica.

En route it became stormy, the moon had set and the boats had over five kilometres to cover rowing to Banda, so perhaps inevitably Cole found himself with less than half his force when he landed just before dawn right under the Voorzightigheid redoubt on the south-eastern corner of Banda—home to ten 18-pounders. The British attacked through the storm, taking the battery in the rear and capturing an officer and 60 men without loss.

The garrison of Banda comprised 700 soldiers supported by 800 militia, concentrated in the main forts of Nassau and Belgica, but also in a number of smaller batteries and redoubts like Voorzightigheid. Luckily for Cole, the Dutch had sent a strong force to the north of Banda in the darkness, assuming the British would land where they had in 1796. Cole, who had gone to sea at age nine and had been fighting for 40 years against first the Americans and then the French, appreciated he was extremely exposed. It was crucial to maintain momentum and make use of the element of surprise, which he still retained. He saw Belgica was the key to the defences of the whole island, and marched straight there with his small force.

The fort's garrison was alerted and opened fire as the British approached the outer ramparts in the early light of the new day. It was still squally, so reloading was difficult for both sides, but using scaling ladders brought exactly for this purpose, Cole's men stormed the outer bastions and ramparts. The ladders were too short for the high inner wall, so they found themselves in a very difficult position; fired on from above and no doubt with the forces from the north of the island on their way back. But fortune favours the brave, and so it was here.

The fort's commander, who lived not in the fort but nearby, now arrived and as the main gate was opened for him the British stormed through in the confusion and quickly captured Fort Belgica and the 40 or so gunners who did not jump the walls to escape. The Dutch commander and ten of his men died in the melee.

95. The inner gate to Fort Belgica. Cole's men had escaladed the outer defences in the gloomy dawn light and arrived at the forecourt shown here, but their ladders were not high enough to scale the inner walls. They were taking fire from above, enemy reinforcements were expected, and the outlook was grim for the attackers. The fort's commander, living in the town, arrived in the confusion and the gate was opened for him. As it opened, the British stormed through, the Dutch commander dying in the fracas, and the garrison surrendered.

Now it was the Dutch who were vulnerable. Belgica was armed with 58 cannon, and from its elevation dominated Fort Nassau and the township. As his frigates worked west into the anchorage off Banda, a battery between Voorzightigheid and Nassau opened fire on them, before it was silenced by cannon fire from Belgica. Cole dispatched an envoy to the Dutch commander in Fort Nassau insisting on surrender or he would destroy the town and storm Nassau, and quickly the Dutch capitulated. It had been a very daring endeavour, the huge risks taken paying off; Captain Cole had taken the Bandas without the loss of a single man.

96. Captain Cole, victor of Belgica, stayed on Banda for some time after the surrender of the Dutch garrison, and was subsequently involved with the campaign in Java, which defeated the main Franco–Dutch forces in the Indies. The residence he commandeered in the township of Banda is signposted.

Later in August 1810, it was decided at Ambon that it was time to hit Ternate again. It was the last of the major Spice Islands under Dutch control. Captain Forbes with troops of the Madras European Regiment boarded the Royal Navy frigate *Dover* under Captain Tucker and arrived off Ternate on 28 August. A landing of 174 men of Forbes' regiment, some Ambonese, and marines and seamen, was made at dawn, out of sight of Fort Kayu Merah and just to the west of it—virtually under Fort Kota Janji, which was apparently unmanned.

Forbes stormed Kayu Merah later that night for three killed and 14 wounded, but the fort then came under fire from a battery called Kota Barro, armed with two 18s and two 12s, between it and Fort Orange. *Dover* stood in and silenced it. Forbes then took Kota Barro and opened fire with its cannon on Fort Orange, with *Dover* joining in.

The Dutch garrison commander, Colonel van Mithmam, had recently put down a developing mutiny among his local troops by strapping the ringleaders to cannons and firing them off, and so saw the British more perhaps as kindred rescuers than invaders. After several hours of this cannonade, at dusk van Mithmam surrendered, the 500-man garrison with 90 guns in seven forts being defeated by a much smaller force.

97. An anonymous post-Spanish view of Gammalamma/Kastella from 1683. While some elements of the Spanish fortress are still visible, most of the walls and ramparts appear to have been demolished.

The British occupation of the Spice Islands this time lasted until 1817. During this period, they transplanted nutmeg and clove seedlings to Penang, Sumatra and Ceylon. The French had already smuggled out spice plants to their colonies, so that by the mid eighteenth century, commercial production of nutmeg or cloves was occurring at Ceylon, Grenada, Penang, Mauritius, Zanzibar, Reunion and Martinique. After more than 3000 years of being the world's only sources, the Spice Islands had lost their monopoly. And consequently, their importance.

Dutch control extended and challenged

98. Kapitan Pattimura led a rebellion against Dutch rule at Saparua Island near Ambon. His followers stormed Fort Duurstede in 1817 and held it for three months until recaptured. Pattimura was tried and hanged at Fort Victoria in Ambon.

There were no further external attacks on the Dutch East Indies until the Japanese arrived in early 1942. That is not to say the interim period was peaceful for the Dutch. Firstly, they had to deal with the powerful forces of nature across this geologically unstable area. Earthquakes smashed bastions and ramparts, volcanos levelled villages and plantations, reefs and storms claimed ships, and malaria and a host of other exotic diseases handed out death relentlessly.

As examples, Fort Revenge on Ai was extensively damaged by an earthquake in 1683 and Fort Hollandia on Banda Besar was destroyed by a similar tremor in 1740 and never rebuilt. Fort Victoria at Ambon was damaged by earthquakes in 1643, 1644, 1673, 1674 and again in 1754. Fort Hollandia on Ambon was smashed by a tsunami in 1674, with most of the garrison swept away. Ternate's volcano, Gammalamma, has erupted 60 times since the Portuguese arrived 500 years ago, and earthquakes there were always common. A major quake in 1740 rendered every structure on the island uninhabitable, and severely damaged Fort Orange. In 1980, a series of eruptions caused the evacuation of 40,000 people from the path of lava flows.

Secondly, the Dutch had to combat an almost endless stream of uprisings, rebellions, revolts and insurgencies across the length and breadth of the archipelago. Somewhat naturally, the peoples of the East Indies resented the Dutch taking control of their spices, trade and revenues and frequently rose up in insurrection.

Just after the British left, and incidentally the only such example, local forces in the Spice Islands stormed a major colonial fort and held it for some time at Fort Duurstede on Saparua Island, near Ambon in May 1817.

Led by Pattimura, a demobilised sergeant from the British Moluccan Regiment, several hundred Ambonese captured the fort after a nine-hour battle, putting the garrison of 19 men to the sword, and killing the resident administrator and his family. A Dutch counterattack by two companies a week later was soundly defeated with heavy casualties, as was the rebels' own attempt on nearby Fort Zeelandia at Haruku in June. It was not until August that Duurstede was finally retaken. Pattimura was captured and hanged in December. Today, he is regarded as an independence hero throughout Indonesia, and his statue stands near the entrance to Fort Victoria, at Ambon, where he met his end.

A description of internal security operations carried out by the Dutch from the seventeenth to the twentieth century is beyond the scope of this book; they are counterinsurgency rather than military operations, and the list really is endless. As an example of the type of operations the Dutch had to constantly perform, Johannes Vingboons' impressive watercolour showing the *Conquest of Loki* in 1652 is instructive.

Four Dutch frigates and several korakora stand off a fortified village on the island of Seram, north of Ambon, representing the standard combination of Dutch and loyal local forces. A landing has been affected and an earthen defensive fort protected by timber palisades has been built on the waterfront to serve as the base for subsequent advances.

Immediately inland, the terrain is extremely rugged, with thick vegetation spread across jagged peaks, some of which reach over 500 metres high. The rebels' defences are set behind the village, with a system of interconnected and mutually supporting stone redoubts, batteries, trenches and emplacements, reaching up to the main fort, crowning the central peak. The defenders are well armed with cannon and muskets and have probably hundreds of men available for defence and counterattack.

99. Fort Duurstede on Saparua, near Ambon, was taken by rebellious locals in 1817, and held out for several months until recaptured by Dutch forces. It was the only major Spice Islands fort ever to be stormed by local warriors. It has an extended perimeter but was held by just 19 men, all of whom died in the battle or were executed after it.

While the Dutch eventually took Loki, there were dozens of similar settlements to subdue on Seram alone. Rebels could easily retreat into the hills, the forts could be rebuilt once the Dutch left, and smugglers brought in new weapons. It developed into an endless cycle of raid, counterattack, massacre and rebellion, and not just on Seram, but throughout a hundred islands across the Indies. There remained a low-level insurgency on Seram against central authority (Dutch, Japanese and Indonesian) well into the 1960s.

100. *Conquest of Loki,* by Dutch artist Johannes Vingboons, appeared in the superlative *Blaeu Atlas* and shows a VOC operation against rebels on the island of Seram in 1652. Note the sophistication and depth of the local defences and the efforts the Dutch need to go to—building the foreshore fort—in order to emplace cannon within range to bring them under fire.
Image credit: ANL/Vienna.

7. Modern battlegrounds 1942–2002

World War II

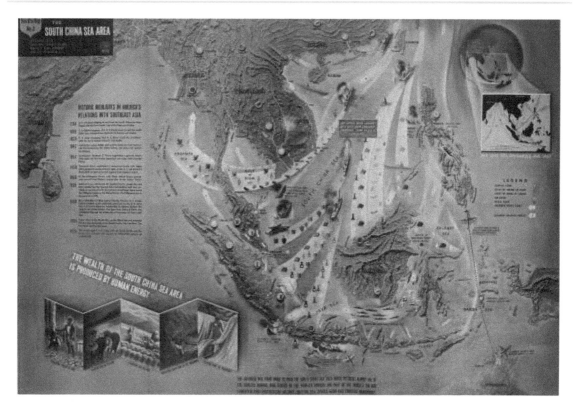

101. 1944 US Navy Department map of South-East Asia highlighting the strategic location and resources of the region as well as the series of battles between Imperial Japan and allied forces in the theatre during World War II. Ambon, the Banda Sea and the Moluccas are visible on the right, astride the air route between the Philippines and Darwin. US Army General MacArthur wanted to recapture the US colony of the Philippines via an invasion from the south, through the Spice Islands; as part of this strategy Morotai was captured in 1944. Eventually however, the US Navy plan to retake the Philippines with carrier task forces attacking west from the Pacific was adopted. Image credit: Paulus Swaen Old Maps.

When war next arrived in the Spice Islands, it had nothing to do with spices, but with the strategic position offered by the Islands. In World War II, it was their location between Australia and the Philippines that was of value. Back in 1898, the US had taken control of the Philippines from Spain. As war clouds gathered in 1941, the Moluccas in the north and the Bandas in the south were insignificant and irrelevant, but Ambon was of vital importance.

Ambon derived its strategic prominence from its location, its superb harbour and the infrastructure the island held. The long Bay of Ambon could safely shelter the largest fleet, and in 1941 the Dutch already had a major naval base, a crucial airfield and a seaplane base there. For the Dutch, Ambon's strategic position held the keys to the eastern flank of their East Indies empire. For the Americans, it stood midway between the new heavy bomber base at Del Monte on Mindanao, and Darwin, terminus of the Pacific reinforcement route from the east coast of the US, and also guarded the southern flank of the Philippines. For the Japanese, aircraft based there protected the resource-rich Indies from attack out of the east, while at the same time preventing US bombers with the range to hit proposed conquests at Singapore, Manila, Java and the Borneo oilfields from operating there. Its location also complemented the planned network of Japanese bases at Kupang in Timor, Kendari in the Celebes, Rabaul east of New Guinea, and the major fleet base at Truk 3000 kilometres to the north-east.

While the Japanese and the Allies both recognised the significance of Ambon before the Pacific War (the Netherlands was occupied by Germany from 1940), the limited military resources available to the Dutch at the time meant that it was only lightly defended. Prior to the outbreak of war, Australia appreciated the threat a Japanese-held Ambon posed to Darwin, and undertook to assist the Dutch in its defence by providing troops and aircraft. Along with Timor and Rabaul, Ambon was identified as one of the strongpoints that would be defended to require the Japanese to fight their way through the island barrier north of Australia. At each outpost a battalion of the Australian Imperial Force (AIF) 8th Division would be posted.[98]

Hence, Gull Force, built around 2/21 battalion and totalling 1100 men, arrived at Ambon from Darwin on 17 December 1941. It came under Lt Colonel Kapitz of the Royal Netherlands Indies Army (KNIL), who also commanded 2800 men of the Moluccan Brigade. Limited air force elements of Australian RAAF Hudson bombers, Dutch ML–KNIL (air force) Brewster fighters, MLD (navy) Catalinas and American USN Catalina flying boats were either destroyed by Japanese air raids starting from 6 January, or

---

[98] For more on the strategic outlook, and this campaign, see *Australia in the War of 1939–1945. Series 1—Army, Volume 4, The Japanese Thrust.*

abandoned the bases soon after. No allied naval forces were available, which handed total sea control straight to the Japanese.

102. Laha Field, Ambon, now known as Pattimura Airport, after the rebel that stormed Fort Duurstede in 1817. A vital airbase in early World War II, it quickly became a target for the Japanese. In mid-January 1942, two Dutch Brewster Buffalos formed the only interceptor strength, and both were shot down in the first raid by carrier-based Zeros. Later, Japanese naval air squadrons using fighters, reconnaissance planes and bombers were based at Laha, and seaplanes and Mavis flying boats flew from Ambon harbour.

Ambon Island was a difficult proposition for the small combined force to defend as the coastline was extensive and the rugged interior traversed with few roads. It was almost two separate islands, joined by a tiny isthmus at Paso, with the Hitu peninsula to the north and the smaller Laitmor peninsula to the south. The focus of the defence was on the Bay of Ambon, which held the airfield, naval wharfs, flying boat base, main town, Dutch headquarters and the main fortifications. It was wrongly assumed that the Japanese attack would be made in the Bay, and so most of the defence forces were deployed around it. Apart from these problems, the Allied forces had little time to coordinate strategy or solve communication issues, lacked aircraft, naval support, sufficient artillery, anti-aircraft guns, machine guns and mortars, had no radios or armour, and had to rely heavily on ambivalent local troops in the Dutch garrison.

While Ambon's old forts Victoria, Middelburg and Amsterdam still stood and were as strategically placed as ever, they were no longer considered militarily useful and played no part in the battle. Somewhat limited modern defences had been built at Paso to guard the pass between the two peninsulas, and at Benteng, south of Ambon town. The latter housed the Dutch artillery HQ and was manned by regular gunners, but armed with just four old 70 mm weapons, albeit in concrete emplacements with underground command and barracks structures. Rather than the fixed coastal guns, the Dutch relied more on two batteries of mobile 75 mm guns, one at Laha and one at Halong, to provide fire support.

103. A Japanese Special Naval Landing Force came ashore on these beaches on the north coast of Ambon on 30 January 1942, and marched overland to attack the crucial airfield at Laha.

By the time the Japanese landed in force at Ambon on 30 January, Borneo had been captured and Sulawesi attacked. Further afield, Hong Kong, Manila, Kuala Lumpur, Wake, Guam and Rabaul had all fallen, and the noose was tightening around Singapore and Java. Two Imperial fleet carriers from the Pearl Harbour attack, *Hiryu* and *Soryu*, provided air cover for the landings, supported by three cruisers and 15 destroyers. A Special Naval Landing Force (SNLF) of battalion size along with some army companies was put ashore on the north coast of the Hitu peninsula (not far from Fort Amsterdam), swept aside the platoon opposing them and split to advance on Paso and Laha Airfield.

104. Ambon War Cemetery, maintained by the Commonwealth War Graves Commission, holds the remains of 2146 Allied servicemen who died in the seas, skies and on land nearby in World War II. Many are Australian soldiers from Gull Force, overwhelmed by the Japanese invasion in 1942.

At the same time, a landing by elements of 228 Regiment of the 38th Division (which had recently captured Hong Kong) was put in at Hutumori on the eastern side of the Laitmor peninsula, and also divided to advance towards Ambon town and Paso.

The Allied command and communication system immediately broke down, and any hope of controlling the battle evaporated. Given the dispersed Allied deployment, lack of motor transport and rugged terrain, effective counterattacks were impossible anyway. Allied positions that put up an active defence were pounded by naval gunfire, dive bombers, fighters and artillery, and by 3 February the last units had surrendered.

Over 300 Australian and Dutch troops were massacred after surrendering, and most of the others died of brutality and mistreatment as prisoners of war.

Ambon was quickly upgraded to a major Japanese base and remained so until the war ended. As a consequence, it was heavily bombed by USAAF and RAAF aircraft operating from the Darwin area, especially in 1944 and 1945. Fort Victoria—central to the township—also suffered much damage. During their occupation, the Japanese also added to the Spice Islands forts by constructing a number of concrete pillboxes and bunkers at various points around Ambon Island, some of which can still be seen today. The most poignant reminder of World War II in Ambon today is the Commonwealth War Cemetery five kilometres north-east of the main town. Here, amid shady jacaranda trees and colourful tropical gardens lie the remains of over 2000 Allied servicemen, including over 350 members of Gull Force.

Compared with battle-scarred Ambon, Ternate had a very quiet war. It was an auxiliary base for Dutch Navy Dornier Do 24 flying boats, three of which were based there in the early days of the conflict. A garrison of 150 troops, headquartered at Fort Orange, provided security. The flying boats were soon transferred to less exposed Lake Tonado near Manado, and had just departed when Ternate suffered its first ever air raid; a Japanese Mavis flying boat out of Palau dropping a few bombs on 17 December 1941.[99] On 7 April, after the main islands of the East Indies had fallen, a Japanese Naval Landing Force came ashore on Ternate at Talangame Harbour and quickly gained the surrender of the Dutch troops garrisoning Fort Orange.[100]

A naval task force—'N' Expeditionary Force—under Rear Admiral Fujita and consisting of a light cruiser, two destroyers, a seaplane carrier, several gunboats and some transports carrying two garrison battalions, met at Ternate after the island was secured, and took undefended Jailolo on Halmahera the next day, before moving on to the conquests of northern New Guinea, capturing Manokwari, Moemi, Seroei, Nabire, Sarmi and Hollandia in succession.

As an insignificant and remote backwater, Ternate stayed clear of the rest of the war apart from some Allied bombing raids, but the island's sultan, Mohamad Jabir, was involved in one fascinating incident. In 1945, concerned that the Japanese occupiers had taken a dislike to him, he went into hiding in a village on northern Ternate, sending word to General MacArthur's new base at nearby Morotai that he needed to be rescued. The sultan was well regarded by the Dutch, and they concurred. A group of Australian Z-Force commandos sailed in and grabbed the sultan, his family, entourage

---

99   *Dutch Do 24 units*, p. 22.

100 For more on these operations, see dutcheastindies.webs.com

and harem, who were then taken by PT boats to Morotai, and on to sanctuary in Australia. The last sultan, Mudaffar Syah (1935–2015), as a ten-year-old boy, was part of this group evacuated from Ternate with Japanese pursuers hot on their heels, and later ascended the throne on the death of his father in 1975.[101]

105. Fort Victoria's battered bastions suffered many earthquakes over the years and became targets for Allied bombing raids later in World War II. More damage was inflicted when the secessionist RMS movement (at the time, the Republic of the South Moluccas; Indonesian: Republik Maluku Selatan, thus RMS) used it as a strongpoint in the 1950s. The Indonesian Army currently occupies the fortress, following behind the Japanese, Dutch, British and Portuguese.

Banda had an even less eventful war than Ternate. The first vice president of post-war Indonesia, Mohammad Hatta, had been exiled there by the Dutch since 1936, and was plucked out by flying boat as the Dutch control over the Indies collapsed under the Japanese onslaught in early 1942. On 8 May 1942—the same day the American forces

---

[101] See smh.com.au/world/the-untold-story-how-z-force-saved-the-sultan-20100423-tj7q.html

in the Philippines surrendered—Japanese troops occupied Banda without resistance. The once legendary capital of the nutmeg islands, with all its decaying fortresses, was not even defended by the Dutch. A tiny force of Japanese was stationed Banda until the end of the war.

Morotai, 200 kilometres north-east of Ternate, had long been a crucial food bowl for the Moluccas, falling under Ternate's loose control from pre-colonial times. It was the only major island in the Spice Islands area recaptured by Allied forces during World War II. Operation *Tradewind* was launched in September 1944 to take Morotai and develop airfields there to support the planned invasion of Mindanao in the Philippines in November that year.

106. Part of the airfield complex at Morotai in 1945.
A few months before, it had been jungle.
Image credit: Australian War Memorial.

Tradewind[102] was by far the largest military operation ever conducted in the entire history of the Spice Islands. It involved 40,000 US Army troops of the 31st and 32nd Infantry Divisions landing almost without resistance from the few hundred hungry Japanese troops on the island at the time. Over 15,000 US and Australian air force personnel and 7000 engineers and support troops landed soon after. The invasion force included an enormous fleet of amphibious craft with a close escort of 28 destroyers and frigates. A squadron of five US and Australian cruisers and ten destroyers provided cover for the invasion, and six escort carriers were available for close air support. Another task force of two fleet and two light carriers pulverised all Japanese airbases within range. Compared to the Japanese invasion force that sheltered in Ternate's harbour on 7 April 1942 for their onward assaults against New Guinea, this fleet was larger by an enormous factor in terms of firepower.

The speed with which Morotai was developed into a massive base was impressive and highlights the enormous resources available to the Americans at this late stage of the Pacific War on what was essentially a secondary operation. Within weeks, a 1500-metre fighter strip had been hacked out of the jungle. Soon two other 2000-metre strips were available with all associated taxi ways and hardstands for 250 aircraft, including 174 heavy bombers. US B-25 bombers flying from Morotai in squadron strength hit targets in the Philippines on 13 October—less than a month after the initial landings. Forty PT boats and several squadrons of fighters and bombers were quickly based there. Wharfs, jetty's, roads, headquarters, accommodation for 60,000 men, a 1000-bed hospital, refuelling facilities, storage and warehousing infrastructure all arose where there had been nothing, and after a few years it all faded back to nothing, although some remains are still visible. Incidentally, the last Japanese soldier to surrender after World War II, Teruo Nakamura, surrendered on Morotai in 1974.

In a notable exception to previous western interventions in the Spice Islands dating back nearly half a millennium, proactive disease control was enacted by the Americans from the beginning. On the very first day of the landings, while fighters strafed the jungle, other aircraft sprayed DDT over the entire beachhead to defeat mosquito-borne diseases, and the taking of anti-typhus and anti-malarial medicine was strictly enforced, leading to an extremely low rate of sickness and disease.

---

[102] See *Australia in the War of 1939–1945. Series 1—Army,* Volume 7, The Final Campaigns.

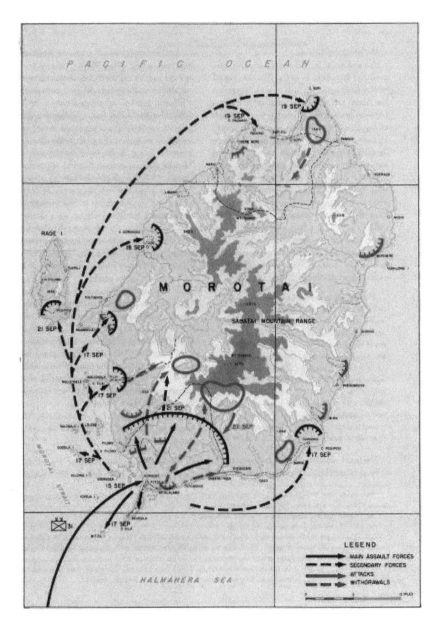

107. General MacArthur's 1966 map showing the initial allied landings and subsequent operations on Morotai from September 1944. While the Japanese forces on the island at the time of the invasion totalled only a few hundred men, it was subsequently reinforced from Halmahera, and fighting continued until the end of the war. Over 65,000 Japanese troops surrendered in the Spice Islands and on Halmahera after the Japanese capitulation.

Post-war chaos

With the surrender of Japan and the end of hostilities in August 1945, Indonesia, far from emerging into peace and stability, descended into chaos. In the final few months of the war, the Japanese had sought to encourage Indonesian nationalism by handing over administrative roles to local elites, forestalling a return of the Dutch colonial administration. These nationalists declared independence on 17 August 1945, much to the delight of most Indonesians.

The Netherlands was itself emerging from six years of German occupation and took some months to dispatch civil and military forces to regain control of its erstwhile empire, and in the interim British Commonwealth troops were sent to take the Japanese surrender and maintain law and order. Australian troops were responsible for Ternate and Ambon and other parts of Eastern Indonesia, where 65,000 Japanese soldiers remained. In Java especially, the Allied forces found themselves under attack from local nationalists and were farcically obliged to rearm and deploy surrendered Japanese formations to assist in restoring control.

When the Dutch returned in force in 1946, they immediately faced a widespread insurgency. In the context of this insurgency, the Spice Islands were somewhat divided. The Moluccas centred on Ternate and Tidore, and the Bandas were staunchly Muslim and not greatly opposed to rule from Java, whereas the significantly Christian Ambonese were in favour of independence. Ambonese soldiers had always formed the backbone of the KNIL (Dutch Indies Army), which increased animosity to Ambonese generally. With Indonesia's formal independence in 1949, it was quickly clear to the Ambonese that their own independence was not on offer.

In response, the Republic of South Molucca (RMS) was declared in April 1950 at Ambon. Its military arm consisted predominantly of well-trained but poorly equipped ex-KNIL soldiers. The new government in Jakarta could not accept this challenge to their nascent authority and dispatched a task force to defeat the rebellion and retake Ambon. In September, they landed several battalions in the north and east of the island (exactly where the Japanese had landed in 1942), and slowly advanced through heavy resistance toward the main town centred on Fort Victoria. The RMS actually had their HQ in the old fortress, and this eventually fell to Indonesian government troops and tanks on 4 December 1950.[103] It was the end of the RMS, although the organisation still exists in the Netherlands among the Ambonese diaspora, still dreaming of their own Spice Islands republic.

---

[103] *Kopassus: Inside Indonesia's Special Forces*, p. 10.

Another rebellion touched Ambon in 1958, when the CIA-sponsored Permesta group based at Manado in Sulawesi also rose against the communist-leaning Indonesian government. War surplus US bombers flown by mercenary pilots attacked government bases on Ambon several times. One of the pilots, American Allen Pope, was shot down and captured as he attacked a government flotilla leaving Ambon to retake Morotai after its capture by the rebels. Pope was tried and sentenced to death, but was later released after pressure from the US.[104]

The final chapter in the history of conflict in the Spice Islands was the intercommunal violence that spread across the islands from 1999 to 2002. While there were many complicating factors, the age-old clash between Islam and Christianity dating back to the Portuguese arrival in 1511 was the prime cause. Central government transmigration schemes that brought thousands of mostly Muslim migrants from other parts of Indonesia to historically Christian areas in Ambon, Seram and Halmahera had built pressure for several years. The influx of armed and trained Islamist fighters from groups like Laskar Jihad in response to the growing chaos exacerbated the situation, and a perceived lack of neutrality from the predominantly Muslim security and police forces only made matters worse.

Eventually, after widespread slaughter, ethnic cleansing and destruction, peace was restored. While intercommunal violence has for now been stilled, the Spice Islands have also witnessed a number of jihadi-type terrorist bombings, most recently in Ambon in 2012.

The Spice Islands today lie close to the confluence of the old British, Dutch and Spanish empires; now the tri-border point where Malaysian Sabah, the Philippines and Indonesia meet. While less contentious than the nearby South China Sea territory puzzle, it remains an area of ongoing concern. Several groups of secessionist Islamic Moros have dominated the Sulu archipelago of the southern Philippines—less than 1000 kilometres north-west of Ternate—for centuries, fighting endlessly against first the Spanish (1578–1898), then the Americans (1898–1942), the Japanese (1942–1945), and finally against the Philippines government (1946 to today). The famous US handgun, the Colt 45, was developed in 1911 to provide more stopping power against enraged Moro attackers during the US campaign here from 1898 to 1913.[105]

In September 2013, elements of the MNLF, one of many Moro rebel groups, launched a major attack on Zamboanga in Mindanao, the Philippines. Only after hundreds of casualties, widespread destruction and the displacement of over 100,000 people were

---

[104] For more on these operations, see *Feet to the Fire: CIA Covert Operations in Indonesia, 1957–1958.*

[105] wikipedia.org/wiki/M1911

the guerrillas defeated by Philippine Army forces.[106] Another mass attack by Islamic fighters took place in Marawi, on Mindanao in May 2017, where hundreds of civilians were killed when the Philippines Army counterattacked, taking several months to clear ISIS–affiliated jihadis.

108. Relics of war remain littered across the Spice Islands from 500 years of conflict. In 1945 an RAAF Spitfire on patrol for Japanese shipping crashed off Kastella, its wreck coming to rest almost on top of the ancient bones of Magellan's *Trinidad* from 1522.

Back in 2013, another group of armed Moro insurgents from Sulu in the Philippines actually landed in Sabah, Malaysia, to press a long dormant claim to the state from the historic sultanate of Sulu. The Lahad Datu incident,[107] as it became known, fireballed into a major clash, with the Malaysian Defence Forces needing to deploy seven infantry battalions and F–18 fighters to evict the rebels, who to this day maintain their claim.

[106] thediplomat.com/2013/09/the-philippines-counting-the-costs-in-zamboanga

[107] thediplomat.com/tag/lahad-datu-incident

The irony of the Moros—who were reportedly once trained and equipped by Kuala Lumpur[108] at Jampiras Island in Sabah in the 1970s to rebel against Manila—now threatening guerrilla war against them in Sabah was surely not lost on the Malaysians.

And it's not just Malaysia and the Philippines that are in dispute over borders in this area. Indonesia was dismayed to lose the claim to Sipidan and Ligitan islands—off Sabah—at the International Court of Justice in 2002, when they were ruled Malaysian. Both countries have also failed to agree on a maritime border in the area, and both sides claim areas of the Ambalat oilfield that has led to naval confrontations as recently as 2009.[109]

Finally, just to the east of the Spice Islands, pro-independence groups have maintained a low-level armed insurgency against the Indonesian state in the two Indonesian provinces of Papua and West Papua since 1965. This conflict is ongoing.

The Spice Islands today slumber in relative peace compared to the carnage and destruction delivered on them in times past by the bestowal of spices across their islands.

What was once a blessing quickly became a curse when Europeans arrived, and many inhabitants of the archipelagos paid with their lives for the world's lust for nutmeg and cloves. Many soldiers, adventurers and traders from the villages of Portugal, the harbours of Spain and the provinces of Holland also paid the price, and lie together with the locals—all collateral damage in the race for spice supremacy.

And while these remote and now-forgotten islands slumber lazily in the tropical sun and the monsoons come and go, and the old stones of the old forts crumble with the drift of the years, the geopolitical fault lines remain close-by to the scent of cloves and mace and nutmeg, and it will surely not be forever that we have to wait to hear that, once again, the Spice Islands are in the wars.

---

[108] *A handbook of terrorism and insurgency in South-East Asia,* p. 229.

[109] thejakartaglobe.com/archive/navy-was-set-to-fire-on-warship/277953

8. Fortress warfare

The evolution of Spice Islands warfare

109. The solid walls, wide ramparts and cannon-armed bastions of colonial forts allowed small garrisons to command much larger numbers of local adversaries. Here are the expansive remains of Fort Nassau on Banda, with Gunung Api volcano in the background. It was one of the largest Spice Islands forts, with a garrison of 150 men.

The first fortifications in the Spice Islands were indigenous, built in pre-colonial times, but details of these are unfortunately vague. Early Spanish and Portuguese observers have given us extended descriptions of all aspects of local life, focusing particularly on how they waged war, their offensive and defensive weapons and their fleets, but made no mention of Spice Islanders using gunpowder and little of their fortifications in the early sixteenth century conflicts.

Firearms, if they had arrived in the region at all before 1500, appear not to have had a significant impact on the style of warfare most commonly practised across the scattered island groups: piracy and maritime raiding. Defending fixed positions against superior numbers of attackers was a losing strategy for local communities because of the casualties their limited populations could suffer. It was more prudent to retreat into hills or jungle and return and rebuild once the attackers had left. There were also few crucial natural assets, like harbours, to defend.

What defences there were probably consisted of earth walls and timber palisades set a little inland and taking advantage of favourable landforms like hills and cliffs. The artwork *Conquest of Loki* (see Figure 100) is instructive on this theme, and although it shows a cannon-armed seventeenth century position, it is likely that forts of similar form existed across the Indies for centuries before this artwork was produced.

Just as Ottoman cannon at Constantinople in 1453 had revolutionised warfare in Europe and sounded the death knell of the high-walled medieval castle, so the advent of modern Iberian artillery had a great impact on warfare in Asia and in the Spice Islands. At sea, standoff gunfire from caravels and galleys could easily destroy lightly-built local shipping, and on land, muskets and cannon emplaced on strong ramparts could inflict gruelling casualties on attackers. Smaller breech-loading swivel guns that could be quickly reloaded with prepared charges were particularly devastating at sea and in forts. And even small cannon could easily breach traditional palisade-type defences.

Mention of the Portuguese attacking substantial, entirely local fortifications in their early ascendancy in the 1520s and 1530s is lacking, suggesting such defences may not have widely existed. Even the earliest Portuguese attacks on fixed defences at Marieco (Tidore) in 1524, Soa Siu (Tidore) in 1529 and 1536, and Jailolo (Halmahera) in 1533 were against fortifications that had been engineered at least partially by the Spanish. The only exception was the local fort at Labuha on Bacan, stormed in 1533, but for which we have no details. At Marieco, the royal settlement was defended by a 'local fort' armed and manned partly by Spaniards. Three attacks by a force of 100 Portuguese musketeers and 1000 Ternatean warriors were repulsed before they broke through, overran the fort, captured seven cannon—from Magellan's ships—and torched the capital.

At Soa Siu five years later, the Portuguese and their allies overcame the defences of the fortified north-facing wall that protected the main township of Tidore, on the east coast, then took the Spanish citadel behind it, and burnt the settlement. This citadel had been built by the Loaisa expedition survivors in 1527 and was armed with ships guns including a full cannon (around a 42-pounder), a culverin (18-pounder) and smaller weapons, emplaced in two stone bulwarks joined by a curtain wall, with another bastion to defend the harbour.[110]

The next major attack, against Jailolo on Halmahera in 1533, involved a lengthy siege by Kastella's Captain Ataide. It is possible that the Spanish and local troops surrendered prior to the defences being overrun by the Portuguese, as the sultan was captured. We know little about the defences of Jailolo at this time, although for later sieges by the Portuguese at the same place—in 1544 and 1551—we know they were very strong, claimed by some as impregnable, and likely engineered with considerable Spanish input.

110. Remains of Kastella showing most of the original diminutive Portuguese fort, with the tower remains in the foreground and the landward wall behind it. High ramparts, muskets and swivel guns were the key to holding such defences against more numerous adversaries, but only in combination with supporting seapower.

[110] *The Spanish fortresses on the island of Tidore 1521–1606.*

Back at Tidore, hoping to prevent the third destruction of the royal residences in a decade, around 1532 the rajah built a fort at Gomafo[111] high up in the hills above Soa Siu and nearly two kilometres inland, accessible only by difficult mountain paths through difficult jungle. The defences did not include artillery and were of no impediment to Galvao as he surprised them from the west in 1536 and, once more, Tidore's seat of power was burnt, the Portuguese moving on from Gomafo to again destroy the township of Soa Siu down on the coast.

Gomafo, an unsophisticated 'bolt-hole'—difficult to reach, remote from coastal attackers and probably encircled by timber palisades—is perhaps a good example of contemporary, wholly local fortifications. It was later rebuilt with Spanish assistance but was once again destroyed by the Portuguese in 1551.

Colonial-era fortifications

The first planned colonial fortification of the Spice Islands, Kastella was started by the Portuguese on Ternate in 1522 and constructed in a similar style to a string of their forts ranging from Morocco to Sumatra. It consisted of two parts: firstly, the citadel including the central tower and inner walls, with two diagonally placed perimeter towers; and then the outer wall structure that enclosed the residential settlement adjacent to the citadel.

The citadel was dominated by a two-storey stone tower (remains of which can be seen today) which served as a fortified command and observation point, and would have had mounted swivel guns that could sweep the ramparts if necessary. Late medieval features including high, narrow walls and high corner towers indicate the Portuguese were initially more concerned with preventing the walls being escaladed rather than breached with artillery. Low and wide modern bastions were later constructed outside the citadel in the 1550s, coinciding with the arrival of cannon from Java and Johore by adversaries of the Portuguese. However, according to contemporary artwork, the next two Portuguese forts, Victoria (1576) at Ambon and Reis Magos (1578) on Tidore, were of a similar obsolete design with high curtain walls and high round towers.[112]

The early design of these three Portuguese forts lacked the modern characteristics that were developing in Europe by the mid sixteenth century. The long series of wars

---

[111]   *Identification of Portuguese and Spanish forts on Ternate and Tidore Islands*, p. 195.

[112]   See the following fort catalogue for more on individual works.

in Italy running from 1494 to 1559 had seen the emergence of a new style of sophisticated, science-based fortification systems, the *trace Italienne*, where low, wide structures less vulnerable to cannon fire superseded high, narrow walls. Additionally, cannon mounted on angled bastions protruding from these walls could command the outer face of adjacent defences but, sited behind sturdy parapets, were difficult to hit with frontal fire. There was no 'dead' ground around a fort that could not be swept by fire. Originally named for the brilliance of Italian military engineers, this style of fortress construction evolved further through the later French and Dutch 'schools' of design.

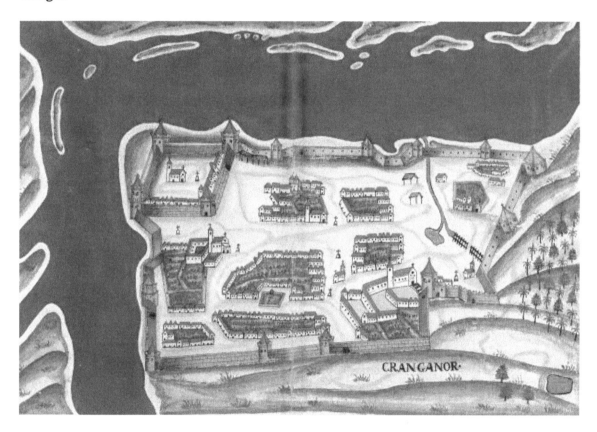

111. *Livro das Plantas de Todas as Fortalezas* was a catalogue of the forts of the Portuguese East by chronicler Antonio Bocarro in 1635, completed at the direction of the viceroy at Goa. Shown here is the fortress at Cranganor, on the Kerala coast of south India, first constructed in 1507. The citadel and adjacent walled township components were similar in layout to those of the Kastella complex.
Image credit: Biblioteca Evora.

Notable characteristics of these 'schools' of Renaissance military engineering, including ravelins, tenailles, covered ways, hornworks, cavaliers, glacis and redoubts, were not found in the Spice Islands forts before the fighting between Spain and the Dutch ended in the second decade of the seventeenth century. With less manpower, more difficult landscapes and less sophisticated opponents who had no siege artillery, the need to develop complex and expensive defensive engineering projects was not pressing at this, the far eastern edge of the world.

Kastella, Victoria and Reis Magos were the only major Portuguese Spice Islands forts built from the foundations up. Apart from the early rudimentary Spanish defences on Tidore and Halmahera, it was the Ternateans who constructed the next series of forts, determined to fortify their island against an expected Portuguese counterattack after the surrender of Kastella in 1575.

Sultan Babullah, ruler of Ternate, proceeded to give the Iberians a fine lesson on how to combine modern fortifications with seapower to control territory. He had Javanese and Malay engineers construct or modify forts at Tacome, Kota Janji and Malayo, and make significant improvements to Kastella. These works were armed with artillery captured from the Portuguese and Spanish and with guns brought in from Java, Aceh and Johore, and manned by hundreds of warriors, many armed with muskets. This impressive combination of a cluster of modern defences fielding abundant weaponry, all held with ample manpower, a supportive local population and a huge fleet of light vessels, thwarted the world's foremost martial power, Spain, for a quarter of a century.

Fort construction

In terms of actual construction, most Spice Islands fortress engineers had little trouble finding a solid foundation in the volcanic rock that abounds throughout the islands. Wherever possible, impervious rock was used on the foundation strata to defeat rising damp.

Wall sections still extant show that a favoured technique was to use rammed earth, sometimes mixed with straw or fibrous grasses, in between the stone-faced inner and outer walls. Bastions were similarly stone-faced and mostly earth-filled. Many of the Dutch and Spanish forts had secure powder rooms located under bastions with arched stonework entries, double doors and rendered stonework internally. The strength of powder room construction has led to several at least partially surviving, including at Fort Nova near Kastella, Fort Tohula, Fort Concordia, Fort Hollandia and Fort Revenge. Stone walls varied greatly in quality. Obviously experienced masons worked on fine detailed sections like entry arches and door surrounds, while the work quality often deteriorates the further you get from the front gate.

The stone used is a mixture of locally quarried volcanic rock and sawn coral from the surrounding reefs, generally laid with mortar, and faced with a rendered coating to provide some protection from the monsoons. Mortar was obtained from burning crushed coral or lime. Some forts, especially in the Bandas, feature distinctive Dutch-style red bricks for door surrounds, which were brought out as ship ballast. The environment was naturally punishing for structures due to consistently high temperatures, extreme rainfall, invasive vegetation and high humidity.

The Dutch, who commenced fortification building in the Spice Islands in 1607 by modifying the local fort at Malayo on Ternate (later Fort Orange), were experts at defensive fortifications after generations of such warfare with the Spanish in their own country during the Eighty Years War. They were skilled at designing, constructing, defending and attacking fortified points, and eventually built the largest number of fortifications throughout the Islands.

The standard template for the early Dutch forts (to 1650) was the quadrilateral with low-angled bastions at each corner and ramparts between; such works were built at Malayo (Fort Orange), Tacome (Fort Willemstadt), Banda (Forts Nassau, Hollandia, Concordia and Belgica), Makian (Fort Mauritius) and Tidore (Fort Mareico). Ignoring smaller forts, only pentagonal Fort Revenge on Ai, in the Bandas, and the later modifications to both Fort Victoria and Fort Belgica, departed from this theme. In size they ranged from Nassau, with a frontage of 130 metres and a garrison of 150, to remote Concordia with a frontage of just 20 metres and a garrison of a dozen.

While such forts were generally not up to the design standards of modern European fortifications, they were sufficient to maintain control over local populations. The Dutch network of forts were components of a wider empire that included powerful naval forces, central political and military commands based on Java, regional garrisons that could lend support, and local allies with their own armed maritime transport.

Against such an integrated system, local armies struggled to overcome well-armed and properly manned Dutch fortifications. The only substantial work ever to be successfully stormed solely by local forces was Fort Duurstede on Saparua near Ambon in 1817, which had a garrison of just 19 men at the time it fell to hundreds of attackers.

On the other hand, European troops storming European-held fortifications started with the Portuguese defeating several Spanish defensive works, as described previously, but accelerated with the arrival of the Dutch. On their arrival in the Spice Islands, they stormed obsolete but resolutely defended Reis Magos (Tidore) in 1605, and again in 1613, as well as the small Marieco (Tidore) in 1613. They failed against the defences of Soa Siu (Tidore) in 1613 and against the new and formidable Tohula (Tidore) in 1614, as the Spanish had failed against Malayo in 1607 and Tacoma in 1609 (both on Ternate) while they were under construction.

112. Fort Duurstede on Saparua showing the extended perimeter ramparts. It was garrisoned by just 19 soldiers who held off several hundred attackers for nine hours before succumbing, illustrating how fortifications greatly reduced manpower requirements—but only up to a point.

Ambon was a crucial base for the Portuguese and the Dutch, and Fort Victoria was a powerful fortification, but apart from stout defence by the Portuguese against several local, Javanese and one Dutch attempt prior to 1605, it changed hands with embarrassing ease in 1605 (to the Dutch), 1796 and 1809 (both to the British). In all three episodes, overwhelming seapower led to a disheartened garrison which led to surrender. The strongly garrisoned, well-armed and expensively updated forts of the Bandas also quickly capitulated to the British when faced with less than overwhelming force, but crucially with no naval support, in 1796 and 1810.

Control of the sea adjacent to Spice Islands forts was thus of vital importance to the survival of fortifications. The Portuguese, relying on annual trading visits rather than on a strong locally based squadron, always had only the most tenuous level of control over the Moluccas, and were fortunate that their local adversaries were slow to acquire decent rampart-smashing cannon. The Dutch, with tremendous advantages of manpower and capital over the Iberians and because of their competent integration of forts and maritime assets, were virtually unchallenged by external forces in the Indies for nearly 400 years. The exception was when their seapower was denuded during the Napoleonic Wars, leaving them vulnerable to the all-powerful Royal Navy.

Similarly, in 1942, when the Imperial Japanese Navy arrived to take the Indies and the Spice Islands, the weak allied naval forces were caught far away, trying unsuccessfully to defend Java.

Contemporary weaponry

At the start of the colonial era in the Spice Islands (1511) effective cannon-armed ocean-going ships were a new global concept, largely pioneered by the Portuguese. Their deployment of caravels and carracks to defeat a numerically superior Mameluke-Indian fleet in 1503 off the Malabar Coast was the earliest example of a blue-water, line-ahead fleet using standoff gunfire; tactics that would dictate naval battles for the next 400 years.[113]

On land and at sea, bronze cannon began to replace wrought iron weapons from around this time. While bronze was more expensive, it was much stronger and did not rust, which made it preferable at sea and in coastal forts. Heavier guns were divided into long powerful culverins, shorter bulkier cannons and stone-firing perriers, which were lighter guns because the less dense stone ball they fired was much less weighty than an iron one of the same size.

Shipboard heavy guns of this early era were mounted on basic carriages or wheel-less wooden sledges, and fired through openings in the bulwarks, or lidded openings in the hull. Much more numerous than the big guns were smaller swivel guns mounted on bulwarks and railings, firing scatter shot or a small ball and used against enemy crews.

As the price of tin and copper which made bronze cannon increased from around 1600, heavier but much cheaper cast iron artillery began to replace bronze guns, especially for the Dutch and English. The beautifully crafted Portuguese bronze cannon became heavily outnumbered by mass produced iron weapons.

Because cannon were smooth bore with no rifling, and because the ball had to be marginally smaller than the bore, they were inaccurate; in fact not much more accurate than a musket, which shot to around 250 metres, though was accurate to less than 100. However, when your target was as large as a ship or a fort, this did not matter so much,

---

[113] For more on this battle, see *Galleons & Galleys,* p. 77.

and any galleon closer than about 500 metres to a properly served culverin (18-pounder) was in mortal danger if it dithered for too long. The stability of fortress-mounted cannon naturally had an advantage over those firing up at them from rolling ships. Large cannon could of course place a ball much further out—Venetians with a 60-pounder at Cyprus in 1570 lobbed some rounds into an Ottoman troop parade at nearly 5000 metres[114]—but it is likely that most land and sea engagements in the Spice Islands were fought between 150 and about 250 metres.

113. The Portuguese observed local Spice Islands warfare and weaponry in detail when they arrived in the early sixteenth century, but made no mention of any local firearms. The advantages of Iberian-style swivel guns, especially on korakora, were quickly apparent, and they began to be produced in Java, Makassar and the Philippines. The Portuguese also sold them to local rulers, often ending up later facing the same weapons.

---

114 *Gunpowder & Galleys*, p.172.

Seapower

For the Portuguese, Spanish, English and Dutch, the ability of ships and forts to interact was always a fundamental part of their colonial strategy. All ships of the time were armed with cannon, and forts often received their armament from the artillery mounted on ships, so it is rewarding to assess what weaponry contemporary vessels carried.

The Portuguese squadrons that rounded Africa, commanded the Indian Ocean and found the Spice Islands in the early sixteenth century were generally composed of two types of vessels: caravels and carracks (or naos). At this time, caravels varied from small 50-tonne scouting vessels mounting six breech-loading swivel guns to much larger ships with 30 or 40 guns,[115] but the bulk of the fleet were in-between these two, likely crewed by 30 men with an armament of four 18-pounders mounted behind gunports below, six falcons (roughly four-pounders) on deck and ten smaller swivel guns on the bulwarks.[116]

Carracks were much larger but slower than caravels, and better able to carry bulky trade goods over oceanic distances while still maintaining a strong armament. Da Gama's carracks that destroyed the Mameluke Red Sea fleet in 1503 off India had a gundeck broadside of six 18-pounders, four bow and stern guns firing balls of about nine pounds, eight falcons in the waist and a multitude of breech-loading swivels on the upper decks for anti-personnel shooting.[117] With such an armament, a single ship outgunned entire fleets in Eastern waters at the time.

Magellan's 1519 Spanish fleet of five small ships with tonnages ranging from 75 to 120 carried around 270 crew and between them shipped an armament of six large cannon (*lombardas gruesos* and *pasamuros*), seven falcons and 58 *versos* (breech-loading swivel guns), illustrating the importance of the latter.[118] Some of these guns were later used to arm Portuguese and Spanish fortifications on Ternate and Tidore. Over time, the load-carrying limitations of the caravel brought about the new concept of the galleon. By 1600, the Portuguese, Spanish, Dutch and English were all building galleons. More seaworthy than the caravel, slimmer and faster than the carrack, the galleon was a manoeuvrable long-range warship that could carry its fill of spices. It

---

[115] *Cogs, Caravels and Galleons*, p. 95.

[116] *Galleons & Galleys*, p. 82.

[117] *Galleons & Galleys*, p. 82.

[118] *Magellan*, p. 94.

mounted heavy guns in the broadside and firing forward and lighter breech-loaders and swivel guns throughout. The Portuguese India fleets fielded 21 galleons as early as 1525.

Drake's *Golden Hind,* visiting the Spice Islands in 1579, was a middle-sized galleon of a couple of hundred tonnes, but larger than the biggest of Magellan's ships, and carried a main armament of 14 demi-culverins (about ten-pounders) below, and six lighter swivel guns on deck.[119] Twenty-six years later, the big 610-tonne English *Red Dragon* which watched the Dutch attack on Portuguese Tidore was much more heavily armed, with two 32-pounders (demi-cannon), 16 eighteen-pounders (culverins), 12 nine-pounders and eight five- or six-pounders (sakers).[120] A 32-pounder was a very big shipboard cannon in the seventeenth century waters of the Indies. By comparison, the VOC's 406-tonne *Amsterdam,* which was one of the ships pounding Fort Reis Magos while the *Red Dragon* watched, carried four 24-pounders, four 18-pounders, 14 nine-pounders and ten smaller guns.

It seems that the weight of cannon on the Portuguese ships gradually decreased from the late 1500s—perhaps due to a lack of large targets requiring ship-killing weapons, and to the expense of bronze cannon which they favoured. By the mid-1600s the perennial problem with Portuguese carracks and galleons when it came to ship-to-ship combat with English and Dutch Indiamen (which supplanted the galleon) was that they were always under-gunned in both quantity and weight of weaponry. Even the largest carracks of over 1500 tonnes carried just 18 or 20 guns,[121] and these were mostly small cannon (six- and eight-pounders)[122] rather than ship-killing 18- or 24-pounders. While the smaller weapons were sufficient for defeating junks and other light Asian craft, they were inadequate against the modern firepower of northern European ships.

A VOC instruction dated 1630 required all Indiamen to be armed with 24 heavy guns (18-pounder or larger) plus smaller guns. When it went down off the West Australian coast on its maiden voyage in 1629, the VOC East Indiaman *Batavia* had an armament of 30 guns. Two 12-pounders were recovered soon after the sinking, while 16 have been brought up in modern times. Most of these are 24- or 32-pounders, though there are some smaller weapons, as expected. From the smaller *Vergulde Draake,* which went down in 1656, a six-pounder and a 12-pounder have been recovered. Interestingly, the

---

[119] *The Artilleryman,* Spring 1990.

[120] *The Merchant Venturers of London,* p. 32.

[121] *Asian Trade & European Influence in the Indonesian Archipelago 1500–1650,* p. 175.

[122] *War and Trade in the Indian Ocean and South China Sea, 1600–1650,* p. 10.

much later *Zuidorp* (1712) and *Zeewijk* (1727) both carried a quantity of small swivels of roughly two-pounder size; the former seven, and the latter six.[123]

The British ships that supported the capture of the Spice Islands from the Dutch in 1797 and again in 1810 were a mix of frigates, ships of the line and smaller craft. At the time, Royal Navy frigates such as the *Caroline* in Captain Cole's little squadron mounted 26 18-pounders on the gun deck with ten nine-pounders and ten 32-pound carronades split between the quarterdeck and forecastle.

114. A Portuguese fusta or galley, depicted by Baptista van Doetcum and appearing in Linschoten's *Iteinerio* around 1596, shows a locally manned, cannon-armed galley widely used by the Portuguese throughout their Asian possessions.

---

123 See *The Armament of Australia's VOC Ships.*

In the archipelagos of the Indies, both Iberian nations and the Dutch also utilised an array of small craft, some to local design, such as prahus, sampans, junks and korakora, and others to European design, principally oared galleys and sailing brigantines. Given the seasonality of the monsoon winds, and the generally light winds of the tropical seas, oared craft such as galleys were extremely useful.

In India in 1525, the Portuguese patrol, communications and battle fleet included five naos, 11 galleons, nine galleys, four brigantines, nine smaller ships and 27 prahus. Galleys were built at Malacca by the Portuguese from 1512 and by the Spanish in the Philippines. Iberian galleys were well armed; at Manila in 1607, the Spanish flagship galley sported a 12-pounder, two nine-pounders, several lighter guns and two stone throwers.[124]

115. Part of the Portuguese fleet from Lisbon to the Indies of 1533, shown in the *Memoria des Armadas*. Visible are a mix of fast, manoeuvrable four-masted caravel redondas as well as a trio of bulky carracks. Main armament for both classes was 18-pounders, the caravels carrying four and the carracks six or more, while all ships also mounted between one and two dozen smaller swivel guns.

---

124 *The Philippine Islands 1493–1898*, Volume XIV: 1605–1609 Artillery at Manila 1607.

116. A cast bronze VOC 24-pounder. Weighing around 2.5 tonnes with a four-metre barrel, it sat on a 500 kg timber carriage and needed a crew of a dozen to serve it properly in fortress or shipborne modes. It could put a ball out over six kilometres at maximum elevation but gunners of the time preferred much shorter ranges.

Of course, the Spice Islanders also understood seapower and they had wielded korakora as their primary offensive weapon since long before the Portuguese arrived. The power of kings was measured in the size of their korakora fleets. Early Portuguese observers noted that Ternate fielded 100 and Tidore 80, and each might be crewed by over a hundred men, including rowers and warriors. They were capable of fast sprints or slower long-range raids, and they did not rely solely on wind. Later versions were equipped with cannon and swivel guns and the warriors were armed with muskets.

117. A group of korakora set off on one of the hongi raids from Ambon in 1786 in this depiction by Petrus Conradi.

Fort armaments

Several lists survive detailing the Iberian cannon available for use in fortresses and at sea in the East, firstly for Portuguese India in 1525,[125] secondly for Spanish Manila in 1607[126] and finally for Portuguese Macau[127] in 1635. While the weapons assigned to the forts of the Spice Islands are not specified, these accounts do give a contemporary glimpse of what was likely to have stood on the ramparts among the islands of nutmeg and cloves, especially as the artillery of Iberian forts of the Spiceries originated in the main from these three locations.

118. A late sixteenth century Spanish cast bronze breech-loader with reloadable chambers. It was swivel mounted, 1.5-m long with a bore of about 5 cm. A crew of two men could fire a couple of rounds a minute while pre-loaded chambers were available, which was an impressive rate of fire for weapons of the time.

A quarter century after the Portuguese arrived in India, there were 1073 artillery pieces in the forts there: 667 of bronze and 406 of wrought iron. These were distributed between the forts guarding the capital at Goa, and other forts at Malacca, Cannanore, Quilon, Calicut and Chaul, as well as galleys and ships of the fleet. Of all the guns,

---

[125] *A Gun-List from Portuguese India, 1525*, Journal of the Ordnance Society, Richard Barker, vol. 8, 1996.

[126] *The Philippine Islands 1493–1898*, Volume XIV: 1605–1609 Artillery at Manila 1607.

[127] *The Defences of Macau*, Appendix 3.

numerically most prevalent were the 680-odd bercos—small breech-loading swivel guns with a two-inch bore firing scatter shot or a small ball, coming with several reloadable iron chambers. They were favourites for mounting on parapets of forts and bulwarks of ships because the ability to change the pre-loaded chambers quickly gave them a fast rate of fire.

Next in number came the 189 falcons—large swivel guns firing about four pounds of scatter shot or a small ball. Third most numerous were the 65 big guns, known as 'camels'. They were carriage-mounted and fired an 18-pound ball. The remainder of the list was a mix of small stone-throwing chambered pieces, six-pounders, 12-pounders, a few 50-pounders and a monster 450-pounder siege gun, probably captured.

Often the superiority of Portuguese firearms is used as an excuse for their victories against huge odds, but this is not necessarily so. At Malacca in 1511 for example, the sultan's forces had over 1000 swivel guns, many more than the Portuguese attackers, but were unskilled in their use.

119. A replica of the 30-pounder St Lawrence cannon, forged by Bocarro in 1627 at Macau. It was a gift to the Imperial Court in Peking, later mounted by the Chinese to defend the Pearl River, and captured by the British in 1841. The real cannon now stands in the Royal Armouries at Fort Nelson in the UK, while this replica is in the Macau Museum.

The gun inventory for the fortress of Pacem on Sumatra may be an indication of what Kastella on Ternate may have been armed with around the 1520s. Pacem had altogether 60 pieces including 37 bercos, 11 falcons, three 12-pounders, four camels and two big 50-pounders. All were lost when the fort fell to the Achenese in 1524, and no doubt fired at the Portuguese in subsequent years.[128]

Eighty-odd years later, Manila, capital of the Spanish East Indies and their most important base in Asia, held in total 71 pieces of artillery, with a further 12 on the city's two defence galleys. There were ten big guns (larger than 18-pounders), 22 medium-size pieces (12- to 18-pounders) with the remainder a mix of the equivalent to Portuguese bercos and falcons. When the VOC captured the Spanish fort on Makian at Taffasoho in 1608, it was armed with one camel, two falcons and 32 bercos, another indication of the popularity of small swivel guns.[129]

Portuguese Macau, the wealthiest city in Asia in the early 1600s due to its control of the Japan–China trade, was heavily fortified after a failed Dutch attack in 1622. In 1635, a report on its defences noted 44 mounted cannon in its nine forts and batteries, plus 18 in reserve. Most of the weapons were in the 18- to 25-pound range, while the largest was a 35-pound culverin.

The remoteness of Macau from Portuguese India, and its dazzling wealth, led to the establishment of its own cannon foundry, by Manuel Tavares Bocarro from 1625. He was the son of a famous Goa-based cannon maker, Pedro Bocarro, who had himself made many pieces of artillery arming Portuguese forts of the East. Bocarro's Macau-made bronze cannon were famous throughout the Orient for their quality and workmanship, and while unfortunately none survive in Asia, one of his foundry's bells ended up on Ternate, and several of his cannon—gifts from Macau to the Chinese and captured in 1841 by the British at the Boca Tigres forts—are on display at Fort Nelson, Portsmouth.

As the Dutch gradually took control of the Indies they were better armed and equipped than the Iberians, and of course, artillery and gunpowder had developed too. By 1800, a fort like Tolukko on Ternate was armed with a 12-pounder, five eight-pounders and three two-pounder swivels. The larger and more important fort at Kalomata fielded two 12s, and four each of eight-, six- and four-pounders. The largest guns on the island were 18-pounders, of which Fort Orange boasted five.[130]

---

[128] *A Gun-List from Portuguese India, 1525*, Journal of the Ordnance Society, Richard Barker, vol. 8, 1996.

[129] *Sent Forth a Dove*, p. 51.

[130] *Naval Chronicle*, Volume 26.

Hand-held weapons

Arquebuses, and the muskets that slowly replaced them from around 1500, used a matchlock system to fire a bullet down a smoothbore barrel. They were sturdy but heavy, and to reload a complex 28-step process taking at least one minute had to be completed while holding the lit match in one hand between thumb and forefinger. Tropical conditions were terrible for properly storing gunpowder and, naturally, such weapons could not be used in monsoonal downpours.

120. A VOC sword from around 1700 with an elaborately decorated hilt featuring the emblem of the VOC. The weapon is part of the collection of the Musee de l'Armee in Paris.

Though the Portuguese initially had the advantage of more modern firearms than their Spice Islands adversaries, the difficulty of reloading and the limitations of using matchlock weapons in a tropical environment meant these often counted for little in a drawn-out engagement. Most skirmishes and battles in the early colonial Spice Islands were decided by the sword, lance, javelin, bow and crossbow, with the musket and swivel gun being the most potent of the firearms.

Magellan's Spanish fleet, anticipating possible battle against forces from his Portuguese homeland, took with it as hand weapons 50 muskets, 70 crossbows, 100 suits of armour, over 4000 crossbow bolts, 1000 lances and 200 pikes, helpfully illustrating the ratio of firearms to earlier weapons and equipment in 1519.[131]

Eighty-seven years later, another Spaniard, Luis Torres in the small galleon *San Pedro,* discovered the strait between New Guinea and Australia that bears his name and sailed on to Ternate where he stayed for three months to support the rebuilding of the Kastella fortress. *San Pedro* was lightly armed with just six three-pounders but also carried 20 muskets, 20 arquebuses, 20 round shields, 20 pikes and 15 halberds, indicating that crossbows and suits of armour where no longer standard equipment by that time.[132]

Local warriors of the Spice Islands at the beginning of the colonial era fought principally with a single-bladed sword, the *pedang,* but also used fire-hardened cane spears and lances that could pierce the chainmail worn by Iberian soldiers. They carried a large shield and often wore padded coats as body armour. From the 1520s they quickly acquired firearms, both muskets and bombards from Javanese and Malay sources, and captured other weapons from the Portuguese and Spanish.

Tactics and organisation

The pioneering role that tiny Portugal played in the Age of Discovery should always be respected. That the Portuguese were able to establish, and for a while maintain, an empire stretching from Morocco to China was a credit to the great men whose vision and determination created that realm: Da Gama, Almeida and Albuquerque. With breathtaking strategic foresight, they established a network of forts, trading posts and naval bases that, for a time, laid a chokehold on the maritime trade between the Atlantic and the Pacific.

---

[131] *Magellan,* p. 94.

[132] *The Voyage of Torres,* p.14.

For over a century though, their most common offensive battle tactic was the infamous headlong charge. Typically, after soldiers and sailors landed from ships on a hostile shore, this played out as a reckless frontal assault in no organised formation against superior numbers, yelling saints' names and brandishing cold steel in the hope that the enemy—who was generally even less disciplined than the Portuguese—would retreat in fear and disorder. Quite often it worked, but if the opponent was placed behind field fortifications of any decency and held their ground, then the Portuguese were routed on the spot, and retired with even greater speed—and casualties—than they had advanced.

They often prevailed against incredible odds simply with willpower and a belief in their own superiority. Examples are Albuquerque's resolve in the extended battle to capture Malacca against well-armed and numerous foes in 1511; Duarte Pacheco's courage and resourcefulness in the defence of Cochin in 1504, defeating an army of 50,000 with just a hundred Portuguese and a few local troops; and Galvao's brilliant 'out-of-the-box' planning and execution of the raid on Tidore in 1536, where he took on thousands of warriors with 120 Portuguese musketeers and some slaves, and emerged victorious.

The Portuguese victories over the Spanish and their local allies in the Spice Islands in battles at Marieco in 1524 and at Soa Siu in 1529 and again in 1533 were all examples of the headlong charge, followed by an escalade of the ramparts. At Jailolo in 1533, because of the strength of the fortifications and the difficult terrain, they had to go through the tedious and lengthy rigmarole of setting up a proper siege with breaching guns behind gabions, trenches and barricades to repel counterattacks, and accumulating stores of powder and supplies. In all these battles, they were supported by hordes of Ternatean warriors to whom the concept of the reckless charge appeared to appeal greatly.

The Spanish were the most sophisticated military power in the world in the sixteenth century and regarded the Portuguese martial effectiveness with some disdain when they became politically united in 1580. However, while the Spanish had previously conquered South and Central America, they had done so against much less sophisticated opponents than those the Portuguese faced in Asia. In their first significant campaign in the Spice Islands, the Spanish tried to take Kastella from the sultan several times without success from 1584 to 1602, using the science of siege warfare.

When they finally did capture it in 1606, it was in a revealing engagement that started with deftly manoeuvred mutually supporting formations of musketeers and pikemen covering the establishment of batteries, but ended in success with a headlong charge and escalade.

Much of the Portuguese problem after around 1570 related not to tactics but to a lack of leadership and proper organisation. Later governors of the Estado da India were, as always, noblemen, but not with the grasp of strategy and tactics that the like of Albuquerque had possessed. They let themselves be blockaded in Goa and Malacca by the Dutch, the two crucial ports they needed to run the empire. And it was not just higher leadership that was an issue. Junior officers often lacked military experience and were more focused on making a name for themselves and accruing spoils as quickly as possible rather than training and professionally leading their men. Only occasionally were there officers who were an inspiration to their soldiers. As their opponents became more competent, Portuguese companies without training could not operate under fire in regular formations, leading all too often to rash attacks that had limited chance of success.

121. Portugal built an empire that extended from Morocco to China with astonishing speed in its quest to secure the spices and trade of the East, but its glory was short-lived and it quickly slipped into decline because it lacked adequate resources, leadership and military organisation to hold onto its gains.

122. Early Portuguese colonial successes were a function of their advanced nautical technology—an astrolabe which assisted in determining latitude, is shown here—their versatile ships, their firepower and their fearless leaders. This combination was, however, not sufficient to maintain their positions without commensurate resources of men, ships, money and guns, which were rarely available in sufficient quantities. Astrolabe from hemisferium.net.

In terms of military organisation, essentially there was none. Astonishingly, the Estado da India fielded no regular, trained military force at Goa until a regiment was established in 1671, by which time the Portuguese position in the East was in terminal decline. Prior to that, loose companies were established for particular operations, and subsequently disbanded. Their deficit in manpower due to disease and desertion contrasted unfavourably with the Dutch, who could rely on masses of Scandinavian and German recruits attracted by the lure of the riches of the Indies. Lack of Portuguese soldiers meant the governor often had to rely on unmotivated local troops, who did at least have the advantage of requiring less pay.

The Dutch, firstly under the VOC, and later the Netherlands state, were more organised than the Portuguese, and applied more manpower to extending their control over the Indies. Always outnumbering the Iberians, by 1700 there were 10,000 soldiers based at Batavia or through the islands under its sway. On arrival in Batavia, they were assigned to one of the fortress bastions, where some training in drill, loading and firing of weapons did occur, and from there they could be posted to regional forts and outposts for years at a time. In all, except for brief periods when the British or Japanese took control, soldiers from the Netherlands stood-to at forts of the Spice Islands for 344 years.

Garrison life

There is little doubt that life for the men manning the forts of the Spice Islands would have been punishingly hard, even by the European standards of the time. Dysfunctional medical care, poor accommodation facilities, rampant tropical diseases, monotonous diet, low pay, boredom, isolation, severe discipline, extreme heat and humidity are just some of the negative aspects of garrison life in the Indies before we even consider warfare.

For the first centuries of the colonial era, to arrive at a fort for duty, soldiers first had to survive the voyage from Europe, which was an endurance test in itself. Portuguese carracks made the journey from Lisbon to Goa in around seven months, packed with sailors, soldiers, friars, administrators and slaves. Leaving the Tagus at the end of the northern winter, they passed south through the maddening steaming calms of the tropical doldrums, rounded the Cape in the stormy southern winter, and arrived around September in India, during the misery of the rainy season. The largest vessels carried up to 200 crew and up to 1000 passengers—mostly soldiers destined for the forts and battlegrounds from Mozambique to Macau—and the majority slept on deck, at the mercy of the extremes of weather.

Exposure, poor food, bad water, terrible hygienic conditions and contagious diseases caused gruesome casualties. Losing half the soldiers on a journey was not unheard of. Storms, shipwrecks, battle and pirates added to the carnage. Many ships disappeared without trace. After three or four round trips to the Indies, the deterioration to the ship's hull and rigging was so severe they were generally unseaworthy, and hulked.

For those that made it to Goa, on arrival, there was no barracks to house them, no system of provisioning and, almost invariably, their meagre pay was far in arrears. They waited at the governor's pleasure until they were dispatched to one of the hot spots of the empire—the burning sands of the Persian Gulf or the far China Seas—where they formed expeditionary forces or were posted to the garrison of one of the forts.

123. The sentry path along the battlements of Fort Concordia on Banda Besar in the Bandas. Concordia was one of the most remote of Spice Islands forts, the coast covered in reefs preventing ships from standing in, a rough track through the hills its only link with other Dutch posts on the island. Even so, the garrison of a dozen or so men would have had to take their turns at patrolling the ramparts, night and day, in all weathers, while those off-duty faced boredom, blasting tropical heat and the dreary monotony of isolated garrison life.

Almost a quarter of a million young Portuguese men sailed to the East in the sixteenth century, but few ever returned.[133] They were divided into several social

---

[133] *The Portuguese Seaborne Empire 1415–1825*, p. 52.

groups. The peasant class *soldadaos* made up the great bulk of the Estado da India's manpower. They served as and when required until death, marriage, incapacitation or desertion. To return to Portugal after a stint of service, they had to receive the governor's permission and pay their own fare, and this rarely happened. Apart from the perils of disease and battle, their pay and whatever they could earn through trading contraband and spices combined with the low cost of existence in the Indies meant *soldadaos* could perhaps sustain a reasonable standard of living, often with slaves and concubines.

124. A forgotten Dutch graveyard on Gunung Api island in the Bandas. It lies amongst the ruins of Fort Colombo just a few hundred metres from the oft-angry volcano after which the island is named. This was a military post, so those that lie here were soldiers at the fort. Casualties from tropical diseases, accidents and sickness always far outnumbered those from battle, and in fact, the garrison at this fort over several centuries never fired their weapons in anger.

They could get permission to leave the king's service if they married a Christian woman, thereby becoming a *casado,* or married settler. In times of crisis—of which many attended the empire—*casados* were of course, liable for military duty once again.

Degredados were convicts from Portugal sent out to bolster the empire's manpower, and consequently enjoyed even fewer privileges than *soldadaos*. Deserters fled punishment or the gruelling life of soldiery, and often found employment with enemies of Portugal throughout the East, but as anywhere, it was a capital offence.

Fidalgos were men of higher birth, seeking a name for themselves in the heady early days of empire, with an eye to a return to Portugal for royal favours once their tour was complete. Others competed for the governor's favour for plump roles. Commanding a fortress or captaincy of a trading voyage were the sought-after positions, where side trading could make a man's fortune in a few short years. Lack of any military experience was no barrier to such a role.

While the concept of upper-class military leadership was prevalent in contemporary Europe, by contrast, the Dutch VOC's classless meritocracy system was much more effective in producing capable commanders, and this showed in the long Portuguese-Dutch War. The history of Portugal's Estado da India is graced with several exceptional land and sea commanders, but these few are outnumbered by a multitude of inexperienced highborns who endlessly slaughtered their men with their own incompetence.

The contrast between impoverished *soldadaos* and their countrymen traders who had the rights to profitable voyages or fort captaincies was extreme. The conspicuous wealth of the successful traders of Malacca, Macau and Goa was legendary throughout the East, and must have seemed obscene to disabled old *soldadaos*, reduced to begging for their existence. For most, the riches of the Spice trade were mirages across the shimmering equatorial seas.

A stint of duty in a fort in the Spice Islands in the sixteenth century or seventeenth century would, however, have been far removed from the plush luxuries of Goa or, later, Batavia. Supply ships came generally once a year to the Spice Islands in Portuguese times, and so for the bulk of their stay, *soldadaos* would have subsisted on local diet: rice, sago and fish. Coconuts, bananas and palm wine (arak) were no doubt highly regarded when they could be had. A metre and a half of rain fell each year at Kastella, spread across the calendar, though with the wettest period from November to June. The hottest month was May, averaging 28 degrees, while the coolest was August, averaging 27. At night it rarely fell below 24 degrees, and the windiest month was January, where the breeze averaged just 10 km/h. Humidity was high all year round. To live through such monotonous tropical conditions in very basic barracks-style accommodation with a boring diet must have been physically challenging and mentally taxing.

The colonial Portuguese were never disposed to extensive military training, and this lack of organised activity combined with the stultifying climate would have quickly turned mere idleness into mind-numbing boredom. Opportunities to participate in raids or exploration would have been keenly sought, if just to escape the tedious monotony of fort life.

Any interaction with locals and especially local women was often limited by the politics of the day. For a significant part of Kastella's Portuguese tenure (1522–75), the fort's inhabitants were targets for local jihadis if they ventured alone beyond the walls. Naturally there are no statistics available, but the incidence of desertion, suicide and insanity would not have been trivial for the Portuguese, Spanish or Dutch garrisons in the Spice Islands.

Disease was of course a much greater killer than battle. Malaria, beriberi, dysentery, dengue fever, typhus and scurvy were all common on the trip from Europe to Asia, or once the soldiers arrived in Asia. Shipboard medical care was often restricted to an ignorant 'barber-surgeon', who in any case was generally without effective medicines. The misguided propensity for 'bleeding' already sick patients only added to casualty lists. At the Royal Hospital for Soldiers in Goa—the main medical station of the Estado da India—in the 30 years from 1600, some 25,000 Portuguese are recorded as dying.[134] This is a telling number for an empire that could only once in this period field a force of 3000 fighting men. As for the VOC, it was 1673 before there was a proper hospital established at Fort Orange, their Moluccan headquarters on Ternate.

For the Dutch soldiers of the VOC, life in the Spice Islands was perhaps more orderly and better provisioned than in Portuguese times, but still extremely isolated. Around 1650, a VOC private at Banda or a sailor on an East Indiaman was paid around nine florins a month,[135] although a large part of this was withheld until the end of their five years of service, as insurance against desertion. What they got in the hand was just enough to survive on, and so they had to earn extra by trading illegally in nutmeg, as was expected of everyone. A master gunner received 22 florins, and a captain 30. There was no pension system.[136]

One German in the service of the VOC, Johann Wurffbain, spent five years in the garrison at Fort Nassau in the 1630s and wrote graphically about some of the amazing aspects of the Indies: earthquakes and volcanos, waterspouts and tsunamis, an enormous snake that ate a slave girl, crocodiles, battles against cannibals and the brutal punishments for transgressions.

Poor discipline and correspondingly severe punishment were always a feature of remote garrisons, both for the Iberians and the Dutch. Insolence to officers, blasphemy,

---

[134] *The Portuguese Seaborne Empire 1415–1825*, p. 131.

[135] Equivalent then to about 16 shillings, or in today's purchasing power, around US$100.

[136] *The Dutch Seaborne Empire*, Appendix II.

drunkenness and fighting were common VOC offenses. Punishments included beheading for murder or desertion, being broken on the wheel for offences against officers, whipping and branding for theft, and running the gauntlet for dereliction of duty.[137] For Iberians particularly, blasphemy was a serious offence that could draw a month in the stocks.

125. One night in 1674, the 40 Dutchmen of Fort Amsterdam's garrison were woken as an earthquake rumbled out of the darkness. Next, a tsunami caused by the earthquake smashed without warning over the bastions, sweeping most of the soldiers away to their deaths.

The most popular pastimes for sailors and soldiers afloat and ashore in the early colonial years were games of chance, mainly with cards or dice, generally accompanied by gambling. Those who were literate and had access to books often read to others to

---

[137] *Voyages to the East Indies,* p. 188.

pass the time, though particularly the Spanish had to be very careful not to get caught with texts proscribed by the Inquisition, which had an active office in Goa from 1560. In the Spanish fleets, the most popular books were about religious subjects, but others about chivalry and adventurous travels to Africa, the Holy Land and the Orient were also common. Telling stories—tall or true—was another pastime, the old hands shocking the new ones with unbelievable tales of sea monsters and strange creatures and bloody battles. Singing, fishing, reciting ballads and playing musical instruments were other ways to alleviate the drudgery of garrison life.

9. Fort Catalogue

Ternate

126. *View of Ternate*, French hydrographer Bellin's 1748 engraving of the orderly Dutch Fort Orange nestled under an exploding Gammalamma volcano. The eruption of 1740 was so violent that every structure on the island was declared uninhabitable, and the fortress badly damaged. This was a quiet period for the Dutch in the Spice Islands; the Spanish were long gone and the British yet to arrive.

In the sixteenth and seventeenth centuries, everyone knew the name Ternate. It was the beacon of the Spice Islands. Deckhands on Arab dhows, sultans in Syria, Portuguese navigators, Levant customs clerks, Venetian senators, Persian harbourmasters, merchants in Hamburg, India and Cairo—all said the name with a glint in their eye. They all knew it meant cloves, and cloves meant riches.

Ternate blasted like a lightning bolt from remote obscurity to a position of incredible wealth and global significance in the space of a hundred years, and after a brief but brutal period of importance and renown, it slowly settled back into insignificance, returning to its original obscurity, as the clove market and its monopoly slipped away. Prior to the Portuguese arrival, Ternate was the pre-eminent of the four regional sultanates, with its arch rival Tidore separated by just a few hundred metres of sea.

Dominated by its very active 1700-metre volcano, the tiny island—just ten kilometres across—was able to support a few thousand people only by importing every necessity and foodstuff. Nothing grew on the island except clove trees. But it was the fruit from these trees that the world was chasing.

In 1512, the Ternateans craftily won the competition to host the newly arrived Portuguese, but this was a victory they would later regret, opening the curtains on a hundred years of violence and conflict. Originally, the sultan had seen the well-armed newcomers as powerful allies in his interminable wars against his neighbours, but he and the other sultans soon found themselves engulfed in a prolonged series of wars to control the spice trade.

The Portuguese fought for several decades with the Spanish before seeing them off but were then themselves bested by the Sultan of Ternate and fled to Ambon. A short time later, the Spanish, who had back in Europe absorbed Portugal, invaded, occupied and fortified all the main islands, with their headquarters on Ternate. The newly arrived Dutch, also keen for spices, fought a series of running battles across Ternate with the Iberians over several decades until they emerged as the victors. They then spent much of the next centuries putting down rebellious sultans, repelling interloping Europeans and trying hard to interdict incessant smugglers.

Today, Ternate with its airport and major harbour is the arrival point for the northern Moluccas and has a fine and varied collection of Spice Islands forts to explore.

Kastella—The First Spice Islands Fort

The oldest of the colonial Spice Island fortifications, construction of Kastella started in 1522 in response to the departure from Spain of Magellan's expedition. The Portuguese monarch, Manuel I, had ordered it built to reinforce his title to the riches of the Moluccas in the face of competing Spanish claims. Antonio de Brito laid the first stone on the feast day of St John the Baptist, giving the fort its original name.

The rulers of Ternate, Tidore, Makian and Bacan had all competed for a Portuguese fort to be built in their domains, seeing a strong Portuguese base as a useful asset in the never-ending struggle for regional mastery. In the end, the fact that Portuguese traders had operated from Ternate since 1512 swung the deal in their favour.

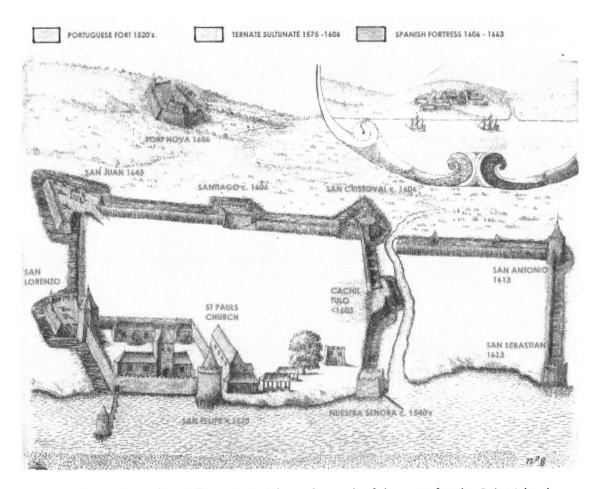

127. A Dutch view of Kastella in 1607, right at the peak of the wars for the Spice Islands. The original artwork has been coloured up to show ownership of the separate construction elements. This remains our best available layout of Kastella.

The location chosen was close to the sultan's court on the south-western coast, but around nine kilometres from Ternate's best harbour at Talangame. Small openings through reefs which fringed the shore at the fort site allowed careful passage by smaller junks and caravels but made it difficult for larger vessels to close and bombard, and these two factors were the principal determinants.

Despite de Brito bringing stone masons from Portugal, construction progressed slowly. Local enthusiasm for the project had died with the previous sultan, materials were hard to obtain, and manpower scarce. And the blasting tropical sun deterred hard labour by anyone. Timbers of the wrecked Spanish *Trinidad*, once Magellan's flagship but captured by the Portuguese and lost off Kastella in a storm, were used in the building process, and its guns supplemented the armament.

128. Remains of Bastion San Lorenzo, looking towards the coast. This bastion stood on the western, inland side of Kastella, replacing or augmenting an earlier high, round column. The central tower is visible in the right background.

Contemporary chroniclers agreed that the early fort was poorly built and militarily ineffective. Gradually the defences were improved, however. Two stone towers were added and the perimeter wall—roughly 60 square metres—was thickened and extended to over five metres in height. Galvao (1536–9) was responsible for extending a mud wall with ramparts and bastions around the Portuguese town that adjoined Kastella. Around 1540, Fernando de Sousa, a Portuguese military engineer and inspector of the fortifications across Asia, had a waterfront bastion, probably Nuestra Senora, rebuilt in stone. Subsequently, another waterfront bastion (probably San Felipe) was built (or rebuilt) in stone.

By 1570, relations between the Portuguese and the Ternateans had deteriorated to open warfare, with the locals laying siege to the fort. That the Portuguese managed to hold the defences for five years suggests a lack of energetic prosecution of the siege by the locals, but also some degree of effectiveness of the walls and bastions, and the weapons with which they were armed. Successive expeditions from Goa and Malacca to relieve the fortress were unsuccessful, and eventually conditions inside deteriorated to the point where the Portuguese were forced to surrender, abandoning their stronghold in humiliation.

Sultan Babullah took possession of a virtual ruin, but he anticipated the return of the Portuguese, so with the help of Javanese and Malay engineers he set about strengthening the defences. The perimeter was greatly extended, walled and provided with a number of substantial bastions. In the 1602 Spanish-Portuguese attempt to batter the sultan into submission, the works were described thus:

> '*for the enemy overlooked, and was strengthened by a stone Cavalier, which is that of Our Lady (later Bastion Nuestra Senora) next to the Sea. Under it was a Ravelin with seven heavy pieces of cannon which did and threatened greater harm to our camp. The Cavalier was all Rampart, four fathoms high and a fathom and a half broad ... On the land side the curtain of the wall ran as far as Cachil Tulo (Bastion), fortified outwards with massy timbers on which there were three large guns, and two on the wall from this Bulwark to that of Our Lady. These forts also had a large number of Falconets and Drakes (swivel guns)*'.[138]

That Acuna, Spanish Governor of the Philippines, was able to take Kastella in 1606 fairly speedily was more a result of the sultan's men fighting outside rather than from the defences. As his companies closed in on Kastella and siege guns were brought up, a force of his bolder troops first reduced some outer defences then, pursuing the fleeing Ternateans, managed to mount the curtain wall. With this, most defenders fled, though a last stronghold in St Paul's church resisted for a time, before also abandoning the fight. The Iberians had their castle back after 30 years. It was the only time in its 500-year history that Kastella was stormed.

Acuna set about improving and modifying the defences, further expanding the perimeter to accommodate a residential quarter, improving bastions and gates, and adding earthworks, all in contemporary style. He also ordered a redoubt built on a small hill above Kastella, commanding the fort and already with some defences, to be completed. This became known as Fort Nova.

Planned as a small three-bastioned quadrilateral—the fourth apex covered by a sharp slope to the nearby creek—its actual form turned out quite different; really a

---

[138] *From European–Asian Conflict to Cultural Heritage: Identification of Portuguese and Spanish Forts in the Northern Maluku Islands.*

small crenelated rampart as shown on the 1607 Dutch artwork. It was completed around 1610 and further refurbished in the early 1640s and 1650s, and then abandoned in 1663 with the remainder of the Spanish defences. Partly due to its existence, Kastella was never seriously threatened, except by the volcano, whose earthquakes no doubt led to the rebuilds.

129. Remains of the Portuguese tower at Kastella. This and part of the north wall were among the first sections of the sprawling complex built.

The Spanish defences were continually improved over time. The emergence of the powerful Dutch Fort Orange from 1607, just ten kilometres away overland, was an incentive. Dutch Admiral van Carden, captured by the Spanish in the Moluccas and for a time incarcerated in Kastella, declared the defences to be invulnerable in 1610. In any case, the Spanish were not troubled for a half century, finally abandoning and partly destroying the work in 1663 when they pulled out of the Spice Islands and returned to Manila.

The destruction has left few remains of the later Spanish defences, although surprisingly several sections of the Portuguese era are discernible. Most prominently, the Portuguese tower from around 1522 is still clearly evident, though ruined. Nearby, a 50-metre stretch of the north Portuguese wall is relatively intact, leading to Bastion San Lorenzo, which is also clearly defined. Inside this wall are the foundations of a number of the internal buildings. While San Lorenzo is only 65 metres from the sixteenth century coastline, the remains of Bastion San Juan are a further 250 metres inland. The foundations of the stone pier and the circular base of the water tower are also apparent now on dry land, illustrating that the sea has receded by around 100 metres, assumedly due to volcanic silting.

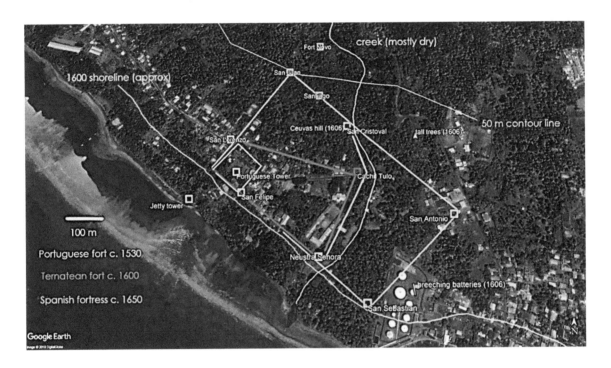

130. A study of the various defence layouts at Kastella overlaid on a modern satellite image. The original Portuguese work was extremely limited, but was soon expanded to enclose the developing township. By the time of its surrender in 1575, it probably enclosed an area similar to the Ternatean fort (in red). Kastella's weakness was the proximity of high ground to the north, from where guns could command the defences. It was to prevent this that Bastion San Juan and Fort Novo were built by the Spanish after 1606.
Image credit: Google Earth.

Finally, a part of Bastion Cachil Tulo is evident, though it has been substantially destroyed by the round-island road which bisects modern Kastella. The wet-season watercourse lying just east of Cachil Tulo has not moved appreciably in 500 years. Of the bastions Santiago, San Felipe, Nuestra Senora, San Cristoval, San Antonio and San

Sebastian and their adjacent walls structures, no remains could be located. But Fort Nova, lost for a century, was found.

Dutch records show that in the early twentieth century Fort Nova's location was still known, but more recent Spanish and Portuguese investigations have not been able to verify its position. In 2012, the author, along with the Regional Director of the Institute of Architectural Heritage, an archaeologist from PDA and Ardi, Benteng Kastella's 'keeper', were able to locate the remains of this little fort on a low, overgrown rise only 100 metres from Bastion San Juan at 00 deg 45'51.8N 127 deg 18'50.5 E.

Not much is left. There are remains of a stone-lined pit that would have served as the powder store, some low wall sections and piles of coral block rubble, but the location ties in with contemporary descriptions, especially the sharp drop-off on the eastern side, its proximity to, and its ability to dominate, Kastella.

Today Kastella's ruins lie forgotten in a quiet, distant corner of Ternate, facing the setting sun from where the galleons used to appear. A monument to the Portuguese defeat in 1575 topped by a huge clove stands in the grounds, with a mosque nearby and a village scattered about. Ardi, a wiry, grinning Benteng 'keeper',[139] can often be found up a coconut tree nearby, maintaining a watch over the jumbled stones and ghosts of the past.

Known today geographically as Kastella, this fort has had several names according to its owners at the time. The Portuguese formally called it St John the Baptist. Colloquially in the sixteenth century it was referred to as Kastella, derived from the Portuguese for 'Castle'. The locals referred to it as Gammalamma after the local town that developed nearby, and the volcano that towered above it. The Spanish, rebuilding it in 1606, referred to it as City of the Rosary. And the Dutch, taking over the ruins in 1663 when abandoned by the Spanish, used a derivative of the local name Gamulamo.

Malayo/Fort Orange—The VOC Headquarters

A Spanish reconnaissance of Ternate from the Philippines in 1584 noted: 'the king [Ternate's sultan] has ... another port called Malayu, surrounded by walls with many bastions and pieces of artillery of small and medium calibre. In this fort are 500 warriors.'[140]

---

[139] Benteng keepers are employed by the Cultural Heritage Department to maintain and secure the old forts.

[140] *From European–Asian conflict to Cultural Heritage: Identification of Portuguese and Spanish Forts in the Northern Maluku Islands.*

A Dutch expedition under Admiral Matleif arriving in 1607 is normally credited with the construction of Fort Malayo, but it would appear that the Ternatean town at Malayu/Malayo was already fortified by this time. Certainly, the Dutch managed to land in the face of the existing Spanish defences some distance away at Kastella and Kota Janji and proceeded to modify the local work into a very powerful fortress in contemporary style. Even before the new defences were complete, Malayo's defenders repelled a strong Spanish attack from Kastella.

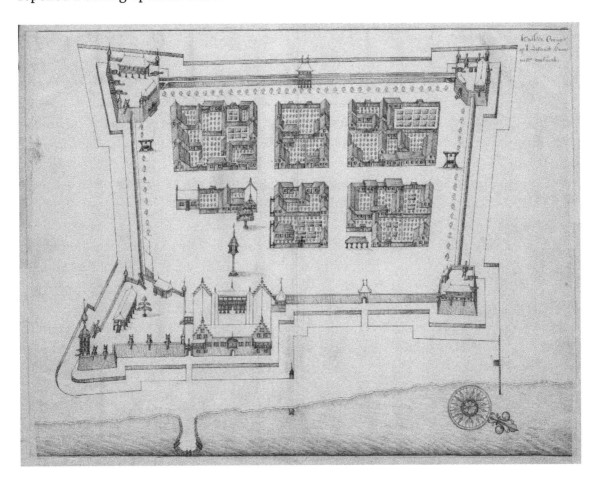

131. Anonymous Dutch rendering from about 1651 showing what a massive fortress Orange was.

During the long wars in their homeland against the Spanish, the Dutch had become expert fortification builders, and Fort Malayo, later Fort Orange, reflected this. Described as a trapezoid with a frontage of 180 metres and a depth of 165 metres, angled bastions at each corner and five-metre fully ramparted walls, it would eventually mount over 90 guns and was fully moated. There were plans in the late eighteenth century to add a cavalier between each of the bastions, but the current footprint shows that this never occurred.

132. The Fort Orange complex today, with Gammalamma volcano behind. Almost drowned in the bustle of Ternate city, Orange is not the dominating fortress it once was.

Despite being a potent defensive work, Fort Orange fell twice, both times to the British, firstly to a seven-week siege in 1801 and then to a combination of marines, landed guns and ship bombardment in 1803. For a time, the Fort was the home of the VOC governors, and was always the residence of Ternate's governor.

Today, Fort Orange sits quite a distance away from the coast; testament to the reclamation that has occurred, as it was originally waterfront. It has lost part of its two western bastions and the intervening wall to a road, but the lengthy ramparts on the other sections can still be walked. Its grounds contain a number of attractive historic colonial buildings which are envisaged to be converted to a Spice Museum at some future stage.

133. While it has suffered from the pressures of its urban location, not to mention earthquakes, Fort Orange retains enough historic fabric to be a prime candidate for renewal.

Fort Tolukko—Local design

134. A view of Tolukko from 1650, looking from the east. By this time the fort had passed from Spanish to Dutch hands and was then the fortified residence of the sultan.

The heritage of many forts in the Spice Islands is disputed and none more so that little Tolukko (or Tolucco). Some reports credit its construction to the Portuguese, but this is unsubstantiated. What is documented is that a Spanish expedition from Manila landed in 1611 and constructed the fort, seemingly to put pressure on nearby Dutch Fort Orange.

Strategically, it dominates one of Ternate's few reef-free landing points (apart from Talangame) and heavy cannon mounted on its gun platform could interdict shipping approaching Fort Orange just 2500 metres away. However, being sited so close to this powerful Dutch fortress, across the island from their other stronghold of Kastella, and in easy range of the guns of passing VOC Indiamen, its utility to the Spanish was always going to be questionable.

135. Tolukko had a facelift in the 1990s. While of questionable authenticity, the attractive landscaping and its picturesque location certainly adds to its allure. It is probably the most visited of all Spice Islands forts.

Soon after construction it was abandoned and quickly in Dutch hands. Renamed Hollandia, it was later handed over to the sultan, whose residence had been lost to the Spanish in the Kastella complex. He then modified the structure as his quarters to local design, giving it a unique indigenous style, at odds with any other European-built fort in the region.

Its guns came into action just once, in 1801. During the British attack on Ternate, their force attempted an escalade of Fort Tolukko, but were driven back and had to settle down to a lengthy siege of Fort Orange.

Today Fort Tolukko is well worth a visit. It is the best extant example of local fortress construction which was at one point widespread throughout the islands. Refurbished and landscaped, it has great views across to the long sweep of Halmahera, as far north as the volcano that towers over Jailolo. Keep in mind when visiting that sedimentation and reclamation have extended the coastline outwards, so that what was once a waterfront fort occupying a tiny peninsula is now around 70 metres inland.

136. Tolukko's quaint dimensions are shown here from above. Four hundred years ago it stood out from the coast on its own small peninsula and the sea lapped where the road now passes under it, but silting and reclamation have left it much further inland.

Fort Kota Janji—Sentinel of the Kastella Road

137. Kota Janji was built to command the route from Talangame harbour to Kastella. In front of the bastions, the land falls abruptly into the sea, and behind the fort is a deep ravine. Acuna in 1606 sent a force of pioneers to climb the slope of Gammalamma volcano in order to outflank the fort.

This fort, located high above and just metres from the strait between Ternate and Maitara, comes under a plethora of names (also Don Gil, St Peter & Paul, Talangame) and with a confusing history. Some reports have it built by the Portuguese, though there is no documentary evidence of construction of any other Portuguese fort on Ternate except Kastella.[141] Similarly, though held at various times by the Spanish and the Dutch, it is not recorded as being built by either.

---

[141] Author's correspondence with Manuel Lobato.

In fact, it is locally constructed, by Ternate's Sultan Babullah sometime before 1585, when the Spanish noted its existence and attacked it unsuccessfully.

138. Looking south, with the Kota Janji fort in the centre of the image and Maitara, Tidore and Makian stretching behind. It is one of the most famous viewpoints in the Moluccas.

Strategically, it crowns the long, climbing ridge that leads west from Ternate's best harbour, Talangame, towards Kastella, meaning that anyone wanting to land big cannon to reduce Kastella needed to pass under its guns.

It is a small all-rampart structure, around 25 square metres, with evidence also of an outer wall. Guns mounted there could command the final approach from Maitara— 2400 metres away—and from Rum harbour on Tidore, but were mostly concerned with the land path up from Ternate's harbour.

In 1606, Acuna's flanking manoeuvre forced the withdrawal of the sultan's troops to Kastella without fighting. Once taken, the Spanish left a garrison and the fort formed part of their frontline with the Dutch, augmented by the later Fort St Lucia. It was abandoned when the Spanish left in 1663. At its peak it mounted six guns and held two dozen men.

Today the site, standing about 40 metres above the sea, has been turned into a tourist attraction and the fort's footprint can be clearly seen. Traces of a second outer wall are also visible along the north side. The round-island road has trimmed the front of the two south-facing bastions. Two large recessed stone-built rectangular pits remain, at least one of them once holding the fort's powder store. The view is spectacular, with a line of volcanos—Maitara, Tidore, Moti and Makian—stretching away to the south.

Kalomata—The conundrum

There is much confusion regarding the Kalomata forts. Some sources maintain that in the seventeenth century, the area between Spanish Kota Janji and Dutch Fort Orange held just one fort, others that there were three. Certainly, today only one survives, labelled Fort Kalomata, by the water on Kayu Merah (Red Wood Cape), the south-east point of Ternate Island looking across to Tidore.

Reimer's 1750s plan for a 'stone fort' shows the 'Post Kajoe Meirah' with its existing structure in light grey outline. This contrasts with an earlier 1622 sketch showing two opposing 'Calomatta' forts sited a distance inland. The uncertainty is compounded by another Dutch view of the Ternate forts also from 1622 which shows a fort labelled as 'Calomatta', which looks suspiciously like Fort Kota Janji.

On the sketch showing two forts toe-to-toe, western 'Calomatta' flies a flag with a diagonal cross, no doubt meant to refer to the Cross of Burgundy used by Spain as both a naval ensign and a land forces standard during the sixteenth and early seventeenth centuries. This suggests the fort depicted is the Spanish St Lucia, built in late 1618 to protect a hill that dominated nearby Spanish-held Kota Janji and in response to the nearby Dutch 'Calamotta' of the same year.

These two Calomattas formed the front line between the Spanish Kastella and the VOC fortress of Malayo, which co-existed just ten kilometres apart for over half a century (1607–63). The Dutch abandoned their 'Calomatta' in 1625, whereby the Spanish left their own and took possession of the vacant Dutch work. Here they remained until their general evacuation in 1663.

We know that in 1642 the Dutch built a fort on the coast over an earlier structure and that this fort—after more reconstructions and redesigns—is the one that can be seen today at Kayu Merah and is named Fort Kalomata, the district of which is however further to the west. What is not clear is if the Dutch Calomatta and the present fort at

Kayu Merah are the same fort. My opinion, based on the differences between the portrayed outlines and tactical considerations, is that they are different works.

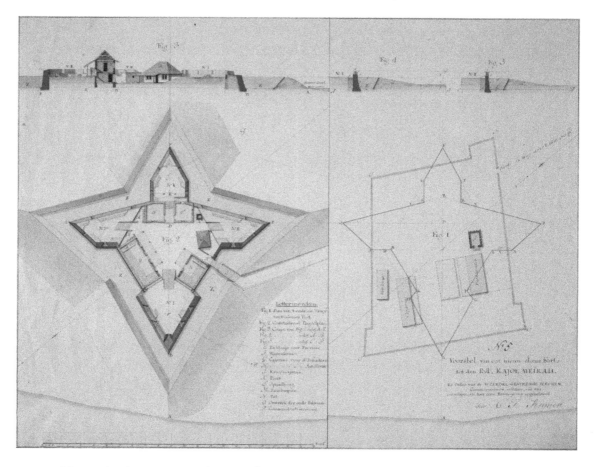

139. Mapmaker/surveyor Carl Reimer's comprehensive 1750s plans and elevations of the fort now known as Kalomata. On the left is the design for the fort substantially as it appears today, while at right the new design is superimposed over the presumably existing Dutch three-bastion oblong which dated from around 1609.
Image credit: Netherlands National Archives.

Certainly, it made sense for the Dutch to emplace guns on Kaya Merah very early in the confrontation with the Spanish after Fort Orange was built in 1607. Firstly, it guarded the land frontier between Spanish and Dutch territory on Ternate; secondly, it could enfilade maritime attacks from Kastella towards Fort Orange; thirdly, it could keep the Spanish harbour at Rum on Tidore under observation; and finally, it had a better view to the south-west than Orange, helping it keep an eye on ship traffic approaching Kastella. There are also some references to a Dutch fort built in this area in 1609.

Combining observations from the ground with contemporary ranges of weapons, I suggest that Dutch Kalomata lay around 500 metres north-west of Kayu Merah, and that Spanish St Lucia lay about 600 metres due north of Kota Janji. In a volatile frontier area, it makes sense for these forts to be self-supporting, and around 600 metres is the maximum functional range for the small nine-pounders that forts like these would have been armed with.

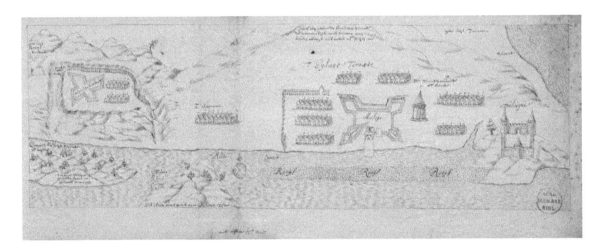

140. An anonymous Dutch sketch from c. 1622 showing two forts on the left labelled as 'Calomatta', one Dutch and one Spanish but neither of them waterfront, as is the case with the modern fort known as Kalomata. Forts Malayo (later Orange) and Tolukko can be seen to the right.
Image credit: University of Leiden.

Later in its life, in 1803, Fort Kayu Merah came briefly into action. The British as part of the Napoleonic Wars occupied parts of the Dutch East Indies. Two hundred marines sought to storm Kayu Merah under cover of darkness, but drifted past on the current. Next day they took the work by escalade and, under cover of guns, landed some cannon which threatened Fort Orange into surrender.

Fort Kayu Merah's walls have been refurbished and it sits by the strait separating the clove twins. No doubt its guns discouraged marauding Tidore korakora from approaching too close to Ternate in days long past. It is well worth a visit. St Lucia's ruins were noted as existing early last century but have now been lost to history. Remains of the Dutch Kalomata—if it is in fact a separate work from the present fort—are also not to be found, the likely locations now part of Ternate city's urban area.

141. A strikingly angled waterfront fort, Kalomata looks across at Tidore and Maitara. Refurbished in the 1990s, it has lost all of its characteristic features except its bare ramparts and bastions. A well, a basic entry portal and some internal stairs are all that remain of what was a state-of-the-art structure filled with barracks, armoury, powder magazines and surrounded by a glacis.

Other Ternate forts

142. The attractive Kedaton is the residence of the Sultan of Ternate and also holds a museum of local history. The small fort of Kota Naka is almost invisible to the immediate right of the Kedaton.

Fort Willemstadt was built on the north-west coast of Ternate island at the village of Tacoma (also Takome) in October 1609 by the Dutch under Admiral Hoen to prevent the Spanish doing likewise, and to control an area of abundant clove yields. As the Spanish refer to a fort of Ternate's sultan at this location in 1606 it seems that, like Malayo, the new fort was built on existing local defences.

The VOC move to locate a fort here attracted a Spanish counterattack a week after rebuilding began, but the defences were sufficiently well manned and sited to repel 80 Spaniards and several hundred local allies—further suggesting that the fort was a substantial work prior to the Dutch arrival.

It was subsequently refashioned in standard VOC style; a four-bastion quadrilateral set on a slight elevation above the village. At its peak it held a hundred-man garrison, but its utility declined quickly and by 1651 it was abandoned and ordered demolished. Traces of its foundations can still be seen, but as elsewhere throughout the Spice Islands, local builders have commandeered much of the coral and stone which once formed the ramparts and bastions.

Kota Naka was a tiny fort built by the VOC in the eighteenth century in the grounds of the sultan's residence. No doubt the intent was to ensure that Company policy was closely followed by the ruler. It would not have needed large weapons to reach the sultan, who held court just metres away. The irregularly shaped rectangle with its volcanic stone walls still stands and, while unspectacular, can be visited with permission, as it remains in the grounds of the Kedaton.

During the Napoleonic Wars, several new defences were added around Fort Orange to provide support against landed troops or bombarding ships. These were named the Kota Barro Battery and Strand Batteries 1, 2 and 3 and lay to the west of the main fortress. The first held two 18-pounders and six smaller guns, while the Strand Batteries fielded a mix of 12-, eight- and six-pounders. The 3rd Strand Battery was also known as the Sultan's Battery, and may also have been the Dutch Voorburg Redoubt, shown on some of Reimer's eighteenth century artwork. All are now assumed to be lost in the urban area of ever-growing Ternate city.

Tidore

Always dominated by its more famous neighbour just to the north, Tidore was like a mirror image of Ternate. Miniature in radius, dominated by a soaring volcano—luckily dormant, unlike Ternate's—it also lacked harbours and any type of cultivation, except for clove trees. Both were ruled by absolute sultans.

While Ternate had gained virtual sovereignty over northern Halmahera, parts of Sulawesi and many of the regional islands, Tidore's influence extended only to the southern part of Halmahera to its east and some of the Papuan islands further east again.

It was unlucky with its strategic alignments, siding with Spain from 1522 to 1545 only to see it lose to Portugal, and then again with the Spaniards against the Dutch from 1606 until their retreat in 1663. It seems the Dutch remembered this, and subsequent regional government and transport infrastructure was always allocated to Ternate rather than Tidore.

Tidore was at one time famed for producing the most plentiful cloves of the greatest quality, and so it was inevitable that it would become a battleground. In the early part of the seventeenth century the Dutch and Spanish fought over several of the forts on Tidore, notably Marieco and Reis Magos, with the Spanish prevailing and the Dutch falling back on Ternate.

With their combination of fortified Soa Siu, other forts at Marieco, Tomanira, Chobo and Rum, and their impregnable citadel of Tohula, the Spanish defences on Tidore were sufficiently intimidating not be seriously threatened after 1615. When the Spanish did abandon the island, they demolished their forts to varying degrees of thoroughness and the remnants were then occupied by the Sultan of Tidore.

143. Flying over Tidore en route to Ternate's airport. Lost somewhere in the township of Soa Siu in the foreground is little Reis Magos fort. Fort Tohula is at the extreme left, but not discernible. Ternate is in the right background. Both islands are dominated by volcanos over 1700 metres high.

Today, Tidore remains in the shadow of much more populous Ternate. The pace is much slower, the streets calmer, the villages more picturesque. A lap around the island on a motorbike takes a couple of hours; allow a couple more hours for fort stops. Most impressive is Fort Tohula, with Fort Torre the only other location where the structure has been rebuilt; the other locations are just scattered ruins, not always easy to find.

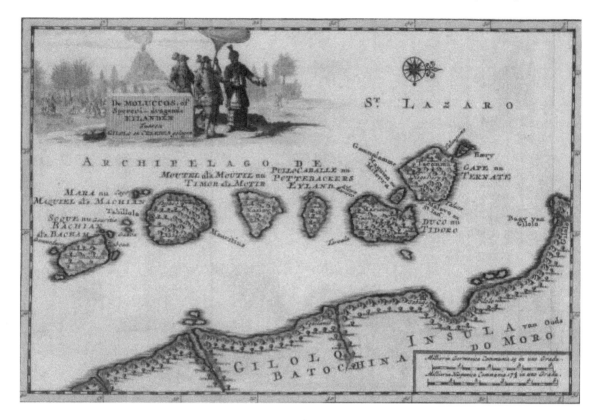

144. A version of a much-copied map of the Moluccas from 1707 with west upwards. Tidore is the second major island from the right. In the background the finery of a sultan, an exploding volcano and clove trees can be seen.

Fort Tohula—The impregnable fortress

Even in its ruined state, today Fort Tohula is a very impressive fortress. Spain's greatest stronghold on Tidore, it was commenced in 1610, but the difficult site delayed completion until 1615. For nearly 50 years it remained the principal Spanish fort on the island, with the name Santiago de los Caballeros.

It's unusual and compact layout, dictated by the hilltop contours, set it apart visually from all other Spice Islands forts. The ten-metre wide entry section sat between two unusually high triangular bastions, with 14-metre and 22-metre frontages. These formed the land-facing defences. Fifty metres away facing east, towards ten kilometres distant Halmahera, was a high circular gun tower of ten-metre radius. Perhaps a 24-pounder sat up here, commanding the sea to west and north, from its 50-metre height able to threaten any vessel approaching Soa Siu, Tidore's main town, in no danger of return fire.

145. Looking north from above Fort Tohula. The semicircular gun platform is in the foreground, and the triangular bastions flanking the entry are at the far end of the complex. As with most Spice Islands forts, the footprint that is evident today is different from how the fort was originally built.

Alone among important Spice Islands forts, Tohula was never stormed, never beaten. Kastella surrendered, Malayo was taken twice, Ambon's Fort Victoria three times. Belgica surrendered once and was stormed once. Kota Janji, Tolukko, Kayu Merah, Nassau, the forts on Makian, Motir, Halmahera and Bacan, all changed hands, often several times.

But Tohula was a tough nut to crack, and after a failed attack in June 1614, the Dutch knew better than to try again. With its near-vertical approaches, massive bastions and towering ramparts it was an intimidating and invincible work. Too high for shipboard guns to elevate, and too steep to ascend in any organised formation, its defences stood the test of time.

146. A fine rendering showing Fort Tohula in its heyday, around 1630.
Image credit: Lucas Kukler.

Some attempt has been made to stabilise the works, rather than to rebuild them, and today the crumbling remains are picturesque and potent. The rugged terrain of Halmahera curves down from north to south across the sweep of the channel, and Tidore's volcano towers over to the west. A few hundred steps bring you up to the landscaped grounds, and the bastions, foundations of internal buildings, powder stores, well, sea-bastion and entry section all remain, though a degree of imagination is required to visualise it.

Fort Reis Magos—Unlucky but plucky

147. A 1607 lithograph by Dutchman de Bry of the Battle for Reis Magos fought two years previously. While there is a relatively modern four-gun battery sited in front, the main defensive work is obsolete and rudimentary, appearing to consist of a weak timber palisade enclosing two round medieval-style towers. Perhaps the artwork is deliberately unflattering to the Portuguese fort because it managed to absorb a tremendous amount of punishment, and the Portuguese very nearly won the battle.

When the Sultan of Ternate took Kastella in 1575, the surviving Portuguese fled to Ambon. Three years later at the invitation of Tidore's sultan they returned to the

Moluccas and constructed Fort Reis Magos on his island, despite them having torched the Tidorean capital three times in living memory. Such were the complex shifting alliances of the Spiceries.

Frustratingly, different accounts have it sited at various distances north of Soa Siu, the exact location of which at that time we are unsure of. Extensive lava flows also appear to have altered the coastline from its sixteenth century form. On the balance of probabilities, it appears that Reis Magos was located between one and two kilometres north of Fort Tohula, and of course, right on the coast. The sultan's court and Soa Siu were likely in 1600 located just north of Tohula, at the very southern end of the modern stretch of development that forms the township.

Contemporary accounts suggest the 60-square-metre fort was poorly designed and constructed, sporting two obsolescent tall round towers and a loose stone curtain wall with narrow ramparts. By 1605, a battery or bastion had been added in front of the walls, with embrasures for four guns.

During the Dutch attack in 1605 its 70 defenders with 11 guns and supported by two small galleons creditably faced 120 cannon on the Dutch fleet for three days of bombardment before a lucky hit destroyed the powder store, forcing the fort's surrender. A combination of forts and galleons had in the past seen off most local challenges, but the Dutch in this case deployed more manpower, more seapower and much more firepower.

Foolishly, the Dutch didn't garrison Reis Magos, and so it was back under Iberian control after Acuna's Ternate victory in 1606. He had it rebuilt and left 100 men there, so it was obviously more extensive than the work shown in de Bry's lithograph. It was bombarded by Dutch ships in 1608 and once more in 1610. In another assault in 1613, the Dutch stormed it with 800 men, the garrison of 50 Spaniards all dying at their posts. They were however unable to penetrate the nearby Soa Siu defences, and after a short while, they abandoned the fort.

With the advent of the invincible Fort Tohula in 1613, the battered Reis Magos faded off into history. No trace could be found of this historic, plucky little fort. Its remains lie under the built-up area of Soa Siu. Outdated, poorly built and lightly armed, it nevertheless faced overwhelming odds twice in its short career and ended up eventually frustrating the enemy both times.

Fort Marieco & Fort Tomanira—West coast sentinels

148. Ternate looms out of the Moluccan Sea, its Gammalamma volcano shrouded in steam and sulphur, with tiny Maitara island on the right. This shot is taken off the modern village of Marieko, Tidore with the tiny fort of Tomanira on a hill just inland from this spot. A large bronze cannon lies below high tide in the foreground, missing much of its barrel, likely spiked and abandoned when the Spanish departed in 1663.

The locality of Marieco (also Marieko, Mareku) on the west coast of Tidore lay close to the best clove trees on the island as well as a small break in the encircling barrier reefs. The royal capital of Tidore had been located there until destroyed by the Portuguese in 1524.

It was to control the west coast and clove groves, and to deny it to the VOC, that encouraged the Spanish to build a fort here in 1609, located in what is today called Ome village. It was a small and limited work. Two angled stone bastions facing the sea with a palisade between, armed with two cannon and manned by just a dozen men. From here you could see the Dutch shipping off Fort Orange, ten kilometres away.

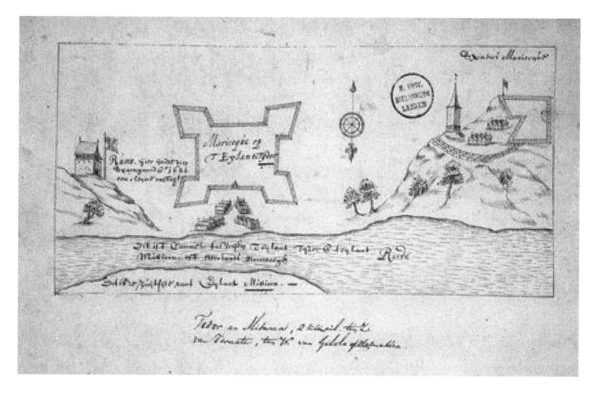

149. From the University of Leiden's Bodel Nijenhuis Collection, this c. 1621 anonymous Dutch artwork shows (left to right) the Spanish fort at Rum, built late 1618, the Dutch Fort Marieco (1609) and the Spanish Fort Tomanira (1613).

As part of the plan to wrest control of Tidore from Spain, in 1613 a Dutch–Ternatean force of 800 men attacked the little fort from korakora after approaching from Ternate at night. Local allies failed to support the platoon on the ramparts, and only one injured Spaniard survived the battle.

The Dutch quickly built a new and bigger Marieco, giving it four angled corner bastions, stone walls, and a palisade enclosing additional buildings and extending to the shore. It mounted 16 guns and held 60 troops. The fact that the ruins in Ome village are more suggestive of the minor Spanish fort than the significant Dutch fort suggests that perhaps the Dutch did not build over the Spanish fort, but in a location further to the south. If so, no trace of its ruins could be found between modern Ome and Marieco villages.

There are references to another fort in the vicinity, Marieco el Chico (or San Jose de Marieco), Spanish-built in 1618. It is possible that this is another name for the fort at Tomanira, however it is described as being some distance inland. If so, it is likely that this was a small fortlet to prevent the Dutch attacking east across the island (north of the volcano) towards the sultan's palace at Gomafo, as Galvao had done back in 1536.

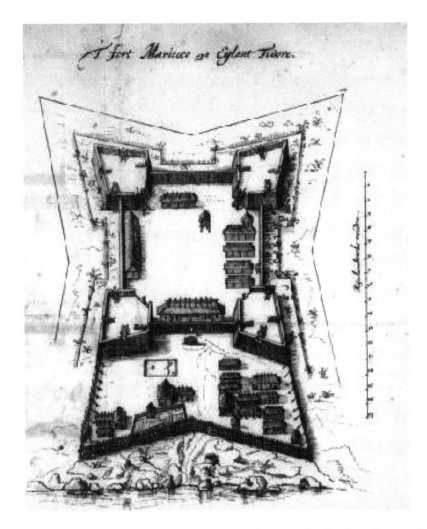

150. The Dutch Fort Marieco, on the west coast of Tidore, built after the much smaller Spanish fort in the same locality was stormed in 1613. Ringed by Spanish forts at Rum and Tomanira, Marieco was abandoned in 1621 and occupied by the Spanish thereafter. Image credit: National Library of France.

The loss of Marieco and the new Dutch presence on Tidore forced the Spanish to construct two additional strongholds to close it in; firstly, Tomanira to the south in 1613, and then Rum to the north in 1618. The latter commanded the crucial anchorage between Tidore and Maitara islands. It seems the Spanish strategy worked, as the Dutch abandoned Marieco in 1621 and it was then manned by the Spanish until 1646.

Tomanira in the 1621 sketch can be seen south of Marieco, set on a steep hill close to the coast, and where it bulges westwards slightly, with two angled bastions, an observation tower, a perimeter wall and some barracks buildings. The tower allowed a direct view to the anchorage in front of Malayo, as well as overlooking Fort Marieco.

Both works were partially destroyed when the Spanish abandoned Tidore in 1663. Today, ruins can be seen of both forts. Spanish Marieco's two western bastions sit separated by a house, on the coast in the village of Ome. Two kilometres to the south on a steep overgrown hill at a height of 50 metres and 250 metres from the shore lie piles of stones and a circular stone-lined well that is all that remain of Fort Tomanira. A bronze culverin missing its muzzle lies below the high-water mark directly below Tomanira's ruins; perhaps it formed part of its long-range armament.

Forts Rum & Chobo—Guardians of the Straits

151. The remains of one of the bastions of the fort at Chobo, last-built of the Spanish Spice Islands forts, in 1643.

The very first colonial Spice Islands fortification was a small storage structure built overlooking Rum harbour where the Spanish survivors of Magellan's fleet unloaded their supplies while they careened the *Trinidad* in 1521. Not far to the south stood the rajah's fortified capital at Marieco, which later had additional defences added by the Spaniards, but was stormed by the Portuguese and Ternateans in 1524.

Much later, two Spanish forts were built to guard the northern approaches to Tidore: Rum on the north-west and Chobo to the north-east. The fort at Rum, known to the Spanish as St Lucas, was built in 1618 as a result of the Dutch occupation of Marieco to the south.

152. A small memorial near the remains of the fort at Rum commemorates the Spanish sailors under Elcano who anchored at this point in the *Victoria* in 1521 and went on to complete the first circumnavigation of the earth.

Rum's defences consisted of a semicircular waterfront battery to prevent adjacent landings, and an observation tower / gun platform on the hill above the battery. The guns here commanded the most protected anchorage across all Ternate and Tidore, where the shelter provided by the point of Tidore and the islet of Maitara created a narrow channel useful in both south-westerlies and northerlies, and which could also link with the Fort Kota Janji guns on Ternate around four kilometres away to close the channel between the two islands to shipping. Additionally, they threatened resupply ships to Dutch Marieco and were able to enfilade korakora fleets heading to Kastella from Malayo. It was a strategic spot.

Like Rum, the Spanish fort at Chobo, built in 1643, was to deter seaborne threats from Ternate and additionally to keep Fort Orange and the harbour at Talangame under observation. It was the last of the major Spice Island forts built. Sitting at an elevation of around 50 metres and about 60 metres from the coral-fringed coast, looking north and north-west, it was well-sited to engage Ternatean vessels approaching the main town of Tidore at Soa Siu.

We have no records as to what size cannon armed Chobo, but quite possibly they were 24-pounders which could happily have sent the occasional cannonball across to Fort Orange, which at 4400 metres range they even had a small chance of hitting.

Both forts where partly demolished and abandoned when the Spanish left the Moluccas in 1663. Subsequently they were occasionally manned by troops of Tidore's sultan.

Today, ruins of both forts can be seen. Little remains of Rum, as the round-island road has unfortunately been built right through it, though the memorial to *Victoria's* circumnavigation nearby is worth inspection. A stone retaining wall still reaches seven metres up from the beach just to the west of the road. At Chobo the fort site is easily identified, though again little remains and its form is difficult to determine. It sits high above the turquoise reefs of the shoreline, just north of the village. Looking at the nearby village structures, it's quite clear where the fort stonework has ended up.

Fort Torre, Gomafo, Soa Siu & Sokanora—Capital defences

Following Magellan's fleet across the Pacific in 1527, the Loaisa expedition illustrated what a hard voyage it was. Only one of the seven ships and around two dozen out of 450 men made it to Tidore, where some survivors of the first fleet still remained. Alarmed at the threat from the Portuguese-Ternate forces, the Spaniards constructed a basic defensive work of loose stone, with two bastions near a stone pier just north of the main town of Tidore, Soa Siu. Its guns—taken from their ships—dominated a break in the reef that formed Tidore's best landing point. This structure is long gone, but probably stood in the rough location of the later Portuguese Reis Magos.

The Portuguese attacked this Spanish fort and destroyed it in 1529, taking 31 cannon and 16 smaller swivel guns, and allowing the 40 odd Spaniards to retire to Jailolo, Halmahera. Other expeditions arrived decimated by the Pacific crossing in subsequent years and reoccupied the Tidore defences, but in 1545, the Spanish again surrendered to their Iberian neighbours and left the scene for half a century.

They were back in 1606—now allied with Portugal—after having taken Kastella on Ternate. They improved the Soa Siu defences and installed a garrison of 100 men, defeating several Dutch attacks, and holding out against the 1613 invasion when the nearby Reis Magos was captured. The north-facing town defences were gradually improved to include extensive walls, ramparts, palisades and a moat, but were not again seriously threatened, and ended up taken over by the sultan in 1663, when the Spanish withdrew.

153. The forts of Tidore, including the sultan's fort-palace at Gomafo, the Portuguese Reis Magos, the Spanish forts and Dutch Marieco are shown superimposed on the *Blaeu Moluccas* map of 1640. North is to the right.

The sultan had his own residence atop the hill at Gomafo. It was sometimes a palace and sometimes a fort, palisaded and at one point equipped with a cannon-armed bastion, but its main defence was the difficulty of the climb up to it.

Where the main Soa Siu defences faced north, the small fort in the local village of Sokanora—south of Tohula—protected the city from the southern approach. The Dutch attacked from here in 1613 after taking Reis Magos, but were repulsed several times.

The town of Soa Siu has expanded north of its original limited extent, and hence most traces of the old bulwarks appear lost to history. The exception is the enigmatic Fort Torre. Pulverised by a lava flow at some unknown date and dubiously renovated in 2014, apparently to a layout dictated by the remaining foundations, Torre is difficult to categorise, because of its form and location.

154. The curious Fort Torre, rebuilt with a square medieval entry tower and a contradicting semicircular protruding bastion. It appears the redesign followed what foundations were still visible, rather than trying to recreate a specific era of the fort's history. There is little that is authentic in the reconstruction. Lava blocks from the flow that at some stage engulfed the fort still litter the site. The view looks WSW towards Tidore's volcano. Gomafo, in the past the sultan's palace/hillfort/hideout, is just visible on the skyline above the semicircular bastion. Galvao attacked Gomafo from the west, passing over the saddle in the right background, then torched Soa Siu town behind the photographer.

Most unusually, it stands 500 metres from the coast, which was almost unheard of for Iberian Spice Islands forts, which survived the threats of more numerous local forces only due to the support of galleons and galleys. As it also lies 2500 metres from Fort Tohula, we can safely assume it was not sited to provide that fort with gunfire support, and therefore pre-dates it, or was built much later. Finally, just to its west, the land slopes upwards, leaving it vulnerable to guns mounted above it, which was something that no self-respecting seventeenth century European fortress engineer would tolerate when siting a work.

The most plausible explanations are that it was either Spanish-built and formed the landward (western) end of the north-facing Soa Siu defences to prevent their line being outflanked; or that it was local-built, guardian of the route up to the sultan's court at Gomafo from the coast, and also of the route across the saddle of the island from the west coast, which Galvao had taken in 1536 to destroy Gomafo and then Soa Siu.

There is reference to a Spaniard, Hernando Torre, building a fort as part of the Soa Siu defences in 1528, but to imagine this as being built half a kilometre inland is dubious. The present form of Fort Torre, however, does provide us with some clues. It is a 30 square metres with no obvious corner bastions but does have a semicircular platform facing south to the Gomafo track at 300 metres distance (i.e. in cannon range). Its entry gate faces south-east towards the township of Soa Siu, also reinforcing the idea that it was part of that town's defences. It is therefore possible that it is a locally built work, completed prior to 1600 or after the Spanish left in 1663, and this possibility is supported by its distance from the coast, focus on Gomafo and unconventional footprint.

Whatever its heritage, Fort Torre commands a decent view over Tidore's main centre and across the channel to Halmahera and is worth a look after an inspection of the more impressive Fort Tohula.

Other Molluccan islands

While Ternate and Tidore were always the most prominent of the Moluccas, there were a number of other islands nearby that were also of varying importance. Some cultivated cloves, like Makian, Motir and Bacan, while others, principally the large islands of Halmahera and Morotai, provided timber, sago, fish and other foodstuffs for the spice sultans, who grew nothing but cloves.

All these peripheral islands fell historically under the suzerainty of either Ternate or Tidore. When the Iberians arrived, the Portuguese allied initially with Ternate, while the Spanish courted Tidore, and the conflict between the two sides spread across the archipelago, along with a mostly fleeting range of fortifications.

Morotai—The sago island

The large island of Morotai, lying north of Halmahera, was also crucial to the Spice Islands because it produced sago in large quantities and its seas teemed with fish. In the sixteenth century there were four settlements on the island. It owed sovereignty to neither Ternate nor Tidore, which were both content to provision themselves from its resources. The population was evacuated to Dodinga on Halmahera by Ternate in the early seventeenth century to escape maritime raiders from eastern Halmahera. It was never fortified by the colonial Europeans, but in World War II, both the Japanese and Americans constructed field fortifications as they fought a lonely forgotten war over its coral-rimmed jungles.

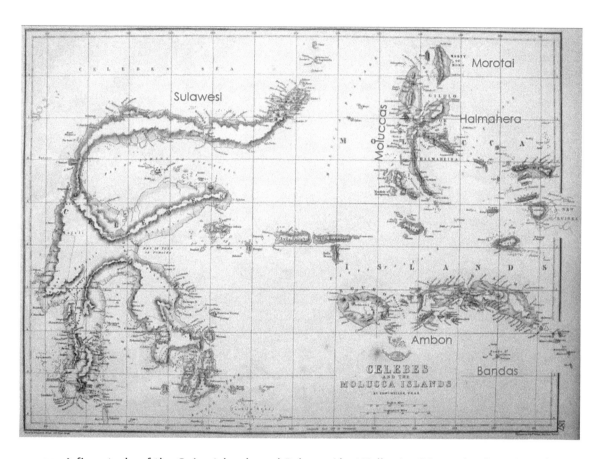

155. A fine study of the Spice Islands and Sulawesi by Weller in 1860. Halmahera is in the upper right quadrant, with its four peninsulas aligned north, south, north-east and south-east. The volcanos of the clove islands lie just to its west. Ambon and the Lease Islands are south of Halmahera and the Banda group are south-east of them. Sulawesi, like a prancing sea monster and surely candidate for the weirdest-shaped island in the world, takes up the western half of the map.

Makian—Gatekeeper of the southern approaches

156. A view of Makian by an anonymous Dutch artist around 1651, showing Fort
Mauritius and the Gnofficquia complex below it. Not shown is the soaring peak of the
islands very active 1357-metre volcano behind the fort.

Makian (also Machian or Macan) was one of the most important islands of the
Moluccas. Larger than either Ternate or Tidore, it also grew more cloves, but never
gained full independence from them and was always controlled by one or the other or
shared by both. Although a Portuguese fort and local defences already existed on the
island, chronicler Argensola describes the Spanish construction of their fort on Makian
in August 1602 (probably on the site of the Portuguese fort):

> '... Furtado erected a fort with all possible expedition, in the most convenient place.
> When finished according to the Rules of Fortification, he put into it a Captain with
> 50 men.'

The incentive to build the fort came from the newly arrived Dutch who, in 1607 under Captain Hermite, stormed this fort with Ternatean allies. It remained in Dutch hands until 1699.

157. Part of one of Mauritius' bastions today. The outline of the fort, with its traditional Dutch four-bastion layout is discernible, along with a well and vaulted powder magazine.

Fort Mauritius was elevated at around 60 metres and was without fresh water, so in 1636 the Dutch had to build a small seaside fort with good access for shipping, called Zeeburgh (also Gnofficquia), to hold water cisterns and trade goods.

On the west coast of Makian, a small Spanish fortlet at Taffasoho, itself built on an earlier Portuguese post, was expanded to a larger stockade with two large and two tiny bastions, while a blockhouse was built at Tabelolo on the extreme south of the island. These forts controlled possible landing places as well as access to the clove trees inland. When it fell to the Dutch in 1608, Taffasoho was armed with an 18-pounder and three dozen swivel guns.

With the decline in importance of the Moluccas in the eighteenth century, all defences on Makian were abandoned and fell into ruin. Remains of all three forts are still discernible, though not impressive. Makian can be reached by a two-hour speedboat ride from Ternate, for which you are advised to bring ear muffs and a gas mask.

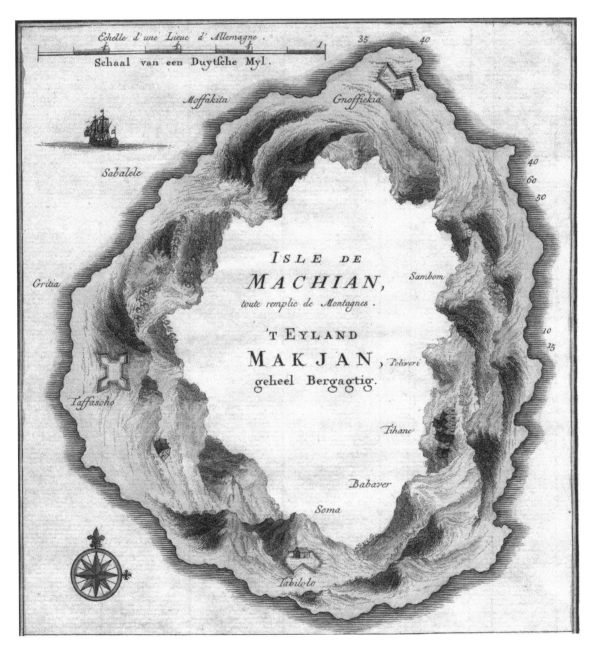

158. An image of Makian by Schley from 1760 showing the small forts of Gnoffickia, Taffasoho and Tabilolo, but curiously not the main fortress of Mauritius, perhaps because it had been partially razed when abandoned in 1699.

Motir—Home of Nassau

Motir (or Moti) was the small island just north of the larger Makian. The Spanish built an outpost here in 1606, and it's probable that there was a Portuguese lodge before that. The Dutch took the Spanish fort in 1607 and subsequently built triangular, three-bastioned Fort Nassau to control the island, commencing in 1609, probably over existing defences.

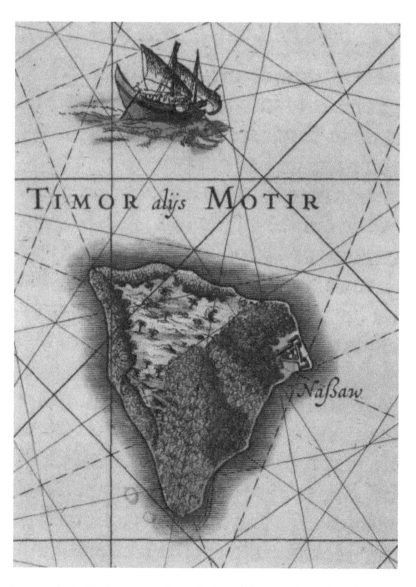

159. A portrayal of Motir showing triangular Fort Nassau from the *Blaeu Atlas* of 1640. North is to the right.

As the Iberian threat declined, the Dutch found that the small platoons at remote garrisons such as Motir were vulnerable to local raiders and, as always, disease, and there was much rationalising. Motir could easily be patrolled by the adjacent bases at Ternate and Makian.

In its heyday, Nassau had three bastions armed with ten cannon and a garrison of 80 men, but its importance faded quickly and in 1625 it was ordered to be demolished. Today, some scattered remains are visible, but much of the coral block that formed the ramparts has been purloined by locals for residential building.

Bacan—Ruler of the Far End

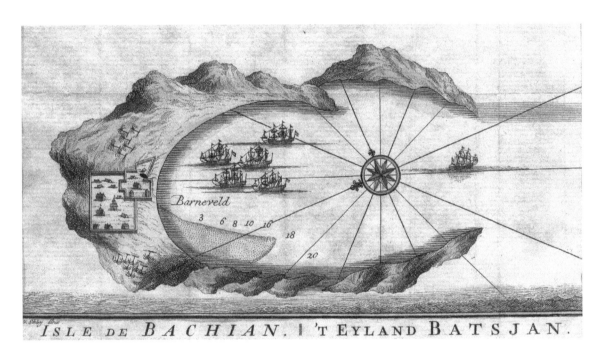

160. A nautical view of Bacan by Schley around 1750, with Fort Barneveld shown at left. A bastion points towards the anchorage, and a stockade extends landward, encasing a small settlement. At an earlier stage, the fort sported four bastions. This was originally a pre-colonial local fort which was then modified in succession by the Portuguese, Spanish and Dutch.

Bacan (also Batjan, Bachian, Bactian) is a large island detached to the south of the main group of Moluccas, around 65 kilometres from the southern-most, Makian. It grew both wild cloves and sago but was underpopulated. Strategically, a fort on Bacan asserted some control over the adjacent southern part of Halmahera and lay on the sailing route from Ambon.

The Portuguese maintained a fortified trade lodge at the principal settlement of Labuha after storming a local fort in 1533 and building atop it five years later. After capturing Ternate in 1606, the Spanish took over this fort but it was then taken by the VOC in 1609 and the garrison and dependents all massacred. This was another hard battle fought between Dutch and Spanish where no quarter was asked for, or given.

The Dutch built an improved fort over the old work, with four stone bastions and a garrison of 50 men. With the Spanish departure in 1663, Barneveld declined in importance, but remained a manned post into the eighteenth century. The fort has been partially refurbished, though with too much concrete, and stands today in reasonable shape, with bastions, ramparts and internal buildings.

Labuha is accessible by flights from Ternate or Pelni ships from Ambon or Ternate.

Halmahera—The great island

161. Part of Halmahera seen from Tidore. Halmahera, which competes with Sulawesi for the world's strangest shaped island, is over 350 kilometres from north to south, while tiny, almost circular volcanos Ternate and Tidore are less than 15 kilometres.

The long coastline of Halmahera (previously also called Gilolo or Jailolo), its extensive hinterland and widely spread villages, had in pre-colonial days always been subject to the contest for control between Ternate and Tidore. In the pre-Dutch days of Iberian influence, with the Portuguese allied to Ternate and the Spanish to Tidore, the island became an extension of the regional confrontation between the two groups.

What was crucial to both sultanates and the garrisons of all Spice Islands forts, was the large stands of wild sago on Halmahera, particularly around the two points on the central eastern coasts where the north-south axis of the island is narrowest. Processed sago was almost pure carbohydrate and available in large quantities; a perfect bulk foodstuff for the soldiers and warriors perpetually focused on warfare and cloves.

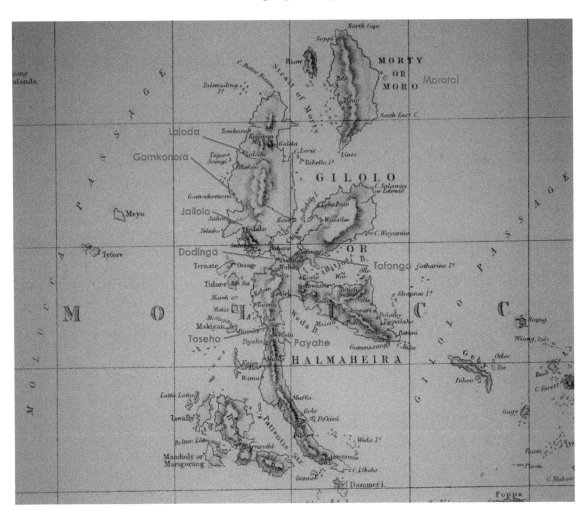

162. The islands of Halmahera and Morotai, showing the location of the major settlements. The clove islands can be seen just to the left of Halmahera. This is part of a map by Weller in 1870.

Generally, Ternate had controlled the northern part of Halmahera, and Tidore the southern, with the front line just south of Dodinga. This village itself was mostly controlled by Ternate, though it was taken by forces from Tidore in 1637, before being recaptured the next year. It was fortified and located slightly inland, controlling the western part of the track across the isthmus, while another village, Tafongo, located on the east coast, commanded access from that side. A small Spanish post was established at Tafongo from 1609, but was very difficult to support and supply, and was abandoned in 1620.

To the south of Dodinga, the narrow strip between Toseho and Payahe was also contested, again, to control quick access to the sago of the east coast. It was generally held by forces of Tidore who were reinforced by a Spanish detachment from 1610 to 1620. In 1641, a Spanish galleon assisted Tidore troops at Toseho to beat off a strong attack by hundreds of warriors from Ternate supported by a VOC East Indiaman, but another attack the following year saw the Ternateans take control.

North of Dodinga, the main settlement of all Halmahera, and one of the original four 'divine' kingdoms of the Moluccas, lay Jailolo (also Gilolo). Perched under its eponymous 1130-metre stratovolcano on a large bay, korakora squadrons of the sultan were well-placed to dominate the northern approaches to the Moluccas. The first Spanish contact was in 1526, and many Spaniards were based there on and off for decades, assisting the sultan in modernising his defences—a substantial fortress on an elevation five kilometres inland—against the forces of Ternate and Portugal.

The Portuguese had to fight hard several times to conquer these defences, culminating in the destruction of the sultanate in 1551. At this last siege, the fortress defences included an outer wall of stone and earth topped with two bastions, an inner wall, 18 cannon and a hundred smaller guns, and numerous local warriors. It took the Portuguese three months to wear down the defences—their longest ever Spice Islands siege.

Following Acuna's victory over Ternate in 1606, after a number of attempts the Spanish took Jailolo and built a small three-bastion stone fort on the coast, named Fort Christobel. Like all European forts on Halmahera, Fort Christobel was vulnerable, difficult to maintain and a disease-ridden graveyard for the small garrisons that were posted there. It was abandoned in 1620. Other settlements further north of Jailolo, including Sabuga and Gamkonora, were also fortified and garrisoned by the Spanish for short periods, but eventually were abandoned to the combined Ternate–Dutch forces.

Ambon and the Lease Islands

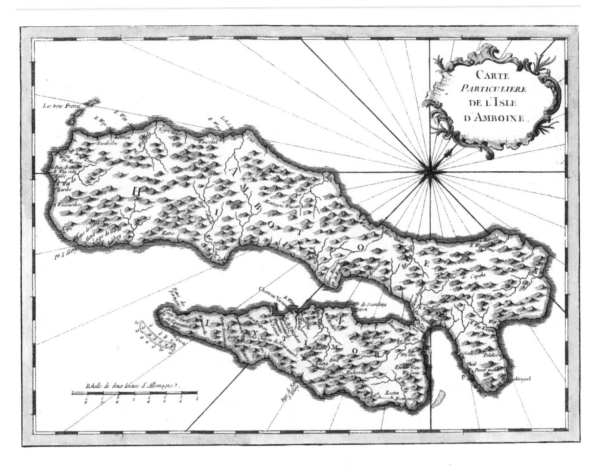

163. The island of Ambon, from a rendering by Bellin in 1761. Note the compass rose below the cartouche shows north-west at the top of the chart. Running due south along the cardinal wind rose from the compass rose highlights 'Chateau Victoria', the original fortress, held successively by the Portuguese, Dutch, British, Japanese and today by the Indonesian Army. The other Lease Islands are to the east of Ambon. The enormous Bay of Ambon is 25 kilometres long, from the southern entrance.

The Lease Islands (sometimes called the Uliassers) are a group of islands south of Seram including Ambon and—heading east—Haruku, then Saparua, and lastly Nusa Laut. Originally, the islands grew neither cloves nor nutmeg, but capital of the group, Ambon Manise—'Sweet Ambon'—had the advantage of a great harbour, a large population and an extensive hinterland which allowed cultivation of foodstuffs for distribution to the other Spice Islands. Located between the clove islands to the north and the nutmeg ones to the south, Ambon was always in a position of strategic significance.

Ambon was also the main focus of Christianity right across the Spice Islands—St Francis Xavier spent some time there—and became an important provider of loyal manpower first to the Portuguese, and later to the Dutch.

164. A statue of Indonesian freedom fighter Martha Tiahahu watches the sunset over Ambon harbour. Born in 1800, she fought with Pattimura at Fort Duurstede, was captured by the Dutch, and died in custody while being shipped to Java as a slave. She was just days short of her eighteenth birthday.

Originally fortified by the Portuguese, Ambon subsequently fell to the Dutch, briefly to the British during the Napoleonic Wars, and later to the Japanese in World War II, who recognised the importance of its enormous harbour. It was also the capital of the 1950s breakaway Republic of the South Moluccas which was subsequently defeated by the central Indonesian government, with the last stand actually occurring in Fort Victoria in Ambon city.

Besides their main stronghold of Fort Victoria, the Dutch built dozens of other forts, watchtowers and blockhouses both on Ambon and throughout the Lease Islands. All the main islands were fortified by the Dutch at some stage for the purposes of controlling local populations, storing spices, repelling Papuan pirates and deterring other European nations.

Excluding Fort Victoria, two bursts of Dutch fort building in the Lease Islands are evident: firstly from 1626, when defences were built or improved on Ambon at Fort Amsterdam and Fort Middleburg, at Saparua (Fort Hollandia), and at Haruku (forts Oma and Zeelandia); and again, in the 1650s when improvements were made to most existing forts and new works were added at Haruku (forts Hoorn, Poorto and Delfft).

Many of the outlying forts were built to a similar blockhouse–and–palisade style as Fort Amsterdam which—much renovated—can still be inspected at Hila on Ambon. Most regarded in Indonesia today is Fort Duurstede, on Saparua, which local hero Pattimura captured when he rebelled against the Dutch in 1817. Some ruined structures can also be seen at Fort Zeelandia and Beeverwijk. The islands east of Ambon can be reached by ferries from Tulehu harbour in eastern Ambon.

165. An anonymous birds-eye view of Ambon, with a portrait of Frederick Houtman—at one time Governor of the VOC—from 1617. Right in the centre is four-bastioned Fort Victoria in its early post-Portuguese stage. A number of Indiamen, korakora and local craft can be seen in the surrounding waters. The other Lease Islands are on the right. Image credit: Rijksmuseum, Netherlands.

Fort Victoria—Battle-scarred relic

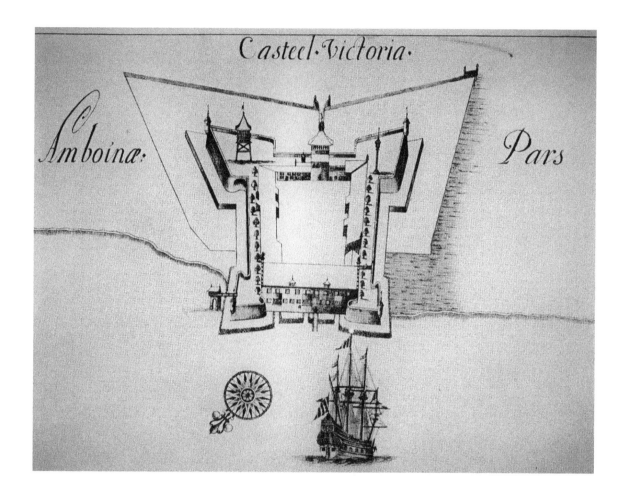

166. A view of Fort Victoria from the harbour approach with a small East Indiaman offshore, around 1651. The scale of the landward defences, extent of internal accommodation and the outer palisaded ditch are evident. There has been only minor modification from the Portuguese layout.

The first lasting colonial fortification on Ambon was built in stone by Portuguese Captain Vasconcelos in 1576, which makes it second oldest of the surviving Spice Islands forts, after Kastella. It was named Forte de Nossa Senhora da Anunciada. There had been a previous Portuguese fortified trading lodge built across Ambon Bay (near today's airport) but it been destroyed in the endless battles against local Muslim forces. The new location commanded Ambon's enormous harbour, which in turn dominated the entire region. The original basic Portuguese work was a small two-bastioned rectangle with the sea-facing defences located near the present bastions Hollandia and Geldrin.

Despite being later upgraded into a reasonably powerful work, the Portuguese fort surrendered without a fight to a Dutch fleet in 1605, although prior to that it had been successfully held against Ternatean and Javanese sieges and a previous Dutch attack. VOC Admiral van der Hagen renamed it Fort Victoria in thanks for the bloodless victory.

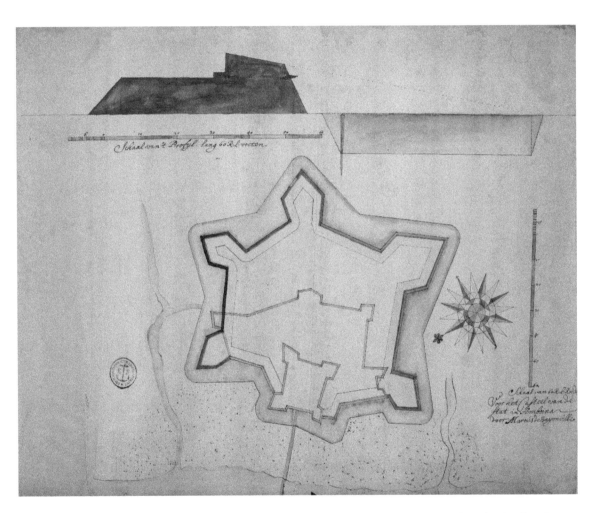

167. Following earthquake damage in 1672–3 the fortress was extended and rebuilt. The scale of the limited original Portuguese footprint is evident in comparison to the new works. This is a plan view of suggested expansion produced in the late seventeenth century. The works were eventually carried out to a similar layout as suggested, but much later.
Image credit: Netherlands National Archives.

After earthquakes in 1643 and 1644, and again in 1672 and 1673, the VOC considered re-siting the heavily damaged work, but in the end chose to rebuild in the same location. The small original four-bastioned rectangle was greatly enlarged over time, culminating around 1780 (after yet another earthquake) into its final fully-moated seven-bastioned polygonal layout. After that reconstruction, Governor van Plueren renamed it Fort New Victoria.

The expense and effort to maintain the defences in the face of successive earthquakes was all for nothing when the fortress surrendered to the British in 1796 without resistance. It surrendered again in 1810 after guns from one of its nearby supporting batteries were captured and turned on it, but as in 1796, it was soon returned to the Dutch.

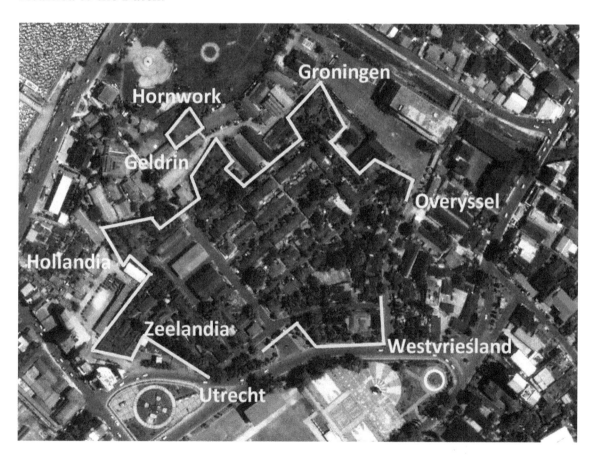

168. The footprint of Fort Victoria with bastions labelled shown on a contemporary satellite view. Originally, the defences were directly on the harbour, but some reclamation has occurred over the years. Indonesia's Pattimura Military District, responsible for the two modern provinces of Maluku and North Maluku, is headquartered at Ambon, with some of the garrison based in Fort Victoria. Image credit: Google Earth.

It then remained in their hands as the administrative hub of their Spice Islands possessions until forces of Imperial Japan stormed the island in early 1942. The Japanese developed Ambon as a major air and naval base and used Fort Victoria as a headquarters, which attracted heavy Allied bombing in 1944 and 1945, destroying much of the town and heavily damaging the fortress. It sustained further damage when forces of the breakaway Republic of the South Moluccas (RMS) used it as a base before being defeated by the Indonesian Army in 1950.

Fort Victoria today is an Indonesian army base and not available for inspection. Even photographing the exterior of the fort is unwise and can lead to trouble with armed sentries. While several of the bastions and walls have been destroyed to accommodate base buildings and Jalan Slamet Riyadi (named after the Indonesian Army commander who was killed retaking the fortress from the forces of the RMS in 1950), the sea-facing bastions and both entry gates still stand, though display the accumulated damage of bombing, battle, earthquakes and neglect.

169. The 'Sea gate' decorated with the crests of Amsterdam, Zeeland, Dordrecht, Rotterdam, Hoorn and Enkhuizen, the founding chambers of the VOC.

On a prearranged tour inside the fortress with senior Indonesian Army (TNI) officers, it was apparent that what remains internally today is a mish-mash of extensions, repairs, alterations, damage—both battle and earthquake—and unsympathetic additions. Powder rooms under the bastions Groningen and Zeelandia were pointed out but not able to be inspected. Other notable features still extant included a number of guerites (sentry boxes) on the bastions and the rebuilt sea gate featuring the six crests of the original chambers of the VOC.

170. The point of Bastion Hollandia today, showing accumulated earthquake and battle damage to the walls and the remaining guerite (sentry box). Originally, a Portuguese bastion stood at this location, dating from around 1576.

Fort Amsterdam—Tsunami victim

171. An attacker's view of Fort Amsterdam. Entry gate is to the left, the first of the sea bastions to the right. The fort was struck by a tsunami in 1674 that swept away most of the garrison.

Fort Amsterdam, at Hila on the northern coast of Ambon, was originally fortified in 1633, on top of a VOC trading lodge dating from the 1600 fleet under Admiral van Hagen. Damaged in a 1644 earthquake, it was rebuilt in its two-bastioned present form in 1644, but again heavily damaged by an earthquake in 1674, when most of the garrison of 40 was swept away by a tsunami that followed the tremor. Later, the three-storey central blockhouse between the bastions was enlarged and heightened.

This 15-square-metre structure has 1.5-metre thick walls, loopholed throughout, with timber floors, internal stairs and an impressive vaulted underground magazine.

In its heyday, Fort Amsterdam fielded 16 guns and 40 men and formed part of a chain of small forts along the north coast of Ambon, including forts Haarlem, Ceith and Lyden, but by 1863 it was abandoned and fell into disrepair. Its form and layout vary greatly from the militarily very effective four-bastioned square forts widely built elsewhere by the Dutch, for two reasons: it was built after the strongest threats from the Iberian powers had subsided; and it was designed and sited more with local rebellion in mind.

During one such rebellion in 1817, supporters of Pattimura attacked the fort, but could not capture it. Fort Amsterdam's importance declined afterwards, until it was finally abandoned in 1863. Early twentieth-century photos show it an overgrown ruin, but during the 1990s it was re-roofed, extensively renovated and is now open for inspection. This type of central blockhouse—reminiscent of the medieval 'keep'—with surrounding low-level outer defences is similar to other now-ruined forts in the Lease Islands at Middleburg, Zeelandia and Beeverwijk.

Fort Amsterdam, about an hour's drive north of Kota Ambon, is reached by crossing the Leihitu peninsula's central spine—reaching up to 900 metres—which provides spectacular views back to Ambon harbour, across the beaches and villages of the north coast and over to Seram.

172. Looking down from the blockhouse at the entry gate. Note the well and the loopholed firing step along the ramparts.

173. Inside the blockhouse at ground level showing the massive timber structural beams, the staircase for access to the upper floors, cobbled floor and embrasures in the 1.5-metre thick walls.

Fort Duurstede—Pattimura's Fort

In the seventeenth century, the VOC established clove plantations on Ambon and in the islands to its east in a bid to reduce the Moluccan monopoly on these still-rare spices. Inevitably, forts were needed to provide internal and external security for these plantations. To facilitate this, around 1626 a stockade was established east of the township of Saparua, which gave its name to the island on which it stood. The fort was rebuilt and expanded following earthquake damage in 1654 and christened Hollandia, but replaced by a new fort closer to the town in 1691. This new fort was named Fort Duurstede.

Built to a unique style and much later than most other Spice Islands forts, Duurstede is a one of a kind. Its two semicircular bastions are crenelated for 28 cannon with another six embrasures along the east-facing ramparts to control the approaches to the bay. Between the bastions are long stretches of three- to four-metre high parapeted walls, complete with guerite sentry boxes, while the inner open space accommodated two large barracks, a commander's residence and storerooms.

Initially, it was manned by just ten soldiers and a corporal, although its coral-stone battlements could hold dozens of guns. Its place in history was assured when in 1817 a local force led by ex-British Moluccan Regiment sergeant Pattimura stormed the ramparts and killed the small garrison. They hoped to foment a wider rebellion but were eventually defeated by a lethargic Dutch counterattack six months later. Pattimura was hung at Fort Victoria.

174. The unusual layout of Fort Duurstede, with its two large circular bastions, was dictated by the constraints of the small peninsula on which it was sited. Restored in 1978 and again in 1995, along with Fort Amsterdam at Hila on Ambon, it is the best of the remaining forts in the Lease Islands.

175. A picturesque location amidst the tropical scenery of the Lease Islands, as well as its capture by Indonesian hero Pattimura, are the drawcards of Fort Duurstede.

176. One of the guerites on the curtain wall showing the profile of the defences including the parapet, banquette and terreplein.

Banda Islands

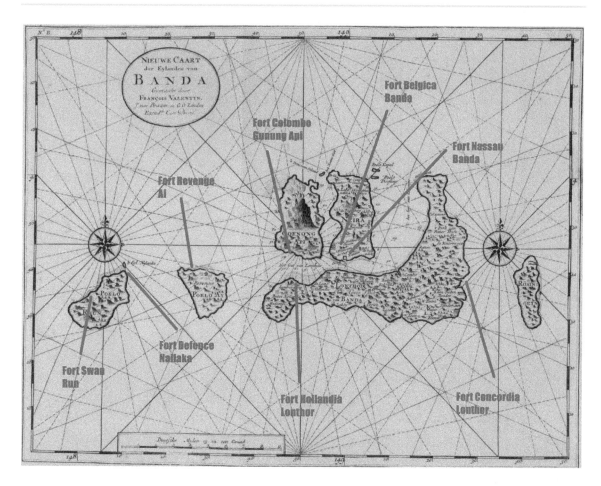

177. The main fortifications of the Banda Islands. All can be seen today, except forts Swan and Defence. The map is a Dutch engraving from around 1725.

It is incredibly improbable that across the entire globe, the only source of nutmeg would be a group of six tiny remote islands in the very far east of the Far East. Adrift in the stunning Banda Sea, the beauty of these islands belies the violence that engulfed them in the seventeenth century, as the Dutch sought to monopolise the nutmeg output, and the Bandanese resisted with equal determination.

The first colonial attempt to build a fortress, by the Portuguese, was abandoned due to the defiance of the Bandanese. The Dutch adopted a much more aggressive strategy, fortifying first Banda's main island (Bandaneira, or just Banda), and gradually the others, and tolerating only subservience. Consequently, a substantial proportion of the indigenous Bandanese population perished in the carnage of the early VOC years.

Just as the Dutch managed to exert full control, enterprising French and British traders managed to smuggle nutmeg seedlings out of the Bandas. Transplanted in other tropical colonies, these crops flourished and dealt the deathblow to VOC ambitions and the Banda economy.

Today, the Bandas retain an aura of mystery, allure and incredible remoteness. As they say in Banda, *'if it was easy to get here, everyone would come'*. Blessed with an endearing local population, outstanding diving and snorkelling opportunities, spectacular scenery, a weight of history out of all proportion to their tiny land area, and an intriguing collection of tropical colonial fortress architecture, these islands are one of the most evocative spots on the planet.

The first fortress built was the massive Fort Nassau from 1609. This was quickly followed by other Dutch forts on the main island, on Ai and on Banda Besar (or Great Banda or Lonthor).

178. A c.1665 oil painting by Vingboons of the main island of the Banda group—Banda or Bandaneira—from the south. The township is to the left, Fort Nassau is in the foreground and Belgica is above and to the right.
Image credit: Rijksmuseum, Netherlands.

The outer island of Run held two small English forts for a short period, before it was traded for Manhattan in a treaty resolving one of the interminable Anglo-Dutch wars in 1667. In the eighteenth century, more minor forts, redoubts, blockhouses and batteries were constructed to keep the locals subdued and deter others, and Fort Belgica was rebuilt into its engaging modern form. All these fortifications failed to stop the British taking over twice during the Napoleonic Wars, after which the islands—having lost their spice monopoly—faded into obscurity.

Fort Nassau—A dark history

Construction of Fort Nassau, the first of the colonial forts of the Banda Islands, was commenced by Dutch Admiral Verhoeven in April 1609. A massive stone-built, four-bastioned quadrilateral, it was situated on the south-west corner of Banda Island to dominate the maritime approaches to the nutmeg capital. Heavy cannon on its bastions could comfortably command the 1700-metre channel to the south down which Java ships arrived, as well as the much narrower passage across to Gunung Api through which vessels from Ambon and the north approached, as well as command the local township. The best, most protected anchorage in all the Bandas lay under its guns.

The Portuguese had commenced a fort in this location back in 1529, but abandoned it after outrage from the Bandanese, leaving just some foundations. The Dutch were initially unimpressed with the position the Portuguese had selected. They were concerned about a hill just to the north that overlooked the site (on which they would later build Belgica) and so started work a distance to the east. They quickly found the site unstable, perhaps swampy and without adequate bearing capacity and reverted to building on the Portuguese foundations.

Before a month had passed, Verhoeven and two dozen of his men were ambushed and killed by the Bandanese nearby, setting the scene for decades of brutality and conflict. Besieged and outnumbered by the locals, the Dutch toiled hard in the blazing heat for several months to complete the work. Initially it held a garrison of 165 men and fielded 26 cannon offloaded from VOC ships. It was in the fort grounds in 1621 that the VOC's most infamous administrator, Governor Coen—who was probably present at the 1609 ambush—took his revenge on the Bandanese, executing 44 of the local chiefs.

This event stains the whole history of Fort Nassau and is vividly remembered by the Bandanese to this day. A series of similar seventeenth and eighteenth century artworks from Nessel, Vingboons, Schley and Reimer show the fort, also known as the *Wasserkasteel,* fully moated, mounting around 30 cannon and with accommodation for a garrison of 150 men. Guerites can be seen at the salient of each bastion and a hornwork was added on the sea side. Vertical timber beams (external counterforts) brace the bastions, a limited defence against the constant earthquakes from nearby Gunung Api.

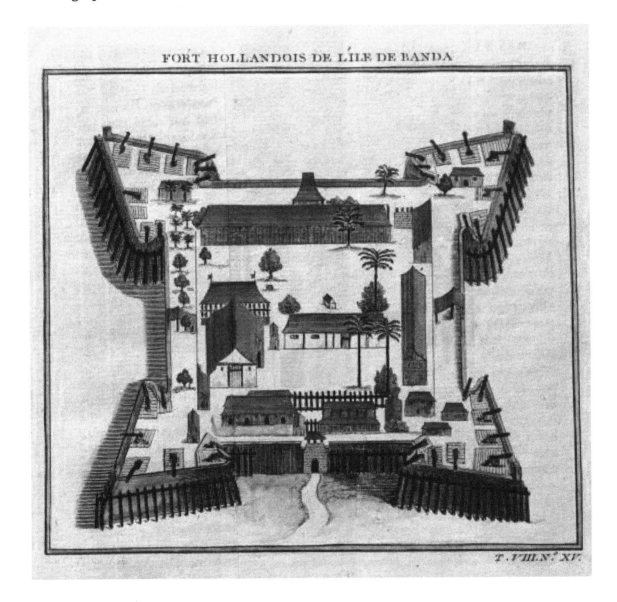

FORT HOLLANDOIS DE L'ILE DE BANDA

179. A 1646 rendering of Nassau by Dutchman Jacobus van der Schley. Notable are the bastions supported by timber beams as earthquake support, the extent of accommodation/storage available in the extensive internal buildings and the mix of carriage-mounted cannon and parapet-mounted swivel guns.

In 1611, concerned that their most powerful fort and headquarters in the archipelago could be threatened by guns emplaced on a 30-metre hill just 250 metres to the north-east of Nassau, the VOC began construction of Fort Belgica on this feature. Much larger than Belgica, Fort Nassau remained the base for the trade activities and spice storage.

180. The inner side of the water gate on the southern side of Fort Nassau. The solid, vaulted brick construction of the 12-metre long passage under the ramparts has seen it survive where much of the fortress is ruined.

Overshadowed by its more glamorous neighbour, Nassau suffered the ultimate indignity when the Royal Navy's Captain Cole captured Fort Belgica by escalade on a stormy night in 1810, and then turned its guns on Nassau to force a general Dutch surrender. Lacking Belgica's commanding location and unique layout and with a tragic history, Nassau has been passed over for restoration funding, and this is apparent in its present state. There is no trace of the hornwork built in the eighteenth century on the southern face. A road has destroyed the two northern bastions (Zeelandia and Delft) and only the southern ones, Admirals Point (west) and Rotterdam (east) remain. The encircling moat ditch has silted over but is still apparent in places. From the western entry gateway around to the Rotterdam bastion the work is partially complete, though of the interior structures, only some foundations are still apparent. Ramparts, casemates, parapets, guerites, barracks, storehouses ... all have sadly passed into history.

181. Like the southern entry, the western passage that leads into the fortress has survived. Note the vaulted brickwork, flagstone floors and arched galleries in the seven-metre tunnel.

Remaining are the arched southern (5 metres wide, 12 metres long, 3.8 metres high) and western (5 metres wide, 7 metres long, 3.8 metres high) vaulted entrance tunnels. Arched red brickwork can be seen in the western entry archway. Even in its present ruined state, the five-metre high and five-metre thick solid ramparts and the 15-metre faced bastions still give an impression of the inherent power and extent of this fortification.

Forever to be associated with the murders of Verhoeven and the Banda chiefs, Fort Nassau will always hold a dark place in history, and a wander through the eerie ruins, looking up at imposing Belgica and across the emerald strait to Banda Besar, does little to assuage the blood-soaked guilt of its grounds.

182. Looking across what was once the parade ground of Nassau, today a sad and forlorn space haunted by ghosts of the past.

Fort Belgica—King of Spice Islands Forts

The most impressive of all Spice Islands forts, Belgica stands tall and proud, dominating the tiny township of Banda—a superb and unique example of tropical colonial fortress architecture.

Built under orders of Governor Both in 1611 partly to awe the Bandanese, its main role was to fortify the hill above Fort Nassau to prevent anyone else—particularly the English—doing the same. Unfortunately for Fort Nassau, 200 years later an English force did storm Fort Belgica and then threatened to bombard the lower fort until it surrendered.

Originally constructed as a standard VOC small four-bastioned quadrilateral, Fort Belgica lay just 200 metres north of the much larger Fort Nassau, at an elevation of around 30 metres. Like Nassau, Belgica also had a weak point: to its north lay another, higher hill and, worried that the English or Bandanese might site cannon there, the

Dutch ended up also fortifying this feature with a small work, referred to on contemporary artwork as 'Banda Redoubt'.

In 1662, following earthquake damage, Belgica was rebuilt in the same square style to hold a garrison of 40 men. Ten years later this poorly built fort was demolished and replaced with the extraordinary castle-like structure which we see today.

The new double concentric pentagonal design, with low-angled outer bastions and a higher crenelated inner wall with tall round towers and extensive casemates underneath, accommodated a 400-man garrison and fielded 58 cannon. It was marginally smaller than Fort Nassau—110 metres between bastion salients compared to 120 metres for Nassau—but incomparably grander.

183. Attractively symmetrical Fort Belgica from the air, showing inner and outer defences.
Image credit: Rumah Banda Museum, Banda.

Belgica is certainly a unique design among Spice Islands forts. While others, notably Fort Revenge on Ai Island, are also of five-bastioned design, Fort Belgica's two separate pentagon systems within the same perimeter make it one-of-a-kind. More noteworthy than the shape however is the use of a high curtain wall with high circular towers on the inner perimeter. It resembles a reversion to pre-artillery medieval style castles, almost as if the outer perimeter has been added to protect an ancient inner construction.

184. Looking west to the very active Gunung Api volcano from one of Belgica's towers, with parts of Banda Besar just visible on the left.

185. Taken from the upper battlements of the inner castle, this view illustrates the profile of the inner and outer defences. The view is SSE with the ruins of Fort Nassau imperceptible on the far right and the island of Banda Besar in the distance.

Despite its unorthodox style, it is very cleverly designed. Although the outer curtain wall and bastions appear to be quite low, when they are scoped, they do an excellent job of preventing the inner walls being hit by gunfire from the majority of the surrounding area.

186. A view from the point of one of the outer bastions across the forecourt to the inner defences. The only entry gate to the inner defences is visible on the right. In 1810, Captain Cole's men were initially caught in this very vulnerable space after escalading the outer wall.

Supposedly a German naturalist, G. E. Rumphius, who lived in Ambon and was engaged by the VOC at one stage as an engineer, had a hand in the mathematics of the design, so perhaps we are indebted to him, as well as the construction engineer de Leeuw, for what many consider to be the most beautiful castle of the Indies.

The rebuilding was completed in 1673. More earthquake damage caused another rebuild in 1795 which was not, however, enough to prevent the fort and its garrison surrendering to a small British fleet under Rear Admiral Rainier—which had already taken Fort Victoria at Ambon—the next year.

Returned to Dutch hands in 1803 (after the British had transferred nutmeg seedlings to their other colonies), Fort Belgica once again came under attack by a British squadron in 1810. Attacking from small boats on a stormy night, several hundred British sailors and marines under Captain Cole first took a shore battery west of Fort Nassau, then a redoubt next to Belgica, finally escalading the fort walls and securing the work in the face of minor resistance. The Dutch governor held out with some troops in Fort Nassau until Cole threatened to storm it and bombard the town, whereupon it surrendered.

Handed back to the Dutch again in 1817, Belgica's and Banda's days of importance were over, and they slipped into tropical obscurity. The fort retained a military function until the 1860s, when it was abandoned. In the early twentieth century the fort was renovated, but it was not until the 1990s that a full refurbishment occurred.

Today, Fort Belgica is a must-visit. Its commanding position, stunning all-round views and fascinating layout combine for a great experience, the most imposing in the region. It has 'Tentative Status' on the UNESCO World Heritage List.

Fort Revenge—Witness to tragedy

Fort Revenge on the island of Ai (or Ay) has a dark past and vies with Fort Nassau for the title of most tragic of all Spice Island forts. Today it is a neglected but evocative testament to the Dutch victory over the islanders in 1616.

The year before, local warriors in a reasonably sophisticated series of defences had been almost overrun before handing the Dutch a stinging defeat and hundreds of casualties. The eventual counterattack under VOC Admiral Jan Lam smashed the Ai defences, destroyed local resistance and the battle aftermath ultimately caused the death of most of the local population, killed or hunted down as they tried to flee to Run. Over the shattered remains of the only settlement on Ai, Fort Revenge was built.

There was no question where to site the fort. Ai is almost completely surrounded by coral reefs, and the majority of the coastline is steep and virtually impassable, except for a small flat section of the northern coast, where the village and fort lie. While the anchorage offshore is particularly exposed to the winds and squalls of the winter northerlies, it provides the only access for larger vessels around the seven-kilometre circumference of the triangular island. Hence, the fort's guns could control the anchorage and the village, which was crucial to prevent the English from rekindling rebellion among the few remaining people of Ai.

Design for this work departed from the previous quadrilateral style. Revenge was a large five-bastioned pentagon, the first for the Spice Islands, and very similar to the layout of the much later Castle of Good Hope at Cape Town. The bastions each had 15-

metre faces and seven-metre flanks, with a curtain extending 23 metres between bastions. Two-metre thick walls reached up to ten metres high enclosed an area of around 500 square metres. Compared to forts Hollandia and Concordia on Banda Besar, Revenge was enormous.

187. Fort Revenge, like Fort Nassau, has a blood-soaked and tragic history which partly explains its present ruinous state. This rendering is from around 1650.

Each bastion was block-faced and earth-filled, with a vaulted powder room underneath. The northern-most bastion—likely the first built—has finely worked quarried stone detailing, though the quality deteriorates in the remaining areas, with rough-cut volcanic and coral blocks. Accommodation and storage were provided in casemates under the ramparts between the bastions, while the entry is through a six-metre arched tunnel. As there was no fresh water available on Ai, stored monsoon runoff had to provide for the long dry spells, and accordingly Fort Revenge was equipped with two large cisterns for this purpose.

188. The decaying entry gate to Fort Revenge. Not surprisingly, the people of the island appear averse to any restoration works. What remains of the extensive 400-year-old fortress is testament to the solidity with which it was designed and built. Apart from centuries of neglect, it has also been struck by several earthquakes. Today, vegetables are grown inside and goats graze on the grassy bastions.

Originally, Admiral Lam left a garrison of 154 men, but no doubt this decreased substantially as the English menace abated and resupply problems emerged. In 1683 the work was badly damaged by an earthquake, but by then the threat of attack had faded. The Spanish had left the Spice Islands and the English had taken Manhattan, New York, in return for vacating the Bandas.

Rebuilt in 1753, the fort housed VOC prisoners and was abandoned next century, though—alone among Banda forts—it did open fire on the attacking British in 1796.

Nowadays, Ai is on the itinerary of tour boats diving the steep drop-offs and colourful reefs just offshore. Views back to Gunung Api across the turquoise waters and golden sands are superb. The curtain walls are abutted by local housing in all directions. Washing hangs on the earthquake-shattered bastions, vegetable gardens adorn the interior and goats graze on the old parade ground. Given the tragic history of the hulking fortress, it is perhaps a testament to the islanders' dispassion that it still stands at all.

189. The scale of the defences are apparent in this shot, which also shows the entry to one of the vaulted, double-doored powder rooms which lay under each of the bastions.

Of the five bastions, just the northern two remain in a reasonable state; the others are stripped of their fabric, crumbling into the interior. Arched powder stores can be discerned under each of the bastions, and the huge cisterns are still visible. A few nine-pounders lie around the ramparts, fighting hard against monsoonal extremes as they have for hundreds of years. It is a surreal experience to wander the battlements, reflect on Revenge's tragic history and the curse of nutmeg, and take in the stunning views out across tropical seas and lush volcanic islands.

190. The forlorn perimeter of Fort Revenge, looking north with the Ai mosque in the background. The cone of Gunung Api volcano is visible in the distance.

Fort Hollandia—Another earthquake victim

Set on a rock platform 30 metres above the channel between Banda Besar and Gunung Api, Fort Hollandia, initially referred to as Fort Lonthar, was built in 1624 to pacify the locals and command the passage leading into Banda from the west. Guns on its bastions loomed large over the village of Lonthor, one of the main centres of Banda Besar, the largest island of the Bandas. Hollandia formed part of a chain of fortlets and watchtowers that eventually encircled the island, signifying the VOC's desire to maintain the control that had taken so long to achieve.

A typical small Dutch four-bastioned quadrilateral, the fort was well designed, the bastion flanks able to sweep the face of the opposite bastion, with no dead ground around its perimeter. Elevated above the reach of ship-board gunfire, the shoreline below it protected by sandbars and shallows, its guns would have posed a credible threat to any hostile sailing vessel in the channel below.

Fort Hollandia was smashed by an earthquake in 1748 and abandoned, though it was again put to use by the Dutch during the British occupation in 1796. It is unlikely that its big guns ever fired at anything in anger.

191. Fort Hollandia from around 1650. A small version of the VOC's standard four-bastion layout.

Well sited and powerful for its small size, Fort Hollandia retains enough of its fabric to stir the imagination, considering the travails it has been through. With 12-metre bastion faces and 12-metre curtains between bastions its internal space is roughly 20 square metres. A vaulted powder cellar with an arched door sits under the north-west bastion.

Today, the adjacent village has encroached and the south-east bastion and eastern wall are gone, while the remainder of the structure is clearly earthquake shattered. Just three metres from the northern entry and obscuring the view of the channel Hollandia once commanded, a house has been built—a disgraceful example of the lack of local control over heritage structures in some of these areas.

192. Gunbarrel view of the village of Lonthor from the battlements of Fort Hollandia. That its guns overlooked the village and mosque was no accident. The threatening symmetry of Gunung Api is in the background.

193. Like Fort Revenge on nearby Ai, the Lonthor locals have no reason to love Fort Hollandia, and its decay is evident. Also similar to Revenge, earthquakes have dealt it more blows than cannon fire, as can be seen from this shattered bastion, crowned by its forest of tropical hardwoods.

Fort Concordia—Last outpost of empire

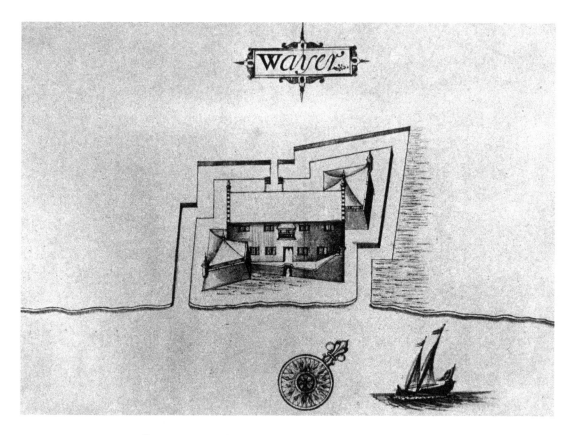

194. A 1650s view of Fort Concordia at Wayer on Banda Besar. The portrayed moat was perhaps an aspiration rather than a reality, as no trace of it could be found.

Fort Concordia is located in the village of Wayer (or Wajer) on the south coast of Banda Besar, separated from the more developed north coast by a range of hills reaching up to 250 metres. This range and the hilly surroundings made land access from the main centres of Lonthor and Celamme difficult. The coast here is fringed by coral reefs, but open to deep water and ocean swells from the south, complicating resupply or reinforcement by sea. There were nutmeg plantations around Wayer and a spice warehouse was located in the village. The original fort's purpose was supposedly to protect the village from 'pirates', though protecting the *perkenier*[142] warehouse and plantations from rebellious slave nutmeg–pickers is a more convincing explanation.

---

[142] Perkeniers were the Dutch plantation managers responsible for managing the slaves to produce the nutmeg crop.

The fort was built in 1630, after any real external threats to the Dutch control over the Bandas had faded. Small and remote, it stood to illustrate the VOC's strength and power to the Bandanese. With the small nearby redoubts Dender (or Morgenster) to the north and Storm to the west, Fort Concordia formed part of a string of strongpoints all around the island aimed at protecting the spice plantations, guarding the slaves working them and intimidating the locals.

195. Looking through the land gate towards the sea gate. Concordia is one of the most remote Spice Islands forts and difficult to get to, but the journey there takes one through some of the prettiest landscapes in all the Bandas.

This was the last outpost of the VOC Empire, sitting as far as you could possibly get from Holland, 14,000 nautical miles, or five months sailing, winds permitting. To be posted to this tiny fort was probably not a positive on one's CV.

Originally, Concordia was a small three-bastioned triangular form, but earthquakes led to a complete rebuild in 1732 into a carbon copy of Fort Hollandia, the standard four-bastioned rectangle. It held a small garrison until abandoned in 1864.

A neat quadrilateral with 12-metre angled bastion faces, three-metre flanks and 12-metre intervals between, the fort looked out to tiny Rozengain Island to the east from seven metres above high tide.

The walls reached up as high as six metres externally and were two-metre thick solid-faced inside and out and earth-filled. Sawn coral blocks were widely used in the construction. There was an arched entry gate north and south and powder rooms under both eastern bastions.

Today, Fort Concordia stands proud but neglected, its form still complete, but its fabric crumbling, quite naturally, considering it is nearly 400 years old and assailed by monsoons and jungle. Its remoteness has protected it, and at least the villagers have had sufficient respect not to build up to its walls, or indeed, inside its grounds. Vegetation is encroaching, including a massive buttress-rooted tree that is taking over the sea wall.

196. A forgotten iron nine-pounder competes with the old stonework of the ramparts to see which will succumb to exposure and neglect first. Seldom visited and down the list for stabilisation funding, Concordia slowly crumbles back into the volcanic earth and tropical forests.

To get to Wayer village it is necessary to take the boat from Banda to Lonthor, then get a motorcycle right along the island, climb up over the passes, and meander on down the south coast. You pass through some of the most picturesque scenery in the Bandas:

nutmeg and kenari groves, quaint villages, tidy cottages. The south coast is particularly stunning, with lush forests and plantations reaching up to the hills and coral reefs fringing the coast. If you have time, a Concordia trip is a day well spent.

Forts of Gunung Api—Volcano forts

197. Remains of Fort Colombo fight a losing battle against the tropical foliage. While this is sobering, the scene here—ruined fortress, forgotten graveyard, jungle reclaiming man's efforts, all beneath a towering and omnipotent volcano and set on a stunning tropical cove—is a decent reward for the journey to make it here.

An impressive, almost perfect and very active 666-metre volcano, Gunung Api towers above the township of Banda from which it is separated by a small channel (the Sonnegat). Scarred by lava flows, stinking of sulphur, regularly venting with anger and often rocked by earthquakes, its forts were never sought-after postings, but they could take ships under fire before the town of Banda could be bombarded, and so the first defences were built from late in the seventeenth century.

Redoubt Kijk-in-den-Pot ('Look in the Pot') was a small, irregular Dutch fort built under the looming mass of the volcano in 1664 under the orders of Governor Van de Vliet. It was located on the south side of Gunung Api to cover the channel to the south across to Banda Besar, down which ships sailed from Java. It lay 1500 metres north of Fort Hollandia at Lonthor on Banda Besar, so between the two of them the forts were easily able to close the channel to hostile shipping.

198. An oblique embrasure shows the more modern style of the most recent rebuild of Fort Colombo.

The location fell in and out of favour with successive governors—sometimes decaying to ruins and then being rebuilt and rearmed. The fort was improved and enlarged a number of times after completion, but destroyed by an earthquake in 1683.

Subsequently rebuilt in the form of a crescent, the footprint of which can be seen today, another period of neglect followed and another battery was built just to the east of it named Battery de Kop (the Head). In 1762, Kijk-in-den-Pot was again resurrected, and at some point renamed Fort Colombo, but in 1769 its guns were transferred across to Fort Hollandia, before it was rearmed once again in 1780. A few years later it fell back into ruin.

Two other small batteries were also built in the far south-western point of the island, named Sibergsburg and Batavia, but they were of no concern to Captain Cole in 1810 as he sailed in from the east and took Fort Belgica with little effort.

Today the overgrown remains of Fort Colombo can be found after a short boat ride from Banda's main pier. It is possible to recognise the semicircular form, the crenelated ramparts and a small overgrown graveyard.

Run & Nailaka—The English forts

199. Nailaka is a tiny sand and coral islet surrounded by stunning tropical seas. Dive boats stop close to the ghosts of Fort Defence to experience the incredible underwater cliffs just offshore. Visibility is up to 50 metres and divers can see species of hard coral, pelagics, eagle rays, turtles, Napoleon wrasse and colourful tropical fish in their thousands as the walls of the island fall away steeply into the Banda Sea.

The small English forts on Run and Nailaka islands in the outer Bandas were built under the direction of the East India Company's Nathaniel Courthope in 1616 and destroyed by the VOC four years later. Although Run produced significant quantities of nutmeg it lacked fresh water and any foodstuffs, making it easy to blockade. So close to the formidable Dutch forts of Nassau, Belgica and Revenge, it was always going to be challenging for the English to hold it without control of the adjacent seas, which they rarely managed.

Run, western-most of the Banda chain, is four kilometres long, lying 24 kilometres from the main island of Banda, while tiny Nailaka is a sand and coral islet just 300-metres long joined to Run at low tide by a rock shelf. The main island is surrounded by strong currents and coral reefs, with jungle-covered cliffs circling most of the coast. The only marginal haven for trading ships was off the main village, located on a small bay halfway along the north coast. As an anchorage, it was exposed to the winter northerlies, but did offer some protection to the trade winds of July and August. The only possible landing points for an attacker were at the village itself, and on the sandy beaches of Nailaka. To prevent a Dutch invasion, Courthope fortified these two key points, but unfortunately, we know very little about the only two English forts in the Spice Islands, and no trace of them remains.

200. Looking north at Run's main village from near the site of Fort Swan, with fishing boats anchored inside the coral reefs. Nailaka is just out of sight, right middle-ground.

Courthope arrived in December 1616 with two ships, *Swan* at 578 tonnes and *Defence* at 406 tonnes and, expecting a Dutch counterattack, wasted no time establishing makeshift batteries ashore. He landed six guns for the two works. Although we have no details of the armament of *Swan* and *Defence,* early East Indiamen of around 500 tonnes normally carried 20 to 30 guns. Two years later, just after dispatching a supply ship to Courthope from Batavia, Admiral Dale landed six cannon from other ships to assist the Jacatra (later Jakarta) sultan—three culverins (roughly 18-pounders) and three demi-culverins (roughly ten-pounders), so perhaps this is suggestive of what may have been offloaded at Run.

One battery, Fort Swan, was situated on an elevation just west of the village facing west and north, able to dominate ships approaching from Java en route to Banda, while the other, Fort Defence, was placed on Nailaka able to fire at vessels approaching from the east. Professionally sited, equipped with a mix of culverins and demi-culverins, properly provisioned and manned and supported by musketeers, even such limited defences could pose a real threat to a smallish attack.

201. It's chilling to reflect that hundreds of years ago blood was spilt over these sands in pursuit of spices. This is stunning Nailaka, looking east towards the main islands.

However, the Dutch at that time in the Bandas were capable of a much more than a smallish attack. A few months before in April 1616, they had overrun the English-supported Bandanese defences of nearby Ai with a squadron of 12 ships and 1000 men. Such an attack would have suffered somewhat from the guns of forts Swan and Defence, but the end result would never have seriously been in doubt.

Nevertheless, the loss of both Courthope's ships to the Dutch and his death while blockade running in 1620, hastened the end for the English base on Run. Isolated and starved, the survivors abandoned the island and the Dutch meticulously destroyed the defences.

Although Swan would have been an excellent site for a minor Dutch fort, the VOC chose never to fortify Run. Eventually, the Treaty of Breda in 1667 formalised the transfer of sovereignty over Run from England to the Netherlands, in return for various other contested Caribbean and North American possessions, including Manhattan Island, which had recently been captured by England. Run for Manhattan!

Today dive boats anchor off the coral walls of Run and Nailaka, the snorkelers and scuba divers oblivious to the tortured history of the golden sands just metres away. No surviving evidence of either fort could be found, testament to the efficiency of the Dutch demolition.

10. Touring the region

202. Travelling across the Spice Islands today can sometimes seem like you've passed through a portal into another world. This is part of Fort Concordia.

The wide sweep of Spice Islands sprinkled across the Molucca, Seram and Banda seas remain remote even today. Not as remote as they once were, certainly, but still relatively difficult to get to and often challenging to traverse. They suit explorers rather than holidayers; travellers with a fondness for adventure rather than resorts.

Ambon and Ternate are the flight hubs for today's Spice Islands, with daily flights from Jakarta. You can also arrive from Makassar and Manado on Sulawesi. Within the region, several small airlines fly between Ternate and Ambon and also to Banda, Labua, Halmahera, Papua and occasionally Timor. You can only fly to Banda from Ambon.

Regional flying in Indonesia is not for the faint-hearted. The archipelagic nation has a comprehensive air network, but one of the world's worst flight safety records. Poor maintenance, dated infrastructure, inadequate training, old aircraft, smoke haze, volcanic dust clouds and tropical weather are all real hazards. Smaller airlines servicing the 'wild East' come and go quickly, and are regularly shut down for maintenance violations by the civil aviation authority, which is itself under-resourced.

203. The Pelni liner *Ciremai* pulls out of the Banda pier—which it dwarfs—and gets ready to use its bow thruster to describe a 180° turn in front of Gunung Api, before heading back down the channel and across the Banda Sea to Ambon.

Flying to Banda from Ambon presents a number of problems, apart from the volcano at the end of the runway. A siren sounds to clear locals and animals from the tarmac when a plane is due, but the airport itself is unmanned, so any cloud cover on approach will result in the flight returning to Ambon. Many other issues can also cause flight cancellations, and it is not unusual to be 'marooned' on Banda when return flights are delayed, cancelled or over-booked. Currently a twice-weekly service operating rather dated Czech-built turboprops haphazardly services the islands. A much better way to travel to Banda from Ambon is the newer fast ferry service which leaves Ambon twice a week during the tourist season and takes about five hours.

Generally, it's probably more convenient to traverse the region by sea if you have time, and in any case, this is the real way to arrive in the Spice Islands, like the navigators of old. The national shipping line, Pelni, runs a fleet of liners throughout Indonesia. These range from relatively new to horribly old, with accommodation from two-person cabins with aircon to sleep-on-the-deck-if-you-find-a-space. The company website shows the various routes, ships of the fleet, classes available, and often the sailing schedule.

204. A line of 'spids' at Rum harbour, waiting to fill up with commuters to zip to adjacent islands like Makian. If you want to see the fort ruins on the outer islands, you will need to take a spid, which is definitely not the most relaxed way to travel. The Spanish galleon *Victoria* anchored just to the right in 1521 before sailing west to complete the very first circumnavigation of the globe.

Shorter range water transport varies widely. 'Spids', fibreglass sweatboxes with twin outboards that leave when full, are most common in the Moluccas, whereas the boats in the Bandas are in less of a hurry. Prices and routes are often fixed, but anything can also be chartered—bargain hard. On land, taxis and bemos are common in most areas, otherwise *Ojeks*—riding on the back of a motorcycle—are possible everywhere.

Luckily, accommodation in the region is easier to manage than transport. Ambon and Ternate have experienced a construction boom in recent years and have a wide range of accommodation, including some four-star hotels. In these cities and elsewhere there are also many *Losmen*-type guesthouses of varying degrees of habitability and pricing. Aircon is recommended after a hard day of equatorial fort touring. Some of the less visited islands have no formal accommodation at all. In general, conditions, services and standards in Indonesia and in the Spice Islands particularly are constantly changing, so proper research is recommended. Naturally, travel insurance and medical evacuation cover are not to be ignored.

205. *Tiger Blue*, a beautiful example of a restored traditional sailing schooner, is one of several such craft available for charter in the Spice Islands.

Undoubtedly the best way to explore the Spice Islands, and a way that deals with both transport and accommodation at the same time, is on a traditional Pinisi schooner, sisterships to the last great sailing fleet of the world. Many hardworking examples of these vessels based out of Makassar still haul bulk cargoes around the 18,000 islands of Indonesia. Some versions, fitted out as tourist/dive boats, offer extremely civilised touring including air-conditioned ensuite cabins. In a two-week charter you can take in both the Moluccas and the Bandas, but the luxury comes at a price.

Retiring to such comfort after a hard day's fort exploring, and sipping a cold sundowner while watching another spectacular sunset behind a looming volcano while the chef tempts you with the aromas of dinner … well, that's really the way to do it!

206. The road to Fort Concordia, on Banda Besar.

Weatherwise, it is difficult to accurately categorise the seasons, because they vary greatly between the northern Moluccas and the southern Bandas and also from year to year. The best season for diving in Banda, when the water is calmer and clear, is in March/April and again in September/November. In terms of temperature and humidity, the months of the south-east trade winds in July and August are usually a degree or two cooler. In Ternate, the rainiest months are April to July, while in Ambon it is May to September, but so close to the equator, it can rain in the Spice Islands anytime, though normally not for too long.

While the region has largely recovered from devastating inter-communal violence in the late 1990s, there remains the potential for disturbances, particularly in Ambon. The Spice Islands remain the flash point between Islam and Christianity in Indonesia, as they have for 500 years.

Generally, local people are tolerant, helpful, curious and friendly, though English is not widely spoken. Indonesian is however one of the easiest languages in the world to pick up in basic form, and any effort will be rewarded.

The Spice Islands forts themselves—and all Indonesian historical architecture—are the responsibility of the Indonesian Bureau for the Protection of Cultural Heritage, which coordinates their stabilisation, maintenance, refurbishment and documentation. All significant forts have a 'keeper' who lives nearby and is paid a nominal wage in return for managing security, collecting admission, escorting visitors, preventing pilfering and trimming vegetation. In a country with many competing budget demands, the funding of the Bureau is less than substantial, and it has a long pipeline of renovation projects awaiting financing.

The selection of target projects, the resolution of work scopes and the execution of those works is not always without controversy, and some past projects have been insensitive to the real identity of the fort. In recent years the government of the Netherlands has also provided some restoration funding.

The best of the forts

In terms of the best forts to see, it depends of course on how much time is available and whether you take in both the Moluccas and the Bandas. Number one on anyone's list should be Fort Belgica, because it is the most iconic of Spice Islands forts—a unique and glorious work of science and art, over 400 years old, and the base for exploration of the endearing Banda Islands. Fort Nassau is close by, and its tragedy and neglect provide a sobering balance to the romance of its more glamorous, loftier neighbour.

A day trip to Run Island and a wander on nearby Nailaka witnesses no forts, but is both a journey across magnificent tropical panoramas as well as a boat ride deep into history; England's very first colony, the long-lost redoubt of the irrepressible Nathaniel Courthope, and a tiny spot of land that was once swapped for Manhattan. The scenery here takes your breath away. A stop-off en route to Run at Ai Island provides another evocative look at a haunting fort of dark tragedy, massive Fort Revenge crumbling away in its shame.

207. Fort Kalomata on Ternate Island.

Earthquake-smashed Fort Hollandia and jungle-wreathed Fort Colombo are also quite easy to inspect in a few hours each from Banda. If time allows, a day's journey to remote, forgotten and captivating Fort Concordia is highly recommended. You will never forget a visit to the Bandas.

At Ambon, you can look—but not too closely—at the battered outer façade of Fort Victoria, but more rewarding are day trips to charismatic Fort Amsterdam on the north coast and Pattimura's Fort Duurstede set amidst the stunning scenery of nearby Saparua Island.

Flying or sailing north from Ambon takes you to the Molucca islands, redolent of cloves and violence, once home of the most sought-after spice on the planet. Ternate itself holds an array of forts, starting with the original, Kastella and its five-century-old ruins facing the setting sun across coconut palms and black volcanic sands. Heading east from there, you come first to tiny Kota Janji with its spectacular line of volcanos south to the equator, and then to the artistic but hollow shell of Kalomata, down on the waterfront at the edge of town. Almost submerged in the clamour of Ternate city is the expansive Fort Orange, perhaps now with its museum. Lastly, the visitor comes to Ternate's intriguing Fort Tolukko, the best surviving example of locally designed Spice Islands fortifications, with sweeping views south and west from its petite gun platform.

208. Fort Tohula on Tidore Island.

A short 'spid' ride to Tidore's Rum harbour from Talangame is an opportunity to inspect the circumnavigators' memorial to Elcano and the *Victoria* nearby, and then circle back past the discarded remains of Chobo en route to Fort Torre, looking over the east coast.

Leave mighty Fort Tohula to last. Climb the 300 steps and be rewarded by a fine view over Soa Siu and east across to the wild far hills of Halmahera. Take in the towering bastions that were never stormed; the town spread under your guns and the volcano touching the sky to the west. Below you in the tiny bay, a Dutch squadron shattered two Portuguese galleons in 1605 and then went on to storm Fort Reis Magos, now lost amidst the cottages of the town before you. Muse about garrison life here 400 years ago, as bored sentries looked past the line of weathered crosses in the graveyard toward korakora pulling out over emerald seas, and the fort captain brings a glass to his eye to watch a Manila galleon glide in under its cloud of canvas. The palms danced in the soft monsoon breeze, the oppressive heat cut a line at the shadows, the storerooms reeked of cloves, and the world is a smaller place just because of those spices and their forts.

Bibliography

Published works

Andaya, Leonard. *The World of Maluku.* 1993

Argensola, Bartolome. *The Discovery & Conquest of the Molucco & Philippine Islands.* 1609

Blair, E.H. & Robertson, J.A. (translators). *The Philippine Islands 1493–1898.* 1903

Bocarro, Antonio. *O Livro das Plantas de Todas as Fortalezas, Cidades e Povoacoes do Estado da India Oriental.* c. 1635

Boxer, C.R. *Four Centuries of Portuguese Expansion.* 1969

Boxer, C.R. *The Dutch Seaborne Empire.* 1965

Boxer, C.R. *The Portuguese Seaborne Empire 1415–1825.* 1969

Brown, Ruth & Smith, Robert. *Guns from the Sea.* 1988

Bruce, John. *Annals of the Honourable East India Company.* 1810

Bruijn & Gaastra. *Ships, Sailors & Spices.* 1993

Chase, Kenneth. *A Global History of Firearms to 1700.* 2003

Clancy, Robert. *The Mapping of Terra Australis.* 1995

Cole, Christopher. *Illustrative Account of Captain Cole's Splendid Achievement in the Capture of the Island of Banda.* 1811

Conboy & Morrison. *Feet to the Fire: CIA Covert Operations in Indonesia, 1957–1958.* 2010

Conboy, Kenneth. *Kopassus: Inside Indonesia's Special Forces.* 2003

Corn, Charles. *The Scents of Eden: A History of the Spice Trade.* 1999

Corney, Bolton. *The Voyage of Sir Henry Middleton to Bantam & the Maluco Islands.* 1606

D'orsey, Alex. *Portuguese Discoveries, Dependencies and Missions in Asia & Africa.* 1893

Danvers, Fredrick Charles. *The Portuguese in India 1481–1571.* 1894

De Figueroa, M.F. *A Spaniard in the Portuguese Indies.* 1512

De Jong, Adrian. *Spice Adventures: Logs of the Gelderland 1601–1603.* 2002

De Jong, Peter. *Dornier Do 24 Units.* 2015

De Morga, Antonio. *Sucesos de las Islas Filipinas.* 1609

Earle & Villiers. *Albuquerque, Caesar of the East.* 1990

Eredia, E.M. *Description of Malacca.* 1613

Estensen, Miriam. *Discovery: the Quest for the Great South Land.* 1998

Foster, William (editor). *The Journal of John Jourdain 1608−1617.* 1905

Fryke & Schweitzer. *Voyages to the East Indies 1676−86.* 1997

Garrett, Richard J. *The Defences of Macau.* 2010

Garton, Robin. *The Guns of the Sacramento.* 1978

Graca, Jorge. *The Fortifications of Macau.* 1984

Grey, Charles. *The Merchant Venturers of London.* 1932

Guilmartin, John Francis. *Galleons & Galleys.* 2002

Guilmartin, John Francis. *Gunpowder & Galleys.* 2003

Hall, Bert S. *Weapons & Warfare in Renaissance Europe.* 1999

Hall, Richard. *Empires of the Monsoon.* 1998

Hanna, W.A. & Alwi, D. *Turbulent Times Past in Ternate & Tidore.* 1990

Hanna, W.A. *Indonesian Banda.* 1991

Henderson, James. *Sent Forth a Dove.* 1999

Hilder, Brett. *The Voyage of Torres.* 1980

Horridge, Adrian. *The Austronesian Conquest of the Sea.* Bellwood/ Fox/Tryon-Upwind (editors). Chapter 7. 2006.

Huyghen Van Linschoten, John. *The Voyage of John Huyghen Van Linschoten to the East Indies.* 1598

Indian Army Intelligence Branch. *Frontier and Overseas Expeditions from* India. Volume 6 Ch XXII. 1910

Jacobs, Hubert. *A Treatise on the Moluccas.* c. 1544

Javellana, Rene. *Fortress of Empire.* 1997

Joyner, Tim. *Magellan.* 1994

Kaufmann, J.E. & Kaufmann, H.W. *The Medieval Fortress.* 2001

Keay, John. *The Spice Route.* 2005

Kirsch, Peter. *The Galleon.* 1990

Kupcik, Ivan. *Munich Portolon Charts.* 2000

Lach, D.F. & Van Kley, E.J. *Asia in the Making of Europe.* Volume III, Book 3. 1993

Linn, Brian McAllister. *The Philippine War 1899–1902.* 2000

Long, Gavin. *Australia in the War of 1939–1945.* Series 1—Army, Volume 7, The Final Campaigns. 1963

Luis Felipe Reis, Thomaz. *Early Portuguese Malacca.* 2000

Meilink-Roelofsz, M.A.P. *Asian Trade & European Influence in the Indonesian Archipelago 1500–1650.* 1962

Milton, Giles. *Nathaniel's Nutmeg.* 1999

Paget, WH. *Frontier and Overseas Expeditions from India.* 1907

Penrose, Boise. *Sea Fights in the East Indies 1602–1639.* 1931

Pires, Tome. *The Suma Oriental.* c. 1515

Pliny the Elder. *Natural History.* c. 77 AD.

Reid, Anthony (editor). *South-East Asia in the Early Modern Era.* 1993

Rocklefs, M.C. *A History of Modern Indonesia since c. 1200.* 2001

Rossfelder, André. *In Pursuit of Longitude.* 2007

Suarez, Thomas. *Early Mapping of South-East Asia.* 1999

Suarez, Thomas. *Early Mapping of the Pacific.* 1995

Tan, Andrew TH (Ed). *A Handbook of Terrorism and Insurgency in South-East Asia.* 2007

Teixeira, Andre. *Fortalezas. Estado Portugues da India.* 2008

Thorn, Major William. *The Conquest of Java.* 1815

Unger, Richard W. (consultant editor). *Cogs, Caravels & Galleons.* 1994

Varthema, Ludovico. *The Itinerary.* 1510

Wigmore, Lionel. *Australia in the War of 1939–1945.* Series 1—Army, Volume 4, The Japanese Thrust. 1957

Wilson, Derek. *The World Encompassed: Drake's Great Voyage 1577–80.* 1977

Wood, A.J.R. *A World on the Move: The Portuguese in Africa, Asia and America, 1415–1808.* 1992

Research papers

De Clercq, F.S.A. 'Ternate: The Residency & Its Sultanate'. 1890

Duivenvorde, Wendy. 'The Armament of Australia's VOC Ships'. 2010

Lobato, Manuel; previously researcher at Instituto de Investigação Científica Tropical, Lisbon.

'The Moluccan Archipelago and Eastern Indonesia in the Second Half of the Sixteenth Century in light of Portuguese and Spanish Accounts'. Research paper. 1995
'A Man in the Shadow of Magellan'. *Revista de Cultura*, Macao Edition 39. 2011
'From European–Asian conflict to Cultural Heritage: Identification of Portuguese and Spanish Forts in the Northern Maluku Islands'. In Laura Jarnagin Pang (editor). *Culture and Identity in the Luso–Asian World: Tenacities and Plasticities.* Singapore. 2012
'Identification of Portuguese & Spanish Forts on Ternate & Tidore Islands'. 2012

Ramerini, Marco (colonialvoyage.com). The Spanish Fortresses on the Island of Tidore 1521–1606.

Rodao Garcia, Dr Florentino University Complutense Madrid. 'Restos de la Presencia Iberica en las Islas Molucas'. 1989

Yves-Manguin, Pierre. Lancaran, Ghurab and Ghali. 'Mediterranean Impact on War Vessels in Early Modern South-East Asia'. In Geoff Wade and Li Tana (editors). *Anthony Reid and the Study of the South-East Asian Past.* Singapore. 2012

Periodicals

The Naval Chronicle (UK)

The Glamorgan Monmouth and Brecon Gazette and Merthyr Guardian 1836: The Late Sir Christopher Cole

The Sydney Morning Herald
smh.com.au/world/the-untold-story-how-z-force-saved-the-sultan-20100423-tj7q.html

The Jakarta Globe
thejakartaglobe.com/archive/navy-was-set-to-fire-on-warship/277953/

The Artilleryman. 'Study of Ordnance may help to determine Drake's California harbour'. Oliver Seeler. Spring 1990

The Great Circle. War and Trade in the Indian Ocean and South China Sea, 1600–1650. C.R. Boxer. Volume 1, No. 2 October 1979

Journal of the Ordnance Society: A Gun-List from Portuguese India, 1525. Richard Barker. Volume 8, 1996

Index

Lightning Source UK Ltd.
Milton Keynes UK
UKHW051218091021
391864UK00003B/44

9 781922 440617